Y0-BCO-328

THE REALITIES OF
MANAGEMENT

THE REALITIES
OF
MANAGEMENT

A View from the Trenches

Royce L. Callaway

Quorum Books
Westport, Connecticut • London

Library of Congress Cataloging-in-Publication Data

Callaway, Royce L., 1934–
    The realities of management : a view from the trenches / Royce L.
Callaway.
        p.   cm.
    Includes bibliographical references and index.
    ISBN 1–56720–315–9 (alk. paper)
    1. Management.   I. Title
HD31. C32   1999
658—dc21   99–10386

British Library Cataloguing in Publication Data is available.

Library of Congress Catalog Card Number: 99–10386
ISBN: 1–56720–315–9

First published in 1999

Quorum Books, 88 Post Road West, Westport, CT 06881
An imprint of Greenwood Publishing Group, Inc.
www.quorumbooks.com

Printed in the United States of America

The paper used in this book complies with the
Permanent Paper Standard issued by the National
Information Standards Organization (Z39.48–1984).

10 9 8 7 6 5 4 3 2 1

I wish to acknowledge the assistance of my wife, Phyllis,
who practically memorized the manuscript;
my children Todd, Stacy, and Beth, for their support and critical review;
my parents, Earl and Carrie, who never lost faith;
my friend Mark, for the literary inspiration;
and Kym, who got the whole thing started in the first place.

The manager administers, the leader innovates.
The manager maintains, the leader develops.
The manager relies on systems, the leader relies on people.
The manager counts on controls, the leader counts on trust.
The manager does things right, the leader does the right thing.

—Fortune Magazine

CONTENTS

Preface   *xi*

1 Introduction   1

2 Managers and Leaders   9

3 Magic Bullets   23

4 Processes and Procedures   47

5 Managing People:
       The People Are the Problem   67

6 Managing the Organization:
       From Bullets to Bubbles   89

7 Virtual Management: Welcome to Oz   111

8 Decisions and Risk: To Be or Not to Be?   133

9   Ethics and Morality: I Cannot Tell a Lie   151

10   Politics: Games and Gambits   171

11   Searching for Intelligence:
         What Were They Thinking   191

12   So What?:
         Observations and Reflections   211

Bibliography   219

Index   221

PREFACE

This is a book about managing and leading based on actual events as seen through the eyes of those responsible for the decisions. There is very little theory here and even less "how to do it" because those of us who are in the trenches know nothing ever works like it is supposed to work. Projects come to ignominious ends for the most trivial reasons, which frequently fall into the "who would have thought" category. The reality of management is that most of what you need to manage effectively is not taught in school. Formal training programs rightfully focus on the fundamentals of what you need to know rather than on how to apply it in a day-to-day environment. Consequently, most managers acquire their management education in the school of "hard knocks."

This book is a series of anecdotes describing mostly real situations, discussing possible decision alternatives, and, more importantly, reviewing the outcomes, both real and possible, of those decisions. All of these scenarios are taken from personal experience or interviews with actual managers who were asked to describe some interesting or common management problems they have encountered. Some of these managers were senior level executives, others were first-level team leaders. These scenarios are either taken directly from those interviews or were fused together to create a composite.

Most managers know the fundamentals of management—that is, how to supervise, budget, forecast, and read financial reports. Therefore, these aspects of management are not really addressed in this book, and when they are relevant, it is assumed the reader is familiar with them.

The issues described here are faced by all levels of management and may appear simple or almost self-evident at first, but it is these subtle and seemingly simple issues that often create the most problems. In these scenarios the problems range from those in which there is little information available to those where there is ample information, but the choices are all equally bad. In some of the scenarios the problem is so simple that only an idiot could make a mistake and frequently we do.

1

INTRODUCTION

Managing has never been an easy task. It was difficult enough when all that was required was planning, organizing, and directing. In those days there was a "boss" who gave the orders, and there were workers who carried out those orders. Slackers and malcontents were summarily sacked and were easily replaced with any of the number of interchangeable workers who were theoretically lined up at the gate. Managers were generally selected on the basis of their conformity to the norm and their adeptness at pleasing the boss. To be a "boss" did not require much training, which was good, because for the most part there was none. Training was not considered necessary, because the new manager was not expected to do much more than keep the lower classes in line and act as a link in the bucket brigade of information flowing from the top to the bottom of the company.

For those managers who felt the need to learn management techniques, improve their existing techniques, or just to fill their office bookshelf, there were always books flowing from learned consultants and academics describing the latest management style or technique. These books almost always promised to bring management success and career advancement to the managers, who immediately implemented these newly minted management techniques. At the very least these books promised predigested solutions; jumping on these bandwagons provided the manager a solution without having actually to think about the situation and formulate an original answer. Additionally, the implementation of these management solutions du jour demonstrated to upper executives the manager's incisive insight and cutting-edge thinking. This is how job enrichment, quality circles, participative management, managing by objectives, and many other milestones on the pathway to effortless success were inflicted on the innocent and unwary. This is not to say these techniques have no merit—quite the contrary; many were and continue to be quite relevant. The issue is that in and of themselves they are limited. Like so many things in life they must be used in moderation and appropriately. All too often the uncreative or unskilled manager turns to these trendy management fads as a substitute for the analysis and creativity required for effective leadership and problem resolution.

On the other hand, some of these trendy books require so much thinking and analysis that it is unlikely very many readers derive much value from them beyond filling their bookshelves with obviously important texts on current management thought. For example, several years ago *The Book of Five Rings* was a very popular and widely recommended text that was regarded as an excellent example of strategic management thinking. *The Book of Five Rings* is in fact a book of Japanese philosophy dedicated to training Samurai warriors in swordsmanship. Like all philosophy, it is not for the impatient or intellectually challenged. *The Book of Five Rings* appeared on many executive bookshelves, and for a while it was quite stylish to refer to the book as if you not only had read it, but *actually understood* it. In reality this book was intended as a contemplative exercise for the Samurai. Consequently, the passages are not only brief, but so abstract that they are unintelligible without considerable thought and reflection by the reader. Precisely how the various lessons might be applied to everyday business management or strategic analysis is unclear, and if any of the lessons *could* be applied it would require significant time and analysis to determine how to apply it. With that level of effort the thoughtful and analytical manager might well have gotten just as much value from contemplating the five coffee rings on his desk.

High-level strategic books like *The Book of Five Rings* are the opposite of the ubiquitous "how to" books, in that they do not address anything very specifically. It is left to the reader to translate, define, and determine how the information is applied and in what circumstances. In general, these books address theoretical approaches to problems and rarely address the realities of day-to-day management. This does not mean books dealing with abstractions and theoretical applications have no place. They can be very valuable, and more managers should be aware of the new developments and theories contained in these books. Generally, these books are not intended as universal solutions, and the concepts and the ideas they put forward are meant to be considered, analyzed, and applied *when appropriate*. Unfortunately, from the time the first book on management was written, people have expected to find immediate solutions to their management problems in a book. As a result of this demand there have always been authors willing to offer the easy pathway to successful management.

A trip to the local bookstore today indicates that nothing much has changed since the first of these books on how to become a successful manager was published. The shelves of most bookstores are still crammed with books that deal with broad issues such as "managing the learning organization," "managing chaotic organizations," "managing with Zen," or a host of similar books with equally enticing titles. Ironically, for the thoughtful manager many of these books contain interesting and provocative information. However, the operative word here is *thoughtful*, because these ideas must be carefully considered and applied sparingly. Too often managers attempt to solve their problems with these ideas, even when the concepts in the book do not apply to their situation. Other books tend to either address problems such as "project management," and "challenges in strategic planning," or they describe management techniques used by successful leaders, such as *Leadership Secrets of Napoleon* or *The Buddhist's Approach to Management Nirvana*. These books often address management and leadership from a broad perspective and rarely provide specific solutions for the day-to-day management problems faced by the vast majority of managers. Even fewer, indeed if any, recognize that the differences between many of the problems faced by the first-line manager and the CEO are largely a matter of scale. When reduced to their essence the problems are essentially the same because they deal with people, processes, trust, ethics, and risk. All of these form the ingredients for decisions, and the difference between Vice Presidents arguing over office location is really no different than two members of the rank and file arguing over a window cube.

Beyond the available books on management and leadership are formal training programs. These training programs are usually found at universities or at corporations large enough to have the resources necessary to implement them. Unfortunately, most of these programs fail to grasp the scope and complexity of management and leadership even though they are frequently advertised as management or leadership training. Why is this? Perhaps it is because lower-level employees or academics, those without actual hands-on management experience, develop them. Neither group has the actual experience of applying their theories to real situations. Rarely do leaders or managers actually develop these programs. Even when they do, the programs are frequently narrowly focused or subject specific. In any case these educational programs tend to be topic related regardless of who develops them. Corporate training programs usually focus on the "how to" of company processes and procedures and rarely, if ever, address the more significant "what if" questions—questions dealing with what happens if a key employee resigns, or a new competitor enters the market, or promised equipment does not arrive on schedule. What should you do? What are your alternatives? What is the probable outcome of those alternatives, or why would a manager select one action or decision over another?

Corporate training programs commonly cover budgeting, pricing, personnel issues, financial management, and other topics that the company managers are rightfully expected to know. The intent of these programs is not just to instruct budding managers in a particular topic but to teach them "how we do things here." Doing things "our way" is frequently perceived as being more important than doing things "the right way" because conformity to the company culture is crucial to the corporation and often a critical factor in promotion. Therefore, the manager in training is taught the company way of planning, budgeting, and personnel administration, with each topic being addressed separately.

These corporate training programs are a two-edged sword. On the one hand they ensure that the company has a pool of well-trained (or indoctrinated) managers who are consistent in their actions, but on the other hand these managers are inwardly focused and actually trained (unintentionally) not to stray off the corporate path and into original thinking. Consequently, the products of these training programs are frequently well grounded in the "how" but lack the "why" of management. The process of management is emphasized while the interrelationships between the techniques, process, decisions, and probable outcomes of alternative actions are ignored. Thus the corporate student is put through a series of rote drills much like learning the multiplication tables, while personalities, motivations, and individual methods are glossed over or ignored entirely. Furthermore, corporate and academic programs rarely fit individual styles of management and even more rarely attempt to teach leadership skills.

As a result the interrelationships between people issues, financial management, resource management, leadership, planning, and all of the other topics that are involved in management problems are not addressed. Instead, each new manager is left to apply them on the job within the context of his or her individual style. For example, one of the most popular styles of leadership is *leading by example* but precisely what is meant by this is not made clear, and the "how you do it" is left to the individual to determine. Most people assume that this means follow my lead, but does it? Does it mean "do as I do, not as I say" or does it mean "do as I say and not as I do"? Could it just as easily mean that the leader demonstrates what is expected? What about *leading from behind?* What does that mean? Does that mean the followers make the decisions and the leader accepts or rejects? Does it mean the leader leads through influence rather than by authority? How do you *lead from behind?* What techniques are employed? Is that leading or *pushing* or perhaps what is meant here is leading through *inspiration?* But how do you inspire people to follow you? Do you conduct pep rallies and hire cheerleaders, or do you preach a vision? This lack of precision and detail regarding the techniques and styles of leadership is the fundamental flaw in many, if not most, training programs, and, as serious as these problems are, there are others and, less obvious but equally important problems.

Corporate programs are usually developed by Human Resources or the educational arms of the companies they serve, but are often motivated or initiated by the successful managers within the company with the objective of passing on their knowledge and experience. The result is the management team creates duplicates of themselves (variously referred to as corporate clones or suits) even though this may not have been the original objective. Nevertheless, the typical corporate training process cranks out managers who are indistinguishable from one another and rarely equipped to think creatively even though they are encouraged *to think out of the box*. However, as most of us know, those managers who take this advice literally and actually do deviate from acceptable thinking and procedures are viewed as mavericks and *loose cannons*, not suited for promotion. Consequently, as the management positions fill with graduates of this program, graduates who think and react in predictable ways, and as those graduates *move up the ladder*, the basic "rightness" of the program is reinforced. The successful graduates all think alike and are successful; therefore, they are reluctant to change the training. After all, "if it ain't broke, don't fix it." Left unchecked this incessant process ultimately creates a corporate culture, which may be successful for a long time. The longer the successes last, the more rigid the culture becomes, and the more difficult it is for the company to meet changing conditions. After all, the Mesozoic Era saw the rise of the dinosaurs. They were hugely successful for millions of years, but in the end they were just dinosaurs, inflexible and unable to change. If left unchecked this cloning process of the corporate managers—the successful corporate culture, and a "we're number one" attitude—ultimately leads to decline. Companies who fail to bring in outside talent or infuse new ideas are at risk of becoming corporate dinosaurs. Actually this is more than just a risk because the world of business is filled with the fossil remains of corporate giants and fossils in the making. It is usually easy to spot these incipient fossils. They move slowly, if at all. They frequently have a policy of "promoting from within," meaning that no new ideas are welcome here. Processes are defined and unchanging because they are unchallenged. Company reorganizations become the corporate version of musical chairs, except no chairs are removed and no new players ever join the game. Meanwhile, the management stoutly maintains that "people are our most important asset" but systematically removes the creative ones who display independence of thought or action. Therefore, the message from dinosaur management is "We want more people just like us." Inbreeding is not healthy in business any more than it is healthy in nature. When you look around and find everything is moving in slow motion, that nothing has changed in years, and that everyone looks alike, you are working for a dinosaur, and a step into the future is probably in order.

On the other hand, the initial training many of us receive starts at the university. Traditional universities focus on single-topic issues such as accounting, organization theory, and communications. These are covered in great detail and ensure that the budding manager is well grounded in the subject. Obviously it is very important that managers are well grounded in the basics. Understanding cost accounting, organizational theory, and communications is important, and the greater the responsibility the more important these things usually become. What are generally lacking at these traditional universities are the reality checks and the interrelationships between these subjects and actual problems. Certainly it can be argued that the role of the university is to teach the basic subjects, not how to apply them, and there is merit in that argument. However, the university has a responsibility to teach *critical thinking* so that students learn to question predetermined answers to universal problems.

Real management problems are almost always a mixture of things ranging from communications to technology, from personnel to politics, and all contain that ever-present *human variable*. Even accounting and engineering problems that appear to be "pure" rarely are. Real problems rarely come in neat packages, are often complex, and frequently require a spectrum of knowledge and experience for resolution, not just knowledge of the topic or discipline, or a rote solution, but the interrelationships with other departments, alternatives, political dimensions, and certainly the financial impact of various solutions. Sometimes these problems can require information on or knowledge of such diverse subjects as history, sociology, or psychology. However, this is not the way training programs are structured or reference material is presented.

Generally, training programs are analytical in nature and structured in such a way that the student arrives at a predetermined "answer." Even when case studies are used, they are frequently constructed so that the "analysis" leads to a "correct" resolution. In real life there are rarely "right" answers and in some cases only "least worst" choices are available, and without that right answer these managers frequently have difficulty finding any answer. Furthermore, it seems as though the more mundane the situation, the more probable the solution alternatives seem trivial, and the less likely the inexperienced manager will react analytically. Yet it is these mundane problems that often impact organizations in the most dramatic and unexpected way. If you have doubts about how trivial decisions and seemingly inconsequential acts can have enormous impact, allow me to provide an actual experience as an example.

Once upon a time a company had an outstanding employee in Harry B. Harry was a brilliant scientist, and his contributions were far greater than his salary. Like many scientific people Harry was motivated more by praise and recognition of his accomplishments than by the salary. Harry thrived on the opportunity to work on complex scientific problems using the best equipment money could buy. Harry enjoyed his work and did not seem to be aware of his worth. However, his superiors recognized that Harry was not just a scientific whiz, he was crucial to the enterprise. Therefore, they regularly gave Harry bonuses, salary adjustments, and frequent one-on-one praise. It was during one of these one-on-one sessions that the Vice President casually mentioned that he was considering awarding company jackets to key employees. Weeks went by, and while the money and praise continued to roll in, the jacket did not. After three months, this very key employee walked in one morning and resigned. His official reason for resigning was he was offered roughly twice his salary by a competitor. Privately, he confided in his colleagues that he really did not want to leave, but he had not received a jacket (total cost: $50). His conclusion was that he was not considered a "key employee" no matter what the Vice President said to him privately. If he were a key employee he would have gotten a jacket, *like everyone else*. Furthermore, the Vice President could not be trusted in Harry's eye, because he made promises that he did not keep, and Harry did not want to work with anyone who lied and did not meet his commitments.

The Vice President was stunned by the resignation. From his perspective he had done everything he could for Harry. He had given Harry a laboratory filled with the latest gadgets. He had sent him to conferences and had given him the freedom to research and reflect. He had provided Harry with thousands of dollars in bonuses and salary. He had heaped praise on him both publicly and privately. He had given Harry anything he asked for. What more could he have done?

Unfortunately, this hapless Vice President did not even remember the comment about the jacket. The fact was, he had never acted on the idea and had never given *anyone* a jacket. Only Harry remembered the comment, which he took as a commitment. When this "commitment" was not fulfilled, he took the failure to give him a jacket as a repudiation of his value as an employee. Because it was obvious that the company did not value him enough to give him the jacket that publicly displayed his value, he felt he had no choice but to resign. To Harry the money and praise were nice, but the jacket was a tangible and visible recognition of his value.

With Harry gone projects began to slip, and customers began to complain. Although no one is irreplaceable, Harry came close, and finding another Harry would be difficult. Clearly the company needed Harry back, so the Vice President asked Harry's former manager to meet with Harry and try to woo him back. Harry's former manager was unaware of the promised jacket or its significance, so when he met with Harry he was astonished that the jacket was even a consideration. He assured Harry that he was a very valued employee and he would have the promised jacket if he would return. Harry came back with a salary increase, but the real factor in his return was the company jacket, which he wore regularly. The fact that many of his colleagues were jealous of his jacket was a bonus. This is an actual example of how a seemingly trivial comment can have vast consequences. The failure to spend $50 on a jacket ultimately cost the company thousands of dollars in late projects and salaries, not counting the impact on customer satisfaction. The fact is that managers are chartered to reward employees for their efforts and that nonmonetary rewards are sometimes more effective than cash. Therefore, managers should be aware that unguarded comments are often interpreted as promises that can lead to costly results if not kept.

In this example the Vice President was an experienced manager, yet in an unguarded moment he made a blunder in personnel management and leadership. Perhaps most employees would not even remember such a casual remark or react so strongly even if it were remembered. Nevertheless, this employee did, and the manager did not take into account the impact that his casual remark would have. Managers with academic training but limited experience are even more susceptible to this type of innocent mistake because they are rarely prepared to deal with ambiguous situations or the human variable. Formal training programs tend to focus on the larger issues, the ones that can be directly measured in finite terms rather than the trivial ones that are ambiguous or considered insignificant. Although the larger issues are very important, the small events can be just as significant and have real impact. This is an aspect of management that is largely unexplored. The small problems, those dealing with cube assignments, time off, and employee recognition, are either ignored by most training programs or discussed only in a generic way. The impact some of these issues might have on the company is rarely measured. Consequently most managers are left to handle the situations as they arise with little or no inkling of the possible ramifications of their decisions. This is painful for all concerned, but it is known universally as "gaining experience," and that is what this book is all about.

2

MANAGERS AND LEADERS

Perhaps it no longer matters how, or even if, managers are trained, because the current trend is to "lead" rather than to "manage." Although it is generally acknowledged that there are differences between these two concepts, what those differences are appears to be generally ignored in the race to convert from the old management paradigm to the new leadership style. The evidence of this trend is all around, and you may not have noticed that leaders are replacing managers at a dizzying pace. It appears that our corporate executives have come to believe that with the stroke of their administrative pen, their unwanted and outdated managers can be magically transformed into that latest and most fashionable organizational trend—*a leader*. It is all so simple. All that is required is to strike the title "manager" from the list of job descriptions and replace it with "leader."

You know how it is. One day you are the department manager—happy as a clam in your little bureaucratic heaven—and the next day you are the "leader" of a new downsized, reengineered, and streamlined team, ready for action and poised to meet the future. As if by magic your department has disappeared, and in its place is this newly constituted team. Of course down in the trenches the new team looks suspiciously like the old department—except smaller. You find that at the stroke of a pen you have been transformed from a manager of resources into a *leader of men* (in the generic sense, of course). But most of us have found in following this metamorphosis that very little has changed. Naturally, the downsizing has left you with a smaller staff, but your responsibilities are the same—well, almost the same—because as the leader you are not only expected to lead this team but also be a part *of the team* (translation: do some work). You and the smaller staff must now do everything you did before plus work more hours to compensate for the reduced staff. Furthermore, as the leader you are expected to lead by example, which means that you have retained all of your old duties, taken on direct responsibilities for certain tasks formerly done by the staff, and added more hours to your work schedule. You find that you not only are doing everything you did before, but you are also an active contributor with tasks of your own. Essentially, as a leader, management has become "an extra duty," something to be done in your spare time as a "background" activity.

This magical transformation of managers to leaders and the associated trimming of "excess" employees is then vividly displayed to the board of directors and stockholders as an example of how the company executives are up-to-date and have the vision necessary to lead the company into the next century. They have eliminated all of those bad old middle managers and their lazy outmoded "B" workers and replaced them with leaders and enthusiastic "A" players. The company is now poised to meet the future head-on—but is it really? (Picture Tess Trueheart tied to the railroad tracks and the future as the oncoming locomotive.) The problem is that changing titles and reducing staff is an age-old management strategy that may have an immediate impact on the bottom line, but without a change in operational methods, it is at best an organizational band-aid. What is required is fundamental structural, cultural, and philosophical change, plus an understanding of the reasons for the changes and a clear vision of the future. The new managers (leaders) must have a clear understanding of how their position has changed and what is expected of them. Without these real changes and an understanding of the impact of the changes, reducing staff and changing titles are merely euphemisms and administrative exercises that may actually hurt the performance of the enterprise more than they help. Therefore, magical transformations of managers to leaders will not work. The new leaders must actually *be* leaders, capable of managing as well as inspiring. This brings us to the very basic question: What distinguishes a leader from a manager?

Now that managers may be found at virtually every level of the corporation, this question takes on much more importance. If there are real differences between managers and leaders, they must be fully understood, because they affect every level of the organization, and the incumbent managers may not have the stuff of leaders. We speak of leadership traits and principles. We talk about managers having *command presence*. We make attempts to distinguish between management and leadership but use the terms interchangeably because the objectives of both appear to be identical. Therefore, the question is: Are they truly different?

Managers

Of course the differences between management and leadership have been a controversy since the concept of "management" was introduced. On the one side are those who believe management is simply a bureaucratic skill that can be acquired by anyone, while "leadership" is a natural trait. On the other side are those who believe that it really does not matter if they are the same or different because both are skills that can be taught, and therefore anyone can be a leader or a manager. There is enough evidence on both sides of this issue to keep the controversy raging as it has for decades.

Before the industrial revolution, "managers" did not even exist. Society was dichotomized into the aristocracy and the lower classes. Those members of society involved in commerce were viewed as "commoners" and money-grubbing merchants neither capable nor worthy of leading. They were men with an eye on the ducat and not on the horizon, unlike the aristocrats, who were genetically programmed for leadership and were leaders by birthright. The aristocrats, due to their nobility, could rise above the demands of ledgers and profits to see the larger picture. I believe it is this dichotomy that lies at the heart of the controversy over leadership and management today. Essentially the controversy centers on the belief that leaders (bluebloods) are born and managers (commoners) are trained. Of course, the French Revolution and the march of history have largely eliminated the aristocrat-versus-commoner dichotomy from meaningful consideration. In fact, one could say the French Revolution vividly demonstrated the inherent risks of leadership. Nevertheless, what remains after the decline of the aristocracy is the residual belief that leaders and managers are different. Leadership continues to be viewed as a natural trait inherent at birth, whereas management skills can be taught to anyone. It is this belief that underlies the focus on management processes and procedures and the association of management with bureaucracy.

What then is a *manager*, and what distinguishes a manager from a leader? Managers are usually viewed as colorless, bloodless bureaucrats who thrive on process and procedure. They are the organizers who, given the objectives and direction, create the plans and processes for every step of the way but seem unable to set the direction or establish the strategy in the first place. Managers are seen as the people who believe that, given the right process, they can use trained monkeys to achieve success. They are the planners who assemble and apply resources but do not motivate or inspire people to action. Managers do not have that aura of electricity and excitement associated with leaders. This is a common view—but is it accurate?

This raises a very basic question: "What precisely does a manager do?" Essentially, management is the process of using people, money, time, and material resources to accomplish the mission and tasks of an organization. This requires the manager to plan, organize, direct, and control these resources. This is the popular view of what a manager does but these concepts are also quite generic and imprecise, which leads us back to the original question: "What does a manager actually do?" As basic as this question is, it really has so many answers that it has no answer at all. Some popular and common roles of managers are:

- Performing the duties necessary for personnel administration
- Mentoring, developing, and training subordinates
- Planning (strategic, resource, marketing, project, etc.)
- Conducting interdepartmental relations
- Establishing and achieving performance goals and objectives for the group
- Monitoring the internal and external situation for changes requiring reaction
- Acting as the spokesperson for subordinates
- Making decisions

Are these the only duties of managers? Certainly not; and at every level there are different ones and even the common ones have variations. For example, at the threshold level of management, we find supervisors, foremen, and similar first-tier managers. At this level the duties tend to be predetermined administrative tasks with a minimal amount of flexibility. The foreman is not expected to establish a vision or objective or to create a strategic plan. Generally, the expectations for a successful foreman are setting an example, keeping employee morale high, and *following orders*. There is little room for judgment or decision-making because the duties are carefully defined as part of a standard job description. It is not a question of "no thinking allowed," but rather none is expected. Nevertheless, the first-tier manager does perform many of the management duties mentioned above; such as, acting as a spokesperson, balancing resources, mentoring, training, and participating in the information bucket brigade.

As you move up the management chain from foreman, to supervisor, to manager, to executive, to CEO, the essential management duties do not vary conceptually. The variations are usually only in the scope and detail. Decisions are made at every management level regarding personnel, resources, plans, and so on, but the latitude of the decision-maker and the impact of the decision grow with each step. Decisions to change direction or deviate from the standard process may be made at the threshold levels, but only if the deviation or change is trivial. Revamping the process or abandoning it entirely is rarely within the scope of the authority of the first-tier manager. But as you move up the management chain, the scope of the manager's authority increases to the point where he or she can determine if the process should be modified or abandoned entirely.

In spite of their critical value to projects and society in general, the names of the great managers of history are largely lost because managers tend to be the "doers" of society rather than the visionaries. Most people realize that the great Pharaoh Cheops did not personally build The Great Pyramid. It may have been his vision but it was thousands of workers, managed by a host of unknown managers, who transformed his vision into reality. The same is true of the Parthenon, the Coliseum, and a host of other instantly recognizable landmarks. On a more contemporary level, most people are at least vaguely aware that film stars do not actually *make* the films they appear in. Somewhere in the background are the producers and directors, who actually manage the resources that produce the film. The actors constitute just one of those resources. However, from time to time these manager/directors also rise to prominence and become more or less visible. Examples of this would be the directors Steven Spielberg, Alfred Hitchcock, and Ingmar Bergman, whose fame may eclipse that of the actors in their films.

In other areas of business we also find managers who become visible, at least for a time. Some examples are Alfred P. Sloan and William Durant, the men who built General Motors, and Frederick Taylor, who created *Scientific Management*. More recently we see names such as Lou Gerstener, Sam Walton, and Ross Perot. Each of these managers has had an impact on our society, although once they become visible they are usually described as leaders. However, only time will determine if these managers are relegated to the footnotes of history like most managers, even though their impact on society is arguably greater than that of many better known people who are destined for the history books as the leaders of society.

Leaders

Perhaps the most distinguishing characteristic between leaders and managers is found in the cliché that "managers do things right while leaders do the right things." However, it should be recognized that stereotypes and clichés such as this exist because they are common and *accurate*. Leaders *are* different from managers in many ways. Leaders have a natural orientation to people, a vision, or far-reaching objective coupled with a strong determination to achieve that objective, and the ability to inspire others to action. From this perspective leadership can be viewed as an art. It is a characteristic that enables the leader to gain the confidence, obedience, loyalty, and respect necessary to accomplish the vision or objective. Leaders invariably have an objective or purpose in mind. Sometimes it is something as trivial as disassembling and reassembling the teacher's car in the gym, and at other times it could be as grand as conquering Europe. It is this *vision* that distinguishes the role of leader from that of manager. It is the *leader* who sees how things *might be* as opposed to how they are. But the vision alone is not enough. Leaders must also have the enthusiasm and drive necessary to convince others to help them achieve their vision. Unlike managers, leaders are usually action oriented, frequently charismatic, and they exude an aura of excitement and electricity that draws others to them like moths to a flame. Leaders have many traits that distinguish them from everyone else. Some of these common leadership traits are initiative, loyalty, and courage, but the ones that stand out are decisiveness and enthusiasm. Although these traits are not guarantees of leadership the absence of them will reduce the effectiveness of the leader. Perhaps the best way to illustrate these leadership qualities is to cite some examples. Certainly the history books are filled with the stories of leaders whose names leap from the pages—names such as John F. Kennedy, George S. Patton, Martin Luther King, Jr., and, more recently, Princess Diana.

John F. Kennedy had charisma and command presence. He was noted for his vision. General Patton was a decisive and inspired leader who set an example and approached everything with enthusiasm. Martin Luther King was a charismatic man of vision who set an example for an entire generation and whose influence lingers still. History books are filled with stories of women who have left an indelible imprint on humankind, but one of the most recent and visible is Princess Diana. She was the type of leader who inspires others through example. She never *asked* anyone to follow her. It was her public dedication to her own interests and beliefs that inspired others to follow her.

Although leaders frequently have grand objectives that are clearly articulated and carefully planned, it is equally common for leaders to have narrow objectives supported by short-range plans and disorganized thinking. These leaders may be less well known, but it is among them that we find cult leaders, entrepreneurs, politicians, the kids down the block who started their own snow removal business, and all too often, unfortunately, gang leaders. Nonetheless, these less distinguished leaders possess the same essential leadership characteristics as their more successful counterparts. What distinguishes them is their lack of long-range planning, organizing, or vision or other *managerial* aspects of leadership.

Although everyone acknowledges that there are leaders in the world and many people are called leaders, it is also commonly known that many so-called leaders are not leaders but figureheads. How can you tell the difference? Obviously this is not easy to do, otherwise the figurehead leader would be ignored. In fact, the figurehead leader may be completely unaware that he or she is a figurehead, but there are factors that indicate that the leader is ineffectual. Foremost among these danger signals is the morale of the unit. Any group, regardless of size, has morale or esprit de corps, which usually reflects the quality of the leadership of the unit. Poor morale is usually characterized by high employee turnover, a lack of attention to detail, sloppy records, bickering, and high absenteeism. A lack of discipline is another characteristic of poor leadership. Usually this lack of discipline is seen in incorrectly applied or ignored processes, violation of dress codes, and a failure to communicate or keep others informed of progress or whereabouts. But perhaps the most telling sign of a figurehead or ineffectual leader is in the overall proficiency of the group. Strong, capable people gravitate to strong, capable leaders. When these people desert a unit or refuse to join the unit, it is almost always a sign that the leader is weak. Over time a unit will reflect the quality of its leadership. A strong, effective leader will build a team of high-quality people because those types of people will want to join the unit, but also because the effective leader will train and mentor them. If a strong leader is replaced by a weak leader, the quality and proficiency of the group will decline as capable people leave and are replaced by weaker ones.

For those of us on the outside, weak or figurehead leaders are usually distinguished as being ineffectual, indecisive, vacillating, and seemingly unaware of the realities. These are certainly not the qualities of a leader, but then what are the characteristics of a leader? Herein lies the problem, because everyone acknowledges that such a thing as *leadership* exists, but there is not a clear consensus on what it is. Leadership is like "quality"; we all know it when we see it but are hard pressed to define it. Although there is no broad concurrence on what leadership is or the characteristics of a leader, the following list represents some possible characteristics of leaders: A leader

- Is creative in ideas and problem solving
- Has a personal style
- Initiates or creates new ideas and approaches
- Focuses on people and is trusted by them
- Inspires people to action
- Has a vision of what could be
- Questions why something should be done
- Challenges authority and the "right way"
- Stands out as an individual

When these characteristics are compared to those of the manager, the distinction between the two becomes clearer. The manager is focused on procedures and meeting the expectations of others. The leader is focused on a vision of an unrealized future and challenges the status quo. Although we might agree on these characteristics, it is unlikely that we could find an individual who embodies all of the characteristics of either a manager or a leader. In actual fact a pure leader is about as rare as a pure manager, and neither probably exists in reality. When we apply these depictions to actual people in real situations it seems apparent that management and leadership are found in different amounts within all individuals and at all levels in the organization.

In fact, as you move up the management chain, the ratio of management-to-leadership skill shifts toward leadership (see Figure 2.1). Management skills are needed more at the lower levels of management, whereas the ratio is heavily weighted toward leadership at the executive level. The important point to note is that neither leadership nor management is 100%, but there is a mix of both at all levels of responsibility.

This does not mean that as one gains leadership or management skills they sacrifice one for the other. What it does mean is that as a person grows in responsibility the amount of leadership required grows proportionately. The need for management ability remains but is reduced in importance.

There are many examples that demonstrate this mixture of management and leadership, but perhaps none is quite as easily observed and understood as that in General George Washington, a remarkable leader and a stunning manager. At the beginning of the Revolutionary War, General Washington was able to assemble a very large army. It could be argued that the soon-to-be Americans were so highly motivated to fight that they would have followed a broomstick dressed up as a soldier. Certainly this newly formed army was motivated to win and would do anything Washington asked. They were facing the British Army, perhaps the greatest fighting force in the world at the time. Incredibly, Washington and these untrained farmers were starting a war with the greatest army in the world with a handful of musket balls and a snuffbox full of powder. At first they acquitted themselves quite well, but as we all know they soon ran out of powder and shot, food, clothes, and shelter. Worse, there was no money to buy these things. The United States did not exist, and even if it did, it was broke. Furthermore, Washington and the other members of the incipient government were viewed by the world powers of the time as little more than a bunch of traitors justifiably about to be hanged by their rightful king. Yet it was through his personal magnetism and raw leadership that Washington managed to keep his little rag-tag army together. He used his personal fortune to pay for supplies and food, nearly bankrupting himself in the process. He was constantly visible, fought shoulder to shoulder with the men, and had more than one horse shot from under him in battle. It was his leadership that kept the Continental Army together. However, behind the scenes Washington was tireless in his pursuit of food, clothing, and equipment. He procured muskets, captured cannons, and got clothes and even uniforms for his men. He enlisted a professional soldier from the Prussian Army, one Baron von

Figure 2.1

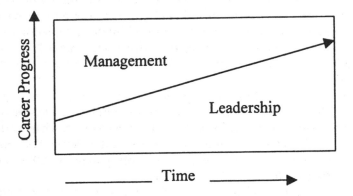

Steuben, to train the Continental Army. Baron von Steuben had trained in the Prussian Army under Frederick the Great, and after the Baron was through with them, the Continental Army was in fact an Army, with discipline, gun drill, and an effective fighting force. Undoubtedly Washington's ability to gather and apply resources, direct efforts and skill sets, and manage all parts of the army to achieve his clear objective speaks well of his management, organizational, and leadership abilities. It is Washington's mix of leadership, vision, and management that formed the foundation of our nation. This is a vivid example of how necessary both leadership and management are to a successful endeavor.

Clearly, to be successful as a manager one must possess some leadership skills, and a successful leader must be able to manage. Management is described as planning, organizing, and directing. Is leadership any different? Every successful leader in history has been an excellent manager or has had the good sense to hire good managers. The fact is, management and leadership are not opposites but simply different sides of the same coin, and like a coin, they cannot be easily divided. Each is required for success. The operative word is "success." The leader and the manager will define success quite differently. For the manager success may be conserving resources, adhering to the plan, conforming to the process, or meeting the objective. For the leader success might be successfully challenging to the plan's objectives, overcoming a competitor, or establishing a new direction.

The problems occur when the leader moves too far from the plan and those he is leading lose track of where they are and what they are doing. In business this usually occurs when a new CEO changes the direction of the company and establishes new strategies without clearly explaining them to his subordinates. Because the vision of the CEO is not clearly articulated, it is not clearly understood by those expected to create it. In their attempts to interpret the vision and direction, the subordinates of the CEO begin to wander off in different directions and establish conflicting objectives. Ultimately the new program and the new direction are a failure, but the failure is actually a failure in leadership triggered by a failure in communications. Leaders are characterized by their ability to conceive a vision of the future and to inspire others to help in the achievement of that vision. However, if the leader fails to communicate that vision to others in a clear and concise manner then the enthusiasm wanes, the followers become confused, and the project fails.

For managers, success might be viewed as attaining the objective, even if it is the wrong objective. Following the plan is seen as paramount, and its timely completion is viewed as "success." These are the managers who become too focused on the process or the plan. This type of manager is seen as pedantic, inflexible, and bureaucratic. All of us have had managers like this. They are the ones who will follow a process or plan with a religious fervor even after the oncoming failure becomes apparent. They lose track of the objective, even if they were originally aware of it, and substitute process and procedure. When the inevitable failure occurs they are always ready with the excuse that they followed the process *exactly* as described, and therefore they are not culpable for the failure. They whine, "I was not the one who failed; it was the process." They use the process and procedures as a shield to deflect criticism and personal accountability.

On the other hand, leaders who are overenthusiastic and too focused on the vision become inefficient, unpredictable, and independent. This type of leader is found in all organizations, but fortunately there are usually not too many of them. All of us have encountered these leaders and at one time or another may have been involved with their hare-brained schemes. These are the leaders whose solution to punctuality is to reduce the number of spaces in the parking lot to less than the number of employees, thereby ensuring that people will arrive earlier to get a parking space. Not only does this visionary leader believe in the validity of this idea, but he is able to convince others. The leader and his adherents are so enthusiastic over this solution to the attendance problem that they convince a large portion of the management team of its merits. Eventually this scheme, accompanied by all of the appropriate business analyses, reaches a manager with enough common sense to see beyond the enthusiasm of the leader, and it dies. Interestingly enough, when this happens the leader that created the scheme is usually seen as the victim of a bureaucratic manager without vision or creativity; but, in fact, this leader was a visionary with no practical managerial skill.

For success, there must be a balance between the discipline associated with management and the inspiration brought by the leader. The resources must be organized in such a way that they can be brought to bear on the problem, but the employees must be inspired to work diligently to make it succeed. Plans and processes must be identified and put in place so that the objectives can be accomplished with efficiency. Once the fundamental structure is in place, the staff must be made aware of the objective, motivated to overcome all obstacles, and prepared to respond to changing circumstances. This delicate balance illustrated in Figure 2.2 is the cornerstone of success.

Managing and/or leading is an art, not a science. Techniques, processes, and methodologies can be taught, but in the final analysis, it is how these are applied that counts. Every manager or leader has a "style," and it is this style that ultimately makes the difference, just as it is with an artist, athlete, or musician. Knowing how to play the piano does not automatically make one a concert pianist. And, not all concert pianists are "great." The same is true of managers and leaders. Knowing the mechanics is important, but how they are applied is everything. Contrast Generals Eisenhower and Patton. Which was the manager and which the leader? Both were effective generals, and each rightfully earned a place in the history books, yet it is the "style" of Patton that distinguishes him as a leader and raises him above the pack. General Eisenhower is credited with orchestrating D-Day and the invasion of Europe. He is viewed as a good general, but I think few would categorize him as a great leader, not because his contributions were fewer than Patton's, but because he lacked the flamboyance and personal style of Patton. No pearl-handled revolvers, no frontline presence, and no charisma—just plodding efficiency and diplomatic skill. Although Patton's defeat of Rommel and the Afrika Corps was dazzling, in the final analysis the conquest of the Third Reich as orchestrated by Eisenhower was significantly more important. Both of these generals were graduates of West Point, where they received the same training in military science and leadership. Yet one emerged as a charismatic leader and brilliant tactician, and the other became a strategist with strong political skills. Perhaps this, as much as anything, demonstrates how leadership is more of an art form than a scientific process.

During his term of office, President Truman was viewed by many as a "party hack," an ignorant bumpkin controlled by a political machine. Many at the time believed his decisions were based on raw politics and were without merit. Yet today President Truman is viewed as one of the great Presidents, a decisive man of vision. What sets President Truman apart from the other capable men who have held the office of President of the United States? Certainly not his political contributions, which were considerable but not beyond what many other Presidents have accomplished. What set President Truman apart was his "the buck stops here" style. His willingness to take responsibility, make decisions, and do what was right, not what was popular, formed the foundation of the Truman "style."

Another more contemporary example of management and leadership is the highly public clash between Ross Perot and Roger Smith, the CEO of General Motors (GM) at the time. Roger Smith was a good executive. He had spent his entire career at GM, climbing the ladder rung by rung. He followed all of the rules, which at GM meant "don't rock the boat." At GM

Figure 2.2

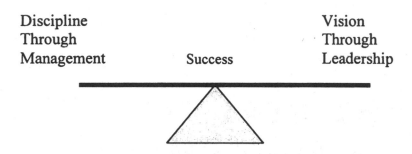

changes and decisions are to be avoided altogether or made slowly when unavoidable. Smith had all of the characteristics of a successful GM manager. By contrast, Ross Perot was an entrepreneur accustomed to making decisions without benefit of thought or analysis beyond his own. Every flaw Ross Perot saw he shouted from the rooftops and demanded instant fixes. He was charismatic with a "take no prisoners" leadership style. The result of this confrontation between the management style of Roger Smith and the leadership style of Ross Perot is well known because the battle was front-page news. But who won? I submit that it was a loss all around. GM needed change and failed to get it. Perot, who had the potential to be a marvelous change agent, wandered off into other activities and slowly changed from charismatic leader to eccentric.

These examples are not intended to say that style is either more or less important than substance but rather to demonstrate that neither is enough to achieve success. Those individuals who achieve greatness have a combination of these skills. Ultimately, the difference between a leader and a manager may be the willingness to take responsibility for failures and the willingness to share successes. Many people are willing to make decisions and assume responsibility, especially if there is little chance of failure, but few are willing to assume responsibility for failure. The history revisionists continue to assert that President Truman did not have to drop the atomic bomb and that this was an expedient but unnecessary way to end the war. Whether that is true or not is arguable, but President Truman never made any attempt to dodge, share, or excuse his decision in any way, and that is what distinguishes him as a leader. This character trait is virtually unheard of among politicians and rare in most corporations.

Most corporate executives cannot tolerate failure or even the hint of failure. Managers associated with even a small failure are often viewed with suspicion and considered to be lacking in the "success qualities" so necessary for promotion. Consequently, most corporations are filled with managers who sidestep, equivocate, and avoid any decision for fear of failure and the associated consequences. These are the garden-variety managers, who attempt to operate in an error-free environment rarely making decisions of any kind. They form committees, examine issues excessively, focus on details, develop models, initiate activities, and leave prior to completion *or blame*. All of us have encountered these managers. Indeed they may be the smart ones, because frequently they are the ones who rise to the top. After all, they have never made a mistake, they are politically correct, and their track record is a string of unblemished successful starts, so who would not promote them? However, often their subordinates would describe these same managers as risk adverse, empty suits taking credit for other people's work. Of course not all of these managers become CEOs, but corporations do seem to breed managers who are cautious and unwilling to take action, make a decision, or take a risk for fear of making a mistake. Therefore, is it any wonder that we commonly find corporate managers constantly looking for more facts, more data, and more time? Time for consultants to review matters, time to create study groups, and time to get a "consensus." The objective is to ensure that the decision cannot be attributed to a "bad judgment call" on the part of one manager and that the risk of a bad decision is shared.

Whether this observation is true or not and whether decisions should be noncontroversial or not, they should not be premature. They must be timely and they must be clear. Indecision and equivocation lead inexorably to failure. The manager who waits for certainty will assuredly be overtaken by events. The trick is not only to make the decision at the "proper" time, but to accurately determine when that time is. Because most decisions are made without having all of the facts, all decisions by definition carry risk. The leader must learn to identify the amount of risk and how it can be minimized while making the decision at the proper time. This is what transforms decision-making from a rote mechanical process to an art form, and it constitutes another characteristic that distinguishes the leader from the manager. Many think of this as style or technique; personally I think of it as courage. Nevertheless, decision-making and risk-assessment are generally viewed as technique and, like all techniques, some do it well, some not so well, and practice always improves it.

It is this quest for the one special management technique that will ensure success that has led to the seemingly never-ending supply of management theories. Each of these, in their own way, contains a grain of truth, yet to date none have provided all of the answers. These various theories and techniques can be compared to a series of musical instruments. Each has a unique style and ability, but when taken together and used as part of a larger activity, they develop a synergy that transcends their individual contributions. This is very much like the real-life management scenario that many of us face every day.

Every management problem in its own way is complex because it is interrelated to all other problems faced by the manager and the company.

Therefore, simple decisions such as whether to give a salary increase or not have ramifications that ripple far beyond the individuals involved. The same is true of budgets, schedules, training, and even the way a decision is made and delivered. To be effective as both a leader and a manager, the leader must be prepared to use the appropriate management or leadership skill for the situation. Because each of the situations is unique, the mix of technique, theory, and style varies as well. It is this variability that is missing from most of the theories, courses, and training programs. Instead, the perpetual quest for the "right" process or "best" technique goes on. Everyone seems to be seeking the Magic Bullet.

3

MAGIC BULLETS

How to manage and lead effectively has been the subject of many books and articles. Academics have labored over this question, managers have documented their experiences, and droves of consultants have coached from the sidelines. Yet this question remains open, and a visit to any bookstore reveals shelf after shelf of books devoted to this subject. Why is this the case? After all of these years of research and experience, why do we not know how to manage and lead effectively? These are not new concepts. After all, management and leadership began with the first organized hunting party.

Visualize the tribe sitting around the campfire discussing the urgent need for mammoth steaks. Everyone agrees that Og is the best and most experienced hunter and therefore the logical one to lead the hunt. After a few successful hunts, everyone agrees that Og should get the best mammoth steaks as a reward for his knowledge and expertise. After a while the discussion phase is gradually abandoned, and Og is simply accepted as the leader and the one entitled to the best steaks. Accepted, that is, until Nog decides that he is bigger, stronger, and just as good a hunter, and as a result he is more entitled to the big steaks. After a discussion involving a few cuffs and bruises and a final "bonk" to Og's head, the tribe has a new leader and the first formal transition of power has occurred. It is now Nog who organizes the hunt, gives the orders, and takes the best cuts of meat. Thus with this primordial "conk" on the head, Nog has placed mankind squarely on the road to civilization, and the foundation of Theory X management has been laid.

As people became more civilized, the need for leaders and subordinate leaders became acute. Gradually, civilized society stratified into the leaders (aristocrats) and the followers (commoners). With some refinements, this has been the basic model for civilization ever since. Armies were organized this way, as were governments and society as a whole. Leadership became hereditary, and the common folk accepted the yoke as their lot in life. Kings ruled by "divine right," meaning that their superior position was ordained by God and a failure to follow their orders was not only treason, it was a violation of God's orders. All law, and thinking in general, was done by the king and his appointees, while the peasants did the work. This hierarchical model was especially valued by the aristocrats, and it lasted until the commoners began to realize that they did all of the work but the aristocrats still got all of the steaks.

As humankind teetered on the brink of the industrial revolution, the common people began to question the need for hereditary leaders who took from them but did not provide anything in return. This question was a revolutionary realization because it triggered a shift in attitudes that reached its peak when the French people dispensed with their superfluous leaders and heads of society in an impressive display of efficiency and dispatch called the French Revolution.

This rather labored and pedantic analogy highlights several fundamentals that cannot be ignored when evaluating management, leadership, and organizations. Perhaps the most fundamental of these is the need for a leader and the hierarchical structure that is inherent in all organizations, even the most enlightened. It can be argued that this is a natural and necessary structure, because it reflects the way most societies operate—not just human societies, but those of the animal kingdom as well. Universally there is a dominant personality or ranking with the majority following. This is really the point of the analogy. From the outset of civilization, humankind has organized itself into hierarchical structures with very specific rules of conduct. Human organizations require a central authority, even when those being ruled delegate it. The problem arises when those in power believe they have a "right" to power because they are superior by birth to those about them. Even after thousands of years, humankind is yet to totally overcome this belief that some are born to lead, but at least the hereditary power of the aristocracy has been erased. Although their titles remain, aristocrats are largely viewed as quaint historical anachronisms.

I am confident that an anthropologist can explain the rise and fall of the aristocracy, but the relevant point is that their decline into irrelevance simply brought us full circle. Once again the Ogs and Nogs of society are free to assert their leadership on the basis of their ability, power, and contribution.

The difference is they are now called managers, executives, team leaders, entrepreneurs, and a zillion other titles that separate them from the herd, which establishes their authority and position in the pecking order of society. The French Revolution was intended to establish an egalitarian society but, alas, that was not to be. Regardless of what we wish, all people are not created equal. Attempts to establish an egalitarian society have consistently deteriorated into dictatorships. The French Revolution collapsed into anarchy and gave rise to Napoleon. The Russian Revolution eroded into dictatorship under Stalin. Egalitarianism does not seem to fit human nature, and hierarchies are always present, even if disguised. However, as George Orwell said in his book *Animal Farm*, some animals are more equal than others. This brings us to one of the most fundamental management theories. Actually, it is not so much of a theory as a description of the then status quo.

THEORY X

The simplest explanation of Douglas McGregor's Theory X involves the concept of "authoritarianism," in which there is a central figure giving orders to everyone else. This authority figure may be a tribal chief, a mighty king, a boss or even a foreman. The title is irrelevant because all of these are really the same position with differing scopes of authority but with the common denominator of power over others. However, it is not this power over others that distinguishes Theory X from other management theories. Rather, Theory X describes the way in which that power over others is exercised.

The strident and often cruel management style characteristic of industry in the nineteenth century carried over into the twentieth. Workers were viewed by the managers as a lazy, shiftless lot, ignorant, unwilling to learn, and hired only to serve the owners ("capitalists" in Marxist Theory). They served at the discretion of the owner or "bosses," whose authority was unquestioned. As we have seen, this form of authoritarian leadership is rooted in classism, and the roots are deep. It was this class-based authoritarian management style that gave rise to Marxism and ultimately to the union movement and organized labor. It was this class orientation that formed the division between "labor" and "management" and laid the foundation for the animosity and mistrust that characterizes their relationship even today. Although this authoritarian management style began to soften with the advent of unions, it was still very prevalent following World War II.

Ironically, it was this class-based authoritarian management style that Douglas McGregor attempted to change when he assumed leadership of Antioch College in 1948.[1] Prior to this, McGregor was a professor of psychology at the Massachusetts Institute of Technology (MIT). McGregor was appalled at how the managers at the time treated their employees. There was no trust on either side. Managers assumed the employees were lazy and shiftless, while the employees viewed managers as evil and exploitive. As a psychologist, McGregor came to believe that these attitudes were not based on reality. He concluded that employees truly wanted to do a good job, and if they were given a chance they would. This opinion was arrived at through his experience and study of psychology rather than management or leadership. Even though he had never managed anything, he came to believe that a leader could operate successfully as an "adviser" and that being "boss" was unnecessary. He believed in the innate goodness of people and their desire to work and achieve.

In any case, McGregor thought that good "human relations" would eliminate discord and disagreement and that decisions should and could be arrived at collectively. He was not the first "leader" to believe in the innate goodness of man or that the exercise of authority and the responsibility associated with it could be avoided. History is filled with descriptions of weak kings, failed generals, and lost empires owing to the inability of the "leaders" to take charge. Perhaps McGregor opted to read *Pollyanna* at the university rather than *The Decline and Fall of the Roman Empire*.

As the President of Antioch University, McGregor attempted to implement his theories of management and avoided exercising his authority as decision-maker, but his tenure was characterized by bickering, indecision, and little accomplishment. To his credit, after a few years in his position as university president, McGregor came to the (by then obvious) conclusion that a leader cannot avoid the exercise of authority. On the basis of empirical evidence, he concluded that someone must make decisions and take responsibility for what happens. This train of thought led him to examine how managers in general viewed their workers, and ultimately he came to the conclusion that managers made certain assumptions about the workers. The first set of assumptions he examined he described as Theory X. These assumptions represented the traditional view of the "command and control" or authoritarian management style that was prevalent at the time. The fundamental assumptions of Theory X were:

1. The average human being has an inherent dislike of work and will avoid it if he can.
2. Because of this human characteristic of dislike of work, most people must be coerced, controlled, directed, or threatened with punishment to get them to put forth adequate effort toward the achievement of organizational objectives.
3. The average human being prefers to be directed, wishes to avoid responsibility, has relatively little ambition, and wants security above all.[2]

McGregor believed these assumptions reflected the prevailing views of management at the time (1960), even though they were not articulated in any formal document or philosophy. Anyone who has had contact with the automotive industry or the union movement can attest that McGregor's conclusions were not only accurate but this management philosophy is still in existence today. Therefore, Theory X describes an attitude about workers that drives an authoritarian conduct based on the belief that the boss is "above" the worker in education and class and therefore entitled to privilege and command. Furthermore, the underlying assumption is that the worker is less intelligent and of a lower class so the boss must coerce the unwilling worker through threats and motivate through punishment. Essentially this management style has characterized virtually every human organization since the beginning of time. It is classism or elitism at its clearest.

However, to be fair, I must say that as the twentieth century draws to a close, this management style and the antagonistic schism between management and labor do appear to be softening. The authoritarian style associated with Theory X has fallen into disfavor, and alternative management styles are being tried. Nevertheless, the basic conclusion reached by Douglas McGregor, that someone has to make decisions and take responsibility, is still valid. Regardless of the style of management selected, there must be a leader or decision-maker to take responsibility for whatever happens. Consensus management simply does not work as a management style. It is time consuming, slow to reach decisions or respond to changes, and generally yields the poor results that McGregor observed.

Thus, Theory X is more of a description of actual management *practice* than a recommended way of managing. McGregor felt the authoritarian style of management that has characterized virtually every human endeavor since the beginning of civilization was inherently wrong, even though it was effective. Wrong not only from a moral standpoint, because it allowed the privileged few to rule over others, but wrong from the perspective of business as well. Because Theory X rests on a negative foundation that workers are neither motivated nor inclined to do a good job, McGregor concluded that the authoritarian style would not provide maximum worker output. He looked for a better way.

THEORY X—REVISITED

Before we move on to McGregor's better way, it may be worthwhile to note that Theory X is neither "dead" nor intrinsically "bad." There are human endeavors where the authoritarian leadership style is certainly useful and may even be the best way. For example, this authoritarian leadership style has been the foundation of armies since their inception. This is because it works and more democratic leadership styles do not. In times of emergency or crisis, it is necessary for the group to immediately react as a unit with the common purpose of self-preservation. It has repeatedly been demonstrated that armies must have discipline, purpose, direction, and cohesiveness. These qualities are best achieved through unquestioned authority, and frequently this authority rests on fear or at least the understanding that unpleasant consequences will follow disobedience. It is highly unlikely the military will ever give up Theory X leadership, nor should they.

Nevertheless, Theory X leadership is certainly on the wane outside of the military or paramilitary-type organizations. Although this authoritarian management is virtually as old as humankind, Douglas McGregor first formally described it as a management theory in 1963. Essentially, it was a description of the way things were and was intended as a contrast to Theory Y, which he felt was a much better method of managing. Whereas the Theory X manager functions like a warlord, the Theory Y manager is more like Mr. Rogers.

THEORY Y

Although McGregor learned the hard way that human organizations require hierarchy and a decision-maker, he did not abandon his belief in a better way. He followed what he believed to be the description of the then current management philosophy (Theory X) with what he hoped would be a new style of management. He believed that if management created conditions in which the members of the organization could achieve their personal goals best by directing their efforts toward the success of the enterprise, managers would not have to closely supervise or control the work environment. The new management style that he proposed called for the integration of individual and organizational goals. This new approach to management he called Theory Y, and its basic assumptions are:

1. The expenditure of physical and mental effort in work is as natural as play or rest. The average human being does not inherently dislike work.

2. External control and the threat of punishment are not the only means for bringing about effort toward organizational objectives. People will exercise self-direction and self-control in the service of objectives to which they are committed.

3. Commitment to objectives is a function of the rewards associated with their achievement. The most significant of such rewards, that is, the satisfaction of ego and self-actualization needs, can be direct products of effort directed toward organizational objectives.

4. The average human being learns, under proper conditions, not only to accept but also to seek responsibility. Avoidance of responsibility, lack of ambition, and emphasis on security are generally consequences of experience, not inherent human characteristics.

5. The capacity to exercise a relatively high degree of imagination, ingenuity, and creativity in the solution of organizational problems is widely, not narrowly, distributed in the population.

6. Under the conditions of modern industrial life, the intellectual potential-
   ities of the average human being are only partially utilized.[3,4]

When McGregor postulated Theory Y, it was a radical view of both the
worker and the manager. Essentially, the Theory Y view of the worker was
the opposite view of Theory X. It called on the manager to view the worker
in a completely different light and to conduct himself in a completely new
way. Thus, Theory Y began to close the gap between management and
labor because it called for them to establish a level of trust and belief in each
other. This was a humanitarian view of management, and McGregor
believed that managers who put faith in their subordinates, by exercising
less control and actually encouraging self-control, would encourage the
workers to be committed to the organizational goals of the enterprise
because this would enable them to achieve their own goals. Interestingly
enough, in his Theory Y McGregor did not redefine management with similar "good" qualities or intentions or how the worker views the manager.
Presumably McGregor felt the manager already possessed this commitment
to the company and its goals. Whether or not the workers would change
their perceptions of managers is not addressed.

This was the first step toward a new management style—one based on the
assumption that workers wanted to work and could be trusted to work without being closely watched. In essence, both Theory X and Theory Y rest on
the assumption that the way people react is largely a reflection of how they
are treated. Therefore, if the manager assumes the workers are a lazy, shiftless bunch that cannot be trusted, that is the type of workers he or she will
have. In effect the workers have risen (sunk?) to his level of expectation.
Conversely, if the Theory Y manager assumes that people want interesting
and challenging work and provides this through individual discretion and
increased responsibility, then those are the types of workers he will have.
Therefore, managers create the type of workforce they have through their
assumptions and actions.

It is worth noting that while Theory Y increases the autonomy and
responsibility of the worker, the central leadership function is retained
through implication. This is true of the hierarchical structure as well, but
the authoritarian "command and control" model is replaced by "worker
participation." With the introduction of Theory Y, the focus shifted from
how to improve worker productivity through negative reinforcement, to
productivity increases through positive reinforcement and worker participation. Suddenly managers were asking workers rather than telling them.
Direct orders were replaced with discussion and consensus decisions. This
shift away from the strict authoritarian style in Theory X and toward the
softer, more human Theory Y style did not produce the anticipated effect.
Relations between management and labor did improve and so did morale,
but the decision cycle increased. Unfortunately, the increase in the decision
cycle was not the only drawback. One of the underlying premises of Theory

X was that workers would not assume responsibility and that they desired security above all. Not surprisingly, attempts to implement Theory Y highlighted the accuracy of this Theory X assumption.

THEORY Y—REVISITED

In corporate America managers who are associated with failures are viewed with suspicion and generally cast aside in favor of those associated with successful projects. For the aspiring executive, Theory Y and its participative approach was a godsend. Bad decisions could be hidden from view, or at least pushed off onto the shoulders of others, while good decisions could be easily claimed. In the worst case, decisions could be delayed until the "correct" answer became obvious. What a marvelous management style for the up-and-coming executive motivated by personal advantage.

Each of us has worked with managers and executives who have risen to power by never making a mistake, taking a risk, or making a decision. These are the anointed of corporate America. Participative management provided a haven for these fast-track executives who did not want to assume responsibility for their actions or decisions. With Theory Y it was virtually impossible to determine who was responsible for anything. In good times it was everyone, and in bad times it was no one.

It seems ironic that the Theory Y management style described by McGregor was unsuccessful when he attempted to implement it at Antioch College, yet when it was formally described as Theory Y it achieved credibility. Presumably his academic credentials as a professor at MIT outweighed his limited management experience as the President of Antioch College. For whatever reason, others attempted to implement this participative management style and had little more success than did McGregor. In practice, problems were discussed endlessly, frequently without any conclusion. Decisions were either not made at all or they were made in exasperation by the leader/manager. Decisions, when they came, were usually late. Managers who attempted to use Theory Y in its pure form usually ended up longing for the return of monarchy, or at least a return to the bad old days of Theory X.

The fact that Theory Y received such widespread acceptance leads to the conclusion that McGregor's failure was apparently attributed to his lack of experience rather than any flaw in the theory. Regardless, Theory Y, the first of many "Magic Bullets" intended to improve productivity through simple management techniques, turned out to be a blank round.

MANAGEMENT BY OBJECTIVES

Management by objectives (MBO) is a goal-setting process. The term was coined by Peter Drucker. It can be viewed as an extension to Theory Y, because it assumes that people have a desire for competence and achievement in their work and they will strive harder and perform better if they participate in setting their goals (objectives). George Odiorne (a leading MBO consultant) defines MBO as:

A process whereby the superior and subordinate managers of an organization jointly identify its common goals, define each individual's major areas of responsibility in terms of results expected, and use these measures as guides for operating the unit and assessing the contribution of each of its members.[5]

The intent is to involve workers in integrating their goals with the objectives of the enterprise while establishing a basis for measuring individual performance. It requires the manager to work with subordinates to establish objectives and responsibilities. Essentially this is a simple process that can be viewed as a feedback loop consisting of these simple steps.

1. Establish overall corporate goals and responsibilities
2. Meet with individuals to set objectives and establish action plans
3. Conduct periodic appraisals and check on progress toward objectives
4. Adjust action plans to accommodate any changes
5. Evaluate the final result

At first glance, MBO is deceptively simple and seems like an excellent way to establish direction, involve and motivate the worker, and provide an objective measurement of performance. Essentially it is just basic project management, yet MBO is not widely used today and is generally regarded as another interesting, but not especially effective, management technique. Like so many management theories and fads, it sounds a great deal better in the classroom and reads a great deal better in a book than it works in practice.

MBO came on the heels of Theory Y and was immediately implemented by the leading-edge thinkers (read: "fad-prone") as a way of adding rigor to Theory Y. With MBO we "participated" and "involved" one another in establishing goals and objectives. Once the action plans were formulated, all that was required of the manager was to sit back and monitor progress. Alas, life has a way of ruining some perfectly good ideas, and it did not take long for the fundamental flaw in MBO to rear its ugly head. Ever since Copernicus shattered the medieval view of a static and unchanging universe, nothing has been the same. Apparently, the management theorists behind MBO did not attend class that day, because MBO relies on a static or steady-state environment. This means budgets are fixed, no one resigns, objectives do not change, corporate goals are steady, and all that is required is a lockstep march into the future. Unfortunately, as many of us know, nothing is ever that simple. Budgets get reduced, travel restricted, suppliers fail, people get sick or resign, executives are replaced, and directions change. All of these things and more can occur within the planning horizon. The result is the action plans are in a constant state of change so progress becomes virtually impossible to measure. For the fast-track manager, MBO is a great management tool because it gives the appearance of a rigorous and objective measure of performance while providing a myriad of reasons for excusing failure. These are the observations of a pragmatist, but even the theorists quickly concluded MBO had a few problems in implementation.

Establishing an MBO program requires a top-down approach with the involvement of senior management, which is not always present. Even when senior management is committed to MBO it requires a great deal of time to establish the objectives and then track the process. Furthermore, the people being measured strive to reduce the objectives to those that are easily attained (remember Theory X assumptions), thereby forcing the senior person to pressure the junior for "more realistic" objectives. This then raises the question: Is the process truly participative or are the objectives being established by senior management, and the process is simply a sham? As important as these criticisms are there still remains a fatal flaw.

Once objectives are established and action plans are approved, those being measured almost always exclusively focus on the objectives, especially if these are tied to monetary incentives. The natural reaction to this startling observation is "of course, that is what MBO is all about." In practice, though, this creates significant problems. In effect, "I was hired to paint the barn, not repair it." Therefore, in the dash to meet or exceed objectives, critical factors may be ignored because they were not included in the original plan and are therefore "out of scope." This is an attitude that is most often associated with teenagers and household chores (you didn't say vacuum under the bed too), but it is also the attitude created by MBO, which establishes a reward-based focus that does not encourage the employee to look beyond his immediate responsibilities or objectives. Consequently, as a Magic Bullet for management, MBO was a misfire.

THEORY Z

Following on the heels of Theory X and Theory Y came Theory Z. As American dominance of world markets began to decline, American managers began to feel the heat from the "Rising Sun." One by one the Japanese gobbled up many American businesses, while others suffered significant erosion of market share or were put out of business altogether. American managers were stunned. Clearly the Japanese had a better way of managing, and if America was to survive we had to find their secret and duplicate it. Suddenly every consultant and academic in the Western world seemed to be winging their way across the Pacific to discover the "secret" of the Japanese success. On their return we were assured that Japanese management techniques were so superior that American business was in jeopardy and the American management style was obsolete. The conclusion was that if America had any hope of retaining even a small market share it was contingent upon American managers adopting the Japanese management techniques. The bookstores were flooded with books extolling the superiority of the Japanese management style. Lifetime employment, just-in-time manufacturing, virtual enterprises, and a host of similar concepts came flooding into American managers from the returning academics and consultants.

It has always been rather amazing how hard-headed American businesspeople cannot resist the fads and schemes of individuals with many letters after their names but few accomplishments under their belts. This is not to say that the Japanese had nothing to offer, but there seemed to be little analysis and evaluation of their techniques. For example, lifetime employment was viewed as one of the strengths of Japanese management. Hardly anyone bothered to analyze the value of lifetime employment or to determine that it had not improved productivity where it was employed. In fact, it could be argued that lifetime employment could result in lower productivity because what would be the motivation to work harder? This lack of analysis was true for just-in-time manufacturing, keiretsu (supplier networks), quality circles, consensus management, and so on. All of these had value but none were magic and none could be employed as they had been in Japan. For example, JIT (just-in-time) manufacturing works well in Japan and has been adopted in the United States, but the geographical scope of the United States places restrictions on JIT that do not exist in Japan. In Japan the distance between supplier and factory averages less than 50 miles, but in the United States the suppliers may be over 1,000 miles away from the factory.

In Japan the workforce has a high percentage of temporary workers who are not protected by the famed *lifetime employment* characteristic of Japanese firms. These temporary workers (largely women) are used as a resource buffer that enables lifetime employment to exist. Although temporary workers are used in the United States, they are not used to the same degree as they are in Japan. Another aspect of the Japanese model that cannot be duplicated in the United States is the famed keiretsu of Japan. These cannot be duplicated in the United States because of legal restrictions as well as cultural differences. Consensus management as practiced in Japan is really a variation of Theory Y and suffers from the same strengths and weaknesses. This is not to say that these techniques do not work in the United States, just that they do not work as well, and many times they cannot be used in the same way as they are in Japan. It took some time before these shortcomings became obvious. After all, at the time the Japanese were hugely successful and seemed to have discovered the secret to effortless management. However, not everyone was blinded by the Rising Sun, and some even began to look critically at the Japanese management style. It was against this

backdrop that Dr. William Ouichi of Stanford University[6] described Theory
Z. Essentially, Theory Z is a critical examination of the Japanese management model, the purpose of which was to determine what could be adapted
to American industry.

The conclusion reached by Dr. Ouichi was that much in the Japanese
model could be utilized by American industry, but not without difficulty.
The basic problem is cultural. Much of the Japanese management style
and success lies in the culture of the Japanese people. For example, Dr.
Ouichi points out that the basis for the Japanese management success is
trust, which is lacking in the Western model. In the Western model, the
relationship between the workers and management is one of mistrust. The
workers feel threatened by automation, new techniques, or efforts to
improve productivity and generally view any change as a threat to their
job security. In the Japanese model, the trust described by Dr. Ouichi is
based on the commitment of the company to lifetime employment. There
is an *understanding* between the workers and the management that the
worker will not be laid off, regardless of the conditions, whereas the temporary workers (mostly women) understand they are expendable.
Therefore, in Theory Z, the first step toward increasing quality and productivity is a recognition by the employees that they are a crucial part of
the enterprise with a vested interest in its success. This means that the
management team must modify its behavior to accept that the workers are
inherently dedicated to the success of the enterprise and can be trusted to
act responsibly. Precisely how this is accomplished is not exactly clear,
although the fundamental premise of Theory Z is that involved workers
are the key to increased productivity.

Another aspect of Theory Z management is its focus on teamwork and
flexibility. This flexibility rests on nonspecialized career paths common in
Japanese firms. Typically, a young professional will have a wide variety of
jobs and responsibilities within the Japanese firm. The result is a team of
generalists with some level of knowledge of most aspects of the enterprise.
This approach has several advantages. Not only does it allow a career path
with several promotions (mostly lateral); it also provides greater productivity. This productivity is achieved through time saved by not having to seek
outside advice or support on a problem. Either the person already has the
knowledge or some other person on the team does.

Perhaps one of the most striking differences between the American and
Japanese management styles is how "objectives" are viewed. In the
American management style the objective is visible, quantifiable, or measurable. These objectives are usually agreed on between managers, organizations, or the responsible parties. They represent the criteria for the
measurement of success. Theory Z, resting on the Japanese view, does not
see objectives in the same way. Theory Z managers are expected to understand the company and its philosophy, and, armed with this understanding,

they are expected to establish their own objectives, with success being measured against overall attainment of the corporate philosophy. Growth and success may be measured in terms of customer satisfaction, financial growth, volume of new business, and so on. However, the key is that these criteria are virtually never handed down from above as quantified objectives, but objectives are established by each manager based on his or her interpretation of the corporate philosophy.

An example of the difference between the Japanese and American perspective of objectives is the view of "quality." For an American, a target of x defects per quantity is a perfectly logical statement. Every American knows the objective is to have zero defects, and the x number is the limit. Anything above this number is unacceptable performance. To the Japanese mind, no defect is acceptable and to even express a tolerance for a defect is unacceptable. They view the zero limit as a target and believe the Americans are actually *trying* to achieve x defects. In actual practice the American limit might represent not only a realistic level of performance but one superior to that attained by the Japanese. This is a cultural matter and illustrative of the difficulties in attempting to move style and technique across cultural boundaries.

Although there is much to commend in Theory Z, as a management style it has never achieved widespread acceptance. The underlying philosophy is sound and segments of Theory Z have been adopted, but as a general management practice it has met its Darwinian fate of extinction. As a Magic Bullet, Theory Z turned out to be the wrong caliber.

MATRIX MANAGEMENT

One of the most popular and enduring management forms is *Matrix Management*. This is actually more of an organizational form than a management style, but to be successful it does require special management techniques. Essentially this is a management form created either by or for schizophrenics. It is a project structure imposed on a functional organization, or perhaps it is a functional structure supporting a project organization. It really does not matter, because in either case the workers hear voices telling them to do things that may be in conflict. Each voice assures them that they are the boss and must be obeyed. This management technique, although popular, is not for the faint of heart.

In this management structure, the workers have several managers, and virtually none of the classic organizational principles apply. There are many leaders, differing objectives, divided loyalties, no clear command chain, and a great deal of stress. Nevertheless, this is a very effective management style for project-oriented companies. Matrix Management was pioneered by the aerospace companies and has been used very successfully in many government projects. Since its introduction, it has been adopted by construction firms and other companies that provide ad hoc support or project-oriented deliverables.

With Matrix Management there are actually two management structures, each requiring different skills. There are managers responsible for the functional area (e.g., engineering, programming, legal) and there are managers responsible for the projects. The projects can be large, such as building a dam, or small, such as installing a new computer network. Although the scope and responsibilities vary, the management style is the same for both.

The functional manager generally controls the human resource in the form of hiring, firing, salary, and the other associated administrative responsibilities. The project manager controls the performance appraisal, scheduling, and other project-oriented activities. The relationship between the worker and the functional manager follows the classic hierarchical structure, but the relationship between the project manager and the worker is very ambiguous. In the simplest view, the functional manager is a "manager," whereas the project manager is more properly a "leader." The manager has authority, while the leader has influence. Although this management structure horrifies the purists, it is very popular and works well in many situations. It does require managers with strong leadership skills and a high tolerance for stress and ambiguity. Managers who require clearly defined roles and responsibilities may find Matrix Management beyond their abilities. Also Matrix Management is no place for Theory X managers. It requires the skills normally associated with Theories Y and Z, because the workers on the project have the option to take another assignment. This distinction between job and assignment is crucial. The functional manager has "jobs," whereas the project leader has "assignments." Consequently, if workers do not like working for the project leader, they can request another "assignment." Project leaders who are difficult to work with, who are overly demanding, or who do not command respect find that they cannot attract the best people, and their projects suffer accordingly.

Although Matrix Management continues to be widely used, it is not an easy management technique. It requires considerable skill, patience, and management time to be effective, and it is not applicable in all situations or organizations. Consequently, it cannot be considered to be ammunition and, therefore, does not qualify as a Magic Bullet.

LONG-RANGE STRATEGIC PLANNING

In the flurry of management theories that followed Theories X, Y, Z, and the others, one of the most widely used was Strategic Planning. Indeed, Strategic Planning is still widely used, even though the rate of change in society today continues to compress the planning horizon. The basic premise of Strategic Planning is that we can establish goals and objectives, identify strengths and weaknesses, formulate critical success factors, and then create strategies and plans to accomplish the goals and objectives. It is all very neat and compact and more or less worked when it was first formulated around 1965.

Strategic Planning was a method of controlling the future through planning. The fundamental assumption was that by analyzing and extrapolating past performance we could forecast and control future performance. Competitors were known, target markets identified, market shares understood, sales forecasted, and everything was projected into the future. In an effort to recognize that there might possibly be some unforeseen change or variable, scenarios were created. These gave the management team a best, worst, and probable set of scenarios with supporting "what if" strategies. This was a grand plan and very reminiscent of the European aristocrats, who divided the world into "spheres of influence" without bothering to ask any of the natives if they had other plans. All in all, Strategic Planning was very neat and clean and effective, until those darn natives got in the way.

Several things combined to bring Strategic Planning into eclipse. This technique rested on a predictable rate of change in an identified set of circumstances. In other words, the planners had to know the future conditions. When these assumed conditions failed to materialize, the plans failed. One of the fundamentals of Strategic Planning was knowing the competition and developing strategies to defeat them. It was rather like the British and the French in the eighteenth century. Everyone knew the rules and fought accordingly, but the ignorant Americans refused to follow the rules. They stood behind trees and did not fight fairly. They also won, which is a frequent outcome for those who choose to be innovators. Thus was the case with Strategic Planning when creative and unexpected competitors entered markets. Suddenly there were more car companies than the Big Three, people in the camera business entered the copier business, companies making computer parts began making small computers, and the list goes on. In short, the competitive environment postulated by the strategic planners and their scenarios did not fit reality. No one was prepared to deal with competitors who did not belong because they were completely *unpredictable*.

As if this were not enough, the rate of change in markets began to accelerate along with the rapid changes in technology. When Strategic Planning was introduced, the plans were established on a five-year planning horizon with a one-year action plan. There was plenty of time to react, and plans were updated annually to reflect changing conditions. These changes were properly planned for and introduced on schedule so that planning cycles were unaffected. Well, mostly unaffected. Computers began to get cheaper, faster, and smaller, and this began to force changes on the planning horizon. The planning cycle had to account for this acceleration in technology so the horizon gradually declined to three years and then two. When the life cycle of technology collapsed to six months, Strategic Plans began to disappear because they ceased to be relevant. By the time the plan was completed, the underlying assumptions were outdated, and the environment had changed.

This is not to say there is no place for Strategic Plans or planning, but it does mean that the way we plan must change. Suddenly some of the concepts described in Theory Z begin to make sense. Goals must be high level, and plans must be flexible. Managers must be prepared to react immediately to changes in the technical or competitive environment. Plans must be short range and specific in support of high-level goals, and they must be bound by guiding principles. It is not that Strategic Planning does not work, but it must be looked at in a less specific way. For example, Poland has been viewed historically by other European countries as a logical target for territorial expansion. Therefore, the classic strategy for expansion was to attack Poland. This type of tightly focused and narrowly targeted strategy is no longer reasonable because it is too specific. Instead, a more general strategy must be formulated, one that achieves the objective of expansion without presupposing Poland as the target. It is this flexibility that must be built into future strategic plans.

Therefore, those managers in search of the surefire easy path to management success must turn to other management philosophies, because this Magic Bullet turned out to be a low-caliber bullet with little impact.

MANAGING BY WALKING AROUND

This is sort of the physical fitness approach to management and is especially suited to managers with short attention spans. Rather than sit in a stuffy room surrounded by facts and figures and boring details, why not stretch your legs, walk around, and find out what is "really" happening? The underlying belief of this management style is that the observant manager can determine firsthand what is happening by watching others work, talking to them about their work, or looking at the results of the work rather than looking at a bunch of summaries and reports.

For the manager of a small business this may be an effective management style, but for the manager responsible for many people, who may be geographically dispersed, this is not a practical management technique. Admittedly, it is very important for the boss to see and be seen, but to rely on direct observation as a management technique is both time consuming and risky. It takes time to walk around and visit the workers at their workstations, and when the social factor is figured in, the amount of information gathered versus the time devoted to gathering it is probably not worth the effort. Furthermore, the information gathered may be biased. Therefore, acting on information gathered by walking around is very risky, and if the information is evaluated and analyzed before action is taken, then it might have been gathered more efficiently in some other way.

Although managing by walking around (MBWA) is not a very efficient management style, it has a great deal of merit as a leadership technique. It is still very time consuming and produces little management advantage, but the effect on morale and productivity can be immense. Invisible leaders do not instill loyalty and are very susceptible to manipulation by others. Therefore, it is important for the leader to be seen by the workers and those in the "trenches." Engaging workers in casual conversation can yield insight into problems, processes, and possible cost improvements. However, these must be carefully evaluated and discussed with others in the management chain before reacting.

In summary, MBWA is an excellent leadership technique but not overly effective as a management style. As a Magic Bullet MBWA is more of a ricochet.

SEARCHING FOR EXCELLENCE

This may be the granddaddy of all Magic Bullets. While Matrix Management is only for the brave, Searching for Excellence is really for the lazy. It is an "armchair" approach to management. The basic premise for this scheme is that through empirical research, you can identify the factors common to excellent companies, duplicate them, and thus become excellent, too. This is a no-sweat, no-strain approach to management and analogous to looking over the shoulder of the smartest kid in class and copying his answers. Of course, this presumes you have the same questions, but then if you were quick-witted enough to see this as a problem, you would not have been suckered into this lazy man's approach to thinking in the first place.

Remember our friend Copernicus and his views regarding the "static" universe that we met a few pages back—well, he is still with us. The conditions at a center of excellence are rarely the same outside of that center. Even if the physical conditions could be duplicated, which is highly doubtful, the personalities and corporate cultures are different. Things change. Each change introduces variables. With each variable come choices. With each choice comes risk. Conditions are not the same. Nothing is static, and neither are the answers. So, yes you can copy off of someone else's paper, but the result may not be the same. After all, if your questions are different, then the answers, by definition, must be different as well. Although this seems obvious, the search for excellence and the "best practices" continues unabated.

But these are merely observations and opinions. How does Searching for Excellence actually work as a style of management? It is simultaneously deceptively simple and quite complex. It begins with the recognition that "we are NOT number one" and that there is a need for improvement. Step two is to identify *what* needs to be improved. This is one of those deceptively easy tasks, because if you can easily identify what needs to change, then why not change it? In reality, identifying specifically what needs to change is roughly akin to determining what is causing your headache. For headaches, the solution is to take an aspirin; for performance improvement you find a role model. The third step in this process is to determine who is the number one performer and attempt to find out how they got that way. Although this also sounds like a simple task, it almost never is. After all, you cannot just call up your competitor and ask him to tell you how he is beating you up in the marketplace. This requires finesse, research, analysis, and frequently calls for a consultant to benchmark the processes you need. Once this is done and the "best practices" have been identified and described, they can then be implemented and you are on your way to being *number two*. This is one of the problems with copying others. The best that you can hope for is to be as good as they are. If you want to be number one, then you must be original and innovative, and you must assume risk. Consequently, searching for excellence and best practices is a "followers" low-risk management technique and not one for the aggressive manager who is seeking market dominance.

Searching for Excellence is certainly not time wasted, but as a Magic Bullet it is in someone else's clip.

MANAGING CHAOS

The world is filled with spectators and very few players. Chaos Management is yet another attempt by the observers to tell the players how to play the game. This is not to say that there is no room for coaches, but advice from the sidelines must be cogent. Too frequently the people sitting on the fifty-yard line are throwing out generic advice like "hit' em harder" or "pass if you can't run." Or, put another way, it is as if the Allied General Staff decided that boiling the ocean was a solution to the U-Boat problem. Interesting but not very helpful.

Chaos Management rests on the foundation of constant change. It is an attempt by the audience to tell the players what they have known all along and that is everything changes all of the time. Nothing is easy when you are eyeball-to-eyeball with the problem. Chaos Management attempts to recognize that change is not only inevitable but constant.

The contemporary manager is faced daily with the challenges of rapid changes in technology, new competitors, constantly changing customer requirements, skills shortages, and too many other variables to count. The key to managing in this dynamic environment is to create flexible organizations that can immediately react to changes. This new organization must be capable of meeting any competitive challenge with new ideas, new technology, innovative market plans, and the supporting dynamic organizational structure.

This looks very simple from the bleachers, but precisely what this organization looks like is a little vague. What are the management skills necessary to lead such a dynamic organization? How do you identify what needs to be changed or how to change it once it is identified? Chaos Management is a real need, but because it is chaotic, it is virtually impossible to define or predict anything in advance. Therefore, it is easy to see that what is required is leadership more than management. Managing is organizing and directing, but leadership is inspiring and envisioning the future. If that future is dynamic, then the vision must be dynamic as well.

The days where the CEO sat like a king at the top of the heap surrounded by his minions stroking him with compliments and feeding predigested information to him are either gone or going very rapidly. Chaos Management requires that the senior leadership turn their attention to the future and to establishing the vision or even multiple visions. Senior executives no longer have the luxury of being the captain of a great ship plowing the sea of competition and unafraid of the smaller vessels surrounding them. That great ship no longer exists. Instead, the captain now finds himself the commander of a flotilla of smaller ships, each with its own captain, and suddenly this flotilla is vulnerable to those smaller vessels, which turned out to be enemy gun boats. In reality these small ships are the strategic business units that make up the enterprise and their captains are the business unit presidents. It is these business unit presidents that are in day-to-day control of operations, while the CEO is the new navigator for the entire fleet. As the navigator, the CEO sets the objective and determines the course but beyond that it is the business unit presidents that make the day-to-day operating decisions.

Consequently, Chaos Management is really not so much a management technique as it is a management style. To actually manage in this chaotic environment requires a complete rethinking of the organizational structure. The new, more flexible structure is flatter and has fewer managers, more leaders, and greatly empowered workers. The senior management team has only loose control over daily operations. Instead, they are focused on the future, but the future can no longer be extrapolated from the past, so new techniques are required to determine that future state. To do this, the senior management team must establish what *they* believe the future will be or what they want it to be. Once this is done, they must establish the strategies and plans necessary to intercept that future with the knowledge and preparation for the changes that will certainly occur in the pursuit of the objective.

This is a completely new view of management and their roles and responsibilities. It requires risk, flexibility, and thoughtful leadership. Many senior management teams may find Chaos Management a difficult technique to master, and others may not believe it applies to their situation. Perhaps it does not, but what if it does? The competitive environment today is very unforgiving, and there is little (if any) time to recover from a miscalculation. Chaos Management is a recognition that companies and leaders who wish to *follow* the industry leaders may find themselves out of the running altogether. To practice Chaos Management requires risk, innovation, and a vision of the future in association with the courage necessary to be a thought leader. This is very difficult for managers who became CEOs by making no decision, taking no risk, agreeing with the boss, and playing low-handicap golf. Chaos Management is not for this type of manager, but then maybe this type of manager has no place in the future.

Is Chaos Management the Magic Bullet that we have all been looking for? It is too early to tell but it is unlikely that there is any more magic in Chaos Management than there was in any of the other management theories that promised the easy path to success. Certainly Chaos Management is not an easy path and it is difficult to tell if it leads to success. This Magic Bullet is still in the clip waiting to be tested.

THE HAWTHORNE EFFECT

It should be noted that none of these management theories appear to have been evaluated against the Hawthorne Experiment conducted in Chicago in the 1940s. Without digressing too far, let me explain that this experiment was an attempt to correlate working conditions to productivity. Various things were tried on a group of workers whose productivity was measured against a control group. At first their working conditions were improved and productivity dramatically improved. Then their working conditions were gradually reduced until the workers were, effectively, working in moonlight, but the productivity still improved. After extensive trials no correlation of any kind was found, but the differences in productivity *appeared* to be tied to the attention and involvement of management. Therefore, in examining all of these management theories, the Hawthorne experiment must be considered, because it might be possible that simply by involving the worker in the process, whatever the process is, one might improve productivity. Higher productivity might be more closely tied to involved managers than to management theories or involved workers.

RULES FOR MAGIC BULLETS

The world of business is filled with both real and aspiring managers who are in a never-ending quest for that one management technique that will ensure their success. There have been many in the past, there are many in vogue now, and there are undoubtedly many more in the publishing houses waiting to burst on the scene. Will any of these prove to be better or more effective than the theories that have already been tried? Probably not, because all of these theories seem to have some common assumptions that are often not articulated but generally lead to limited success.

1. These theories seem to assume that human behavior is predictable.
2. They use analysis of previous facts and results to forecast future results.
3. Many theories rest on assumed motives (e.g., people are basically good/bad).

4. Conditions previously observed will continue as observed.

5. There are a limited number of variables to consider.

The fact is that management and leadership are people-oriented skills and thus are subject to an infinite set of human variables. Any individual or group of individuals will react differently to the same set of conditions. Consequently, each new theory must be evaluated. Following is a series of observations that might be used in this screening process. Management theories seem to fall into these general groups, each with their own characteristics.

1. The Rules of Excellence

Some theories provide a series of steps leading to excellent performance. These are almost always based on the past performance of a leader. The assumption is that if these simple steps are followed then success is ensured. The flaw in this thinking seems obvious, because the theory was founded on the past success of the leader so the best that can be attained would be parity. Furthermore, this assumes two things; first, your competitor will not read the book, and, second, the leader will not change or innovate.

2. The Rules of Simplicity

Some theories are like psychics—they give the impression of being very specific when they are actually generalities or perhaps more properly, banalities. These are the theories that expect the manager to seize upon the strengths of the organization and to exploit every opportunity. At the same time the manager is warned to overcome internal weaknesses and to avoid all threats. In the words of Madame Gamboni our Psychic Adviser, we are told this is our lucky day. We have the opportunity now to increase our wealth and to grow professionally, but we must be wary of our insecurity and self-doubt. Furthermore, there is someone in the background working against us, so we must be very cautious if we are to realize the opportunities before us.

What is missing from the theories that fall into this category are any ways to identify strengths, weaknesses, threats, or opportunities. However, once we have identified these then the theory is sure to work. Of course, if we have failed to do this properly then the theory will not work. Madame Gamboni was right again.

3. The Rules of Engagement

Some management theories simply ignore the realities of the lives of most managers. The Managing By Walking Around theory is an excellent example of this defiance of reality. These theories expect the effective manager to assume so many additional burdens that it is impossible to be effective. These theories expect the manager to participate in every meeting; to participate in worker rallies; to present rewards; to walk around and be seen; to talk to everyone while continuing to plan, direct, organize, and administer to everything in sight. For the experienced manager these theories seem like the product of a diseased mind but more commonly they come from the lips of theorists rather than real managers.

4. The Rules of Clarity

There are some theories of management and organization that are so complicated and convoluted that they have limited value even if they are understood. These are the theories that deal with "thought leadership," "thinking maps," "learning organizations," "the democratic corporation," and so on. On the plus side most of these theories are interesting and provocative, but how they can be applied or used is usually very vague. Rarely is anything specific offered regarding how to apply these theories or the actual structure of the organizations they propose, much less how to manage people in these new organizational forms. Generally these theories are published by prestigious universities in very large and impressive books destined to adorn the bookshelves in numerous offices worldwide.

5. The Rules of Change

These rules apply to some of the newest theories because the current trend in management thinking is to be prepared for constant change. These theories call on the manager to create flexible organizations capable of quickly reacting to the changing conditions of the marketplace. The manager is called on to be "nimble" and innovative and to seize opportunities. Of course, none of these theorists explain exactly what this new organization should look like, what changes are good, or precisely how to react to this rapid change. Certainly the competitive environment today is extremely dynamic, and the prudent manager must be prepared to react quickly. However, not all change is good nor all competitors wise, but these new theories just urge the manager to be prepared. How to be prepared or what to do is largely ignored.

6. The Rules for Low IQs

The bookstores are filled with books purporting to teach managers (in as few words as possible) the secrets of (*fill in the blank*), how to manage in (*fill in the blank*) minutes, or the (*fill in the blank*) steps for effective management. There is nothing wrong with these kinds of books, and they are highly popular. In fact, they have sold millions of copies. The probability is you have read one or more. Do you think others in your company or department might have read these books also? The problem with the pop-culture management styles and theories is that if you attempt to use them everyone knows what you are doing. That may or may not be a problem, but what advantage have you gained? Have you established a competitive edge? Are you more effective as a manager? The problem with pop-culture management is that it is popular, used by everyone, hardly creative, and rarely enduring.

In conclusion we can see that there are no rote answers to any given problem, and because there are no "answers," no one management theory is the "Magic Bullet" that everyone seems to be searching for. Yet, none of these theories is wrong because all have some truth and some value. There really is not any one solution or management technique that covers every situation, and it is unlikely there ever will be. What is required is that the manager is aware of the *possibilities* and selects the appropriate theory at the appropriate time.

However, this lack of precision in the area of management theory has not gone unnoticed. Because we cannot select the Magic Bullet that ensures success, it is clear we must bring rigor and discipline to whatever technique we decide to use. Therefore, it is necessary to establish the proper process and/or procedure and then it will not matter what management theory is used. So, next we explore the most recent Holy Grail of management, the standard process.

NOTES

1. Douglas McGregor, *The Human Side of Enterprise* (New York: McGraw-Hill Book Co., 1960), pp. 33–34.

2. Ibid., pp. 33–34.

3. Ibid., pp. 47–48.

4. Ibid., pp. 47–48.

5. Harvey & Brown, *An Experiential Approach to Organizational Development* (Englewood Cliffs, New Jersey: Prentice Hall, 1992), pp. 417–423.

6. William Ouichi, *Theory Z: How American Business Can Meet the Japanese Challenge* (Reading, Massachusetts: Addison Wesley Publishing Co., 1981).

4

PROCESSES AND PROCEDURES

Just as management and leadership have been with us since the beginning of civilization, so have processes and procedures. There has always been the right way, the wrong way, and your way to do something. This attitude of self-assurance is so prevalent that it is virtually part of our culture. Nevertheless, most people recognize there is a process for most things, even if the process is not written down. Perhaps the best illustration of this is the family recipe book. The recipes for your favorite dishes are usually written down somewhere, but how often are these consulted? Quite commonly the best ones are, more or less, memorized, and the quantities are estimated rather than measured. In this case there is the right way, the wrong way, and Mom's way, which we all know is the "best way," no matter what the written process says.

Undoubtedly, the very first process and procedure was for building a fire. Our friend Og was sitting around some dried moss while chipping flint for his newest invention, the spear, when an errant spark ignited the moss, and fire was born. Thus, the association was made between flint, moss, and fire and at a stroke the standard process was born. Og now knew how to select flint, manufacture spear points, and consistently make fire. Thus, the first manufacturing and quality control process was born. (Arguably the first process was the birthing process, but I owe allegiance to my male antecedents.)

Since those primitive beginnings, humankind has been surrounded by processes, with each process intended to make life easier by reducing the amount of effort involved and producing a predictable result—chip flint, tie to stick, throw at game, eat dinner. So from these simple beginnings of consistent processes for fire, hunting, and spear making, other processes came into being and grew in complexity as society progressed. These early processes often took the form of religious ceremonies and rituals, and as mankind became more civilized these expanded into various customs and codes of behavior. In some cases these processes became quite stylized and very rigorous, especially in the areas of religious procedures and royal protocols. For example, groveling before royalty, special garments for priests, kneeling for prayers, covering the head in church, and the list goes on. Society itself rests on processes and procedures that are frequently described as law, custom, and etiquette. Many of these processes and procedures were (are) quite dehumanizing, but processes and procedures reached their epitome with Henry Ford and his assembly line.

The assembly line reduced the human being to a mechanical part of the process, indistinguishable from the machines he served. No thinking was required, no judgment needed, and no discussion encouraged. Every action was defined, almost choreographed, and any deviation punished. The objective was to build things fast, cheap, and alike. In his film *Modern Times*, Charlie Chaplin satirized the assembly line and underscored its repetitive process as both dehumanizing and exploitive. In this film, the machines, the process, and the bosses are dominant, and the worker is a servant—a servant not to the bosses, but to the machines. The worker is shown as a victim who is punished by the machines (through malfunction) for deviations in the process. Through this rigorously defined process, the worker became part of the machine, tantamount to a human widget. In the mass manufacturing process, the machines were the constants and the workers were as replaceable as any other part of the machine. Slowly the pendulum has swung away from these dehumanizing processes that were so prevalent during the first half of the twentieth century. Much of this change can be attributed to the rise of the knowledge worker and the spread of computer-based technology, which creates and is creating general-purpose machines, whose revenue-generating potential is dependent on the operator. Not the operator's knowledge of how to operate the machines, but rather how to utilize the machine to generate flexible and everchanging results. Processes are still present, but now the machines increasingly serve their human operators, whose knowledge creates the value.

With thousands of years of experience, one would think that mankind in general and managers in particular would have mastered the art of defining and using a process. Yet, one of the most difficult things facing management today is how to define and use a process. The fact is that most people are not "process oriented" but are "task oriented." Given a job to do, they simply start, usually by breaking the effort down into what they perceive to be the appropriate series of subordinate steps or tasks and then executing them in an arbitrary or at least in their definition of a *proper* sequence. In these situations each person uses his or her own logic to define the steps and their order of execution. This is characteristic of the *master/apprentice* relationship, in which the master had learned, perhaps from another master, the precise process required to yield the desired quality product. This process was used for arrowheads, ship building, pottery, and virtually every other craft until the industrial revolution. The apprentice was expected to mimic the master in the *monkey-see, monkey-do* theory of process design. However, even with the Monkey model each master had his own definition and sequence of the steps that defined his *technique*. Rarely were these steps formalized, even when they were wildly successful. Consequently product quality varied, and frequently the process was reinvented when the master died, materials were changed, or variations were required. This failure to document processes and to constantly reinvent them is such a common occurrence that it is called "re-inventing the wheel," presumably because we have been doing it ever since the wheel was invented. Why do we humans resist following a process?

Perhaps it is understandable that the dehumanizing processes associated with the assembly line would be resisted, but generally these are not the processes that are ignored. Instead, the everyday processes intended to make us more productive, error free, and more efficient are ignored. Simple things such as backing up data files, filling out request forms, following communications procedures, and so on, are the processes and procedures that are rarely documented and even more rarely followed. Yet it is these simple, repeatable processes that improve productivity and determine the quality of our output that subsequently leads to profits and customer satisfaction. Therefore, is it any wonder that companies continue to place such stress on repeatable processes?

The fast food industry is viewed as a service industry that is devoted to standard processes that yield a standard quality product. It really does not matter which McDonald's you go to; the product is the same because the process (and ingredients) for creating the product is the same. McDonald's epitomizes the standard or "McProcess" with each step in the production of the product carefully described and orchestrated. The objective of the McProcess is to produce a standard product by setting cooking times, ingredients, and assembly procedures, and by defining the "standard service." However, many see this McProcess as a method of achieving universally standard but consistently mediocre products and service. This effort to standardize the process begins with the employee. The employees are in uniform (Theory Z) and are expected to greet each customer with the standard smile and greeting in an effort to provide not only a consistent product but a consistent quality of service as well. Alas, while the product is the same, everyone knows the service varies from McDonald's to McDonald's, because just like everyone else, Ronald McDonald gets frazzled, and the standard service and greeting can sometimes be delivered without the smile or usual civility. "Welcome to McDonald's" can sound friendly, perky, happy, rude, or even angry. The words are delivered from the same script but under different circumstances and by different people. Therein lies the problem—the diversity of people. So much for the standard process.

Until we become a society completely dominated by robots, we are stuck with that most glorious but also most inefficient and unpredictable machine—the human being. Therefore, one of the objectives of the standard process is to minimize that uncontrolled variable—the human. This effort to minimize the human element creates a dilemma. On the one hand we want to humanize the workplace and provide personalized service. On the other hand we want that service to be of a consistent quality, and the only way to do that is to standardize the delivery process. Unfortunately, the more rigorously we define the process, the more we dehumanize it. However, if it is left undefined, then the consistency and quality of the product or service become unpredictable. It may get better or it might get worse.

The challenge for management is to determine not only if there should be a process or procedure, but how standard it should be. On the surface this does not look like much of a problem, especially to those who do not have to actually follow the process. There are many people who are convinced that standard, repeatable processes can substitute for management skill. The assumption seems to be that conditions are constant or at least predictable with some degree of certainty and that every process can be defined and repeated. The underlying belief is that a standard process can be used to eliminate the variables introduced by the surrounding conditions and the customer. Of course, this is an erroneous assumption, but the fundamental belief persists that all processes are repeatable and, if followed, will result in consistency. Perhaps this is true, but sometimes the process itself is part of the problem.

Even a cursory examination of normal conditions will show that some problems are the result of a poor process, while others are the result of no process, and still others are the result of an unenforced process. The trick, of course, is in determining what the problem is and if it is related to any of these conditions. This is not as simple as it sounds. It is very easy to sit back and critique situations gone awry; after all we have a much better view up here in the observation booth. We know from the outset that the problem is a lack of communication, lack of leadership, lack of process, lack of discipline, or a lack of whatever. However, in the field things are hardly ever quite that clear. The processes are rarely written down, and the problem is not always obvious. Worse, events are often clouded by a lack of information or confusing input, so the decision or course of action is often not easily discerned.

To illustrate this point, we have the following situation, which is one commonly encountered by managers. This example is very confusing and difficult to follow, but it is also a real example and a common one at that. In reading this you may find it difficult to follow and at the conclusion feel you were not given enough information. That is probably true, but as is often the case, managers are required to find solutions and take action, often with less than all of the necessary information.

CUSTOMER COMMUNICATIONS

In this example, the Project Manager has responsibility for developing a complete warehousing system for a national home delivery restaurant business. This effort includes meeting with the customer, understanding the problem, establishing the requirements, and then developing the various solutions and reports. Relations with the customer are excellent, and one of the Team Leaders (A) has an excellent rapport with the customer chief information officer (CIO) to the point of establishing a personal friendship. Everything has been going well and everything is pretty much on schedule.

During the previous week, Team Leader B, who has responsibility for developing the Spoilage and Loss Report, met with the customer CIO to review her requirements for the report. The CIO made it very clear to Team Leader B that there will always be spoilage when dealing with fresh ingredients, so the report does not need to address spoilage in any detail. What the CIO is especially interested in knowing is the amount of loss from damaged goods reported by each vendor. Therefore, the CIO has directed Team Leader B to modify the spoilage report to eliminate the overall totals by warehouse but focus on reporting by vendor.

At the weekly project review meeting, Team Leader B begins her update of the Spoilage and Loss Project by discussing the requirements she has received from the customer. Team Leader B indicates that the project scope will be modified to reflect the elimination of the spoilage reporting by warehouse, *as requested by the customer CIO*. Before she can finish her report, Team Leader C interrupts by saying that Team Leader B has misunderstood the requirements.

Team Leader C says he met with the CIO earlier in the week to discuss another matter, but during that discussion the CIO expressed concern over the amount of perishable and damaged goods being delivered to the warehouses. She clearly stated to Team Leader C that she was looking forward to the completion of the Spoilage and Loss Project because it would provide a comprehensive summary of the spoilage and loss rates at each warehouse. Team Leader C states that the CIO was not interested in the report including *spoilage by vendor*, but she was interested in knowing the total amount of spoilage.

This difference of opinion regarding the requirements prompted a spirited discussion regarding precisely *what* the requirements are. Before this point can be clarified, Team Leader A states that in an impromptu luncheon discussion with the CIO, a completely different view was expressed. The CIO indicated that she was looking forward to the completion of this project because it would finally provide a clear view of the spoilage and losses by vendor and by warehouse. The CIO was very emphatic about this so it is clear that both Team Leaders B and C have misunderstood what the requirements are. Furthermore, Team Leader A recommends to the Project Leader that the requirements be amended to reflect this more detailed view and that the project be redirected to incorporate this larger scope.

Was this scenario confusing? Did you have trouble understanding precisely what the problem is and why there is a dispute? Did you have to go back over the material to understand the problem? Welcome to the real world of management where this problem also would have had time pressure and would have been just one of dozens of problems, many of them more urgent and even more complicated. For our purposes, this problem is taken out of context so it is actually much easier to follow than if it were encountered amid all of the noise and distractions created by other daily problems and issues. This allows us to separate it from the usual clutter of crises and routine and to scrutinize it as a stand-alone problem.

On reading this example, some of you management Gods and demi-Gods may have concluded that this situation does not apply to you. It is a simple problem at the Team Leader level and does not relate to the important problems normally addressed on Olympus. Please press on, because I believe the lessons in all of these real examples apply to all levels of management. It is my firm belief that the problems encountered in the executive suite are the same as those encountered in cubicle rows and only the details vary, not the concepts. However, before we examine the lessons, let us look at the action alternatives.

Clearly, the project manager is faced with the problem of whom to believe and what to do. There are several obvious possibilities.

1. The project manager can immediately "get all of the liars into one room" by scheduling a meeting with the Team Leaders and the customer for the purpose of clarifying the requirements. This assumes that each Team Leader has some portion of the truth and the customer may be unsure of precisely what she wants. This meeting would permit a reexamination of the requirements and give everyone an opportunity to restate the project scope and definition.

2. The project manager can schedule a meeting with the customer and Team Leader B. Because Team Leader B is responsible for developing

the actual spoilage report, it is imperative that he be absolutely sure of what is expected at the conclusion.

3. Another and ever-popular alternative is to delegate the problem. The project manager can listen to the quarreling and bickering until he loses patience and then direct the responsible Team Leader (B) to "deal with it." End of problem. (A hidden advantage to this solution is that if required later it can always be reported that we have embarked on a "Search For Excellence." Who could fault that?)

4. Another possibility is to take no action at this time. Instead, the project manager can acknowledge that there is a problem, but it is not serious enough to take any immediate action. The customer has provided Team Leader B with requirements, and the project can proceed until the situation clarifies itself.

As usual none of these is a standout, but depending on your point of view some are worse than others. For example, alternative #4 is a wonderful answer for the fast-track manager who desires to appear decisive without actually being decisive. By taking no action and "waiting for the situation to clarify," the manager has made a decision that buys time for him/her to get more information, to sidestep the issue altogether, or to off-load the decision on to someone else. For those action-oriented managers interested in getting the job done, alternative #4 may be the least attractive, because it has a high potential of wasting manpower and causing re-work. In effect, by waiting for the situation to clarify, the manager is refusing to deal with a confusing and difficult problem. By ignoring it, he hopes it will disappear. It will not.

For some managers, especially in context with other problems, this problem may seem to be more of an annoyance than a real problem. In this case, the Project Manager can very reasonably tell Team Leader B, who is responsible for "dealing with it," and then move on to more important problems. In all of the management books this is called "delegation" and "empowerment." What these books rarely state is that to *empower* means that the power to make the decision has been delegated, and the manager who delegated the power must live with the result. Empowerment is a very effective tool, and the more senior the manager the more effective and necessary the tool. For some managers, delegation and empowerment are used interchangeably; but they are actually quite different. Delegation means the subordinate is granted the authority to make the "correct" decision. Of course the subordinate is never told what the correct decision is—that is the "empowerment" part. If the result is positive, the senior manager has "empowered" the subordinate and may take credit for a positive outcome but can hold the subordinate responsible for any ensuing disaster without shouldering any of the responsibility. After all, the subordinate was empowered. Back in the old days when you delegated something and it blew up, the superior was held accountable; with empowerment the failure rests with the subordinate and success is shared with the manager. Once you get the hang of it, empowerment is really superior to delegation.

Therefore, delegation may be used as a tool for avoiding responsibility and raises the question—Is it a good alternative in this case? Perhaps it depends on how the delegation is handled. Simply telling the Team Leader to "take care of it" is not really effective delegation. In this instance, it is tantamount to deciding that there is no problem and the responsible team leader is free to take whatever action deemed appropriate. To be effective, the manager must give some direction regarding what is expected and how to proceed.

Perhaps the most direct way to resolve this problem is to arrange to "get all of the liars in one room." This brings all of the parties together so that the issue can be discussed and a common direction can be established. This is simple and elegant and would probably resolve the immediate problem, but there is actually a larger problem. In fact, there is a *much larger question* that has not been addressed. And that question is—How did this mess occur in the first place?

There are two obvious answers. First, every team leader in this situation interpreted informal conversations as serious requests for change. This displays a serious lack of process, discipline, and clearly defined roles and responsibilities. In this example, no one seems to be aware that hallway conversations and tangential remarks do not constitute "official input" or change requests. So at the most basic level, we see that there is a lack of a process governing change or change control.

There also seems to be some confusion regarding roles and responsibilities or at least everyone's understanding of them. In this example, Team Leader B had responsibility for establishing the requirements and developing the report. Team Leader C picked up some tangential comments in a meeting on a different subject. Although these comments may be of interest to Team Leader B, they do not represent anything other than "interesting comments." For the Project Manager to give them any credence at all undermines Team Leader B. Team Leader A is a personal friend of the CIO and is also repeating informal comments. Worse, this Team Leader takes a very aggressive and proactive position regarding these informal comments from the CIO. Again, this indicates that the roles and responsibilities among the team leaders are either not clearly defined or not clearly understood.

The second obvious problem is even worse. That is, a change control process either does not exist or exists and is being ignored. This means that there is a lack of discipline that is creating confusion over roles and responsibilities that could easily lead to an uncontrolled expansion of the effort and the ensuing financial impacts. Even in environments where there is commitment to formal processes, this type of conversation is not uncommon, especially if there is good customer rapport. Information is willingly provided in an informal way, and this is passed on informally in the spirit of "good communications." The result is that the established process is ignored and, at the very least, valuable time is wasted. In the worst case, the scope is modified without further corroboration relative to what the requirements actually are or the costs associated with the modified scope. (This is usually known as losing money.)

This was a simple example at the Project Manager level, but it is a common problem. At this level the problem is more easily discerned and resolved. However, at more senior levels the problem itself may be less precise. One of the most common problems at all levels of management is a clear understanding of the objective. Unfortunately all too often as problems grow in complexity, the focus gradually shifts from the primary objective to solving a tangential problem, and the original objective becomes blurred and then lost. This is a very common problem and is almost always the result of not having or following a change control *process*. This change control process is equivalent to a ship's compass and captain's log. By following the process, the project manager knows where they are, where they are headed, and the changes in direction they have taken and why. Without this change control process, the project manager quickly loses sight of the objective as problems arise, changes are requested, and verbal agreements are forgotten.

Although change control processes are useful at all levels of the enterprise, they are not always used, at least not used in any formal manner at higher management levels. Suppose the discussion was between the CIO, the CEO, and the CFO (chief financial officer) discussing modifications to the budget based on discussions with a client who appears to have changed direction. Executives at this level are rarely constrained by processes or procedures, standard or otherwise. The operative word here being "constrained," meaning that these executives might not follow a formal process to control the budget and strategies, even if they exist. However, at the executive level, even though operating process and procedures for the enterprise may not be written down, there are some formal processes that cannot be avoided.

In some cases federal law, especially in the areas of employee treatment, securities, taxes, and the like, determines these processes and procedures. In most cases the laws are so specific that the executive has no discretionary authority at all. At a more mundane level, executives are expected to follow the corporate custom in terms of dress, protocols, and labor relations. Certainly there is some discretionary latitude in these, but a great deal less than one might think. Although processes and procedures exist at the senior management level, they usually do not dominate the daily routine as they do lower down in the organization

This is not an argument for constraining senior executives with rigorous processes, but it is a reminder that a clear understanding of roles and responsibilities, self-restraint, and some discipline is required at all levels, and these need to be self-imposed at the highest levels. The fact is there must be rules (processes), and they must be followed, otherwise chaos and confusion reign. All companies have processes, both formal and informal, but in those instances where the process is not followed or enforced, redundancies, duplications, increased costs, and a variety of similar problems ensue. This is what is behind the drive to establish and implement standard repeatable processes. Unfortunately, there is another side of this coin. What do you do if the processes and procedures are scrupulously followed and you are still left holding the proverbial bag? Again the problem is with people—you just cannot rely on them to do what you want, expect, or predict. On the one hand we establish processes to ensure consistency of output, but on the other, we want and need flexibility in order to ensure our ability to meet changing conditions. Therein lies the problem.

Processes and procedures are important management tools, but they cannot do the job by themselves. Following the process does not always yield the result expected by the customer or promised by the vendor. Generally project definitions, contracts, and commitments are viewed by the parties as being very clear-cut, for example, paint the barn. Painting the barn seems rather simple. We have procedures for specifying time, quality, color, and approval. A contract is written and specifications, including color, are agreed upon. We proceed to paint the barn according to the requirements. Once the job is completed, the customer inspects the completed barn with its new coat of red paint. Yikes! The barn was supposed to be RED, not CRIMSON!! The customer is angry and refuses to pay because you did not fulfill the contract. The barn is painted crimson when he specifically stated that he wanted the barn painted red, and that is what the contract says. The contractor can pull out the contract, and there it is, the barn is to be painted red. Yes indeed, the contract specifies red, we agreed on red, and the barn is red; now the contractor demands that the customer pay up! At this point the customer grabs the nearest empty paint bucket, waves it under your nose and points out the paint is clearly labeled "Crimson Sunset," and the word "red" does not appear anywhere on the can nor does Crimson Sunset in the contract. And so it goes. We had a procedure and followed it, but it did not prevent a problem. Naturally we can argue that the process itself was flawed because nothing was mentioned about the process for color selection or progress inspections. Although the color "red" was specified, the term itself is vague because "red" is a generic term and therefore vague by definition. This, of course, is the pivotal point. The contract did not specify the color by manufacturer or color code or even the name used by the manufacturer. Therefore, when the customer points out that the name on the bucket is Crimson Sunset, which in his opinion is not the *red* he had in mind, the problem arises, because *the meaning of red is open for interpretation.*

What this example illustrates is lack of a process for defining, accepting, and changing specifications for the output of a project. In this case there was a procedure for writing a contract, but there was nothing beyond that. There was no process for customer concurrence on the *actual paint color* to be used. There was no process for progress reporting, and, presumably, there was no process in place to effect change had the discrepancy been detected. Instead, the contract was signed, and the interpretation of the color "red" was left to the discretion of the project manager, who selected the paint color and painted the barn according to the contract but not according to the customer's expectation. But this was a trivial example intended to illustrate the point that processes may appear to exist but may be incomplete in practice. What about an actual example?

In this example the vendor has been contracted by a company to develop a Distribution System. The contract is signed, requirements are submitted, and development is about to begin. The contract specifies that the company is responsible for providing acceptance criteria so that the acceptance testing can be performed on completion of the project. This prompted the following exchange of memos between the vendor and the customer.

To: Customer

From: Vendor

The proposal between Vendor, Inc. and Customer Company calls on us to conduct an acceptance test for the Distribution System prior to becoming operational. Before we can complete our system design and project plan for the Distribution Systems Project, we need acceptance criteria from Customer Company. This acceptance test would be performed by Customer Company at the conclusion of our testing phase and would use the acceptance criteria as a basis for the test. If our product satisfies the acceptance criteria, then Customer Company will accept the Distribution System as completed and operational.

Presently we are in the process of finalizing our project plan and designing the system, but we need your acceptance criteria and agreement that you will accept the product if it meets that criteria before we can complete our plan or design. You are requested to provide this information and agreement at your earliest convenience.

The response to this inquiry was not long in arriving.

To: Vendor

From: Customer Company

We have discussed your request for acceptance test criteria and an agreement to perform the acceptance test. I have endorsed your letter agreeing to perform the test and hope this is satisfactory. We discussed your request for acceptance criteria but are unsure if we have the information necessary for a detailed response.

Based on our understanding of the agreement, Vendor, Inc. has agreed to streamline our distribution operation, retaining all of the administrative structure but revamping or modifying some or all of the computer-based systems in order to make them more compatible and efficient. If this understanding is correct, then our basis of acceptance would be that the new system would improve and expand the existing functionality. The response times would not be less than what we currently experience, and our communications abilities would be enhanced. Our acceptance test would essentially be a verification of these items. If the new Vendor, Inc. system meets these criteria, we will accept the system for implementation.

We are very excited about this project and are looking forward to working with you and all of the Vendor, Inc. team.

Certainly good relations exist between the customer and the vendor, and both are sincere in their efforts to meet the commitments outlined in the contract. The vendor has explicitly stated what they require to move forward, and the customer has responded. Specifically, the customer has agreed to accept the new system if it meets all of the existing functionality plus more. The response times would be improved over the existing times, and overall communications would be improved. All that remains is for the project to be completed and tested. The management control process was used, and it worked—an excellent example of how processes and procedures can be used as management tools.

For some, the next step is obvious—get on with the project. There are only three things that have to be accomplished—expand the functionality, improve the response times, and improve communications. These are relatively simple tasks and can be easily accomplished. The customer has agreed *in principle* with our project and will conduct the acceptance test at the conclusion of the project. We have a contract and the customer's agreement in writing, so there is no reason not to proceed. As strange as it may sound, some managers will take the customer's letter at face value and plunge ahead with the project. I would like to say that this course of action is usually restricted to the novice and neophyte. I would *like* to say that, but unfortunately I cannot.

Consider that the contract was not developed in a vacuum. It followed all of the normal review procedures and was scrutinized by lawyers and various managers, all of whom are senior to the project manager. Many managers would simply accept everything at face value and move forward, because to do otherwise would be tantamount to telling the senior executives that they made a mistake. Some managers have the courage to do that; many more do not. Consequently, the normal sequence of events is for the project manager to recognize that there are a few problems with the phrasing and expectations, but to move forward with the project nevertheless. This is done in the mistaken belief that these *difficulties* can be worked out as we go along. They almost never are.

To the grizzled veteran of corporate combat, there are more than a *few* problems here, but let us address three really obvious ones. What constitutes improved functionality? For that matter, what is the current function-ality? If you do not have a firm idea of what the current level of functional-ity is, how can you expand it? Even if we know the existing level of functionality, what is meant by "expanded"? Does this mean: *new functions, greater volumes, improved information flow*, or what? Has anyone agreed on any of these things? Having the legal department review and approve the contract is not adequate, because they can only review the legalities, not the content. Therefore, even when some legal panjandrum reviews everything there is still room for disputes, so you can only imagine what awaits our intrepid project leader at acceptance time.

Also, according to the agreement we are committed to improving response times. Even if these response times are known and carefully writ-ten down, what constitutes improvement, and how is it measured? To the vendor it may seem obvious that even a 1% change would be an improve-ment, so anything he can do above what is currently being experienced is within the parameters of acceptance. Of course, the customer undoubtedly anticipates some "noticeable" improvement, and his acceptance hinges on some visible "clock time" improvement. Furthermore, the customer appar-ently expects improved communications, but, again, improvement is not specified, much less what communications are being referenced. This could very easily be tied to the response times and functionality, but just as easily it might reference communications with the suppliers or employees. Whatever the correlation is, it is not mentioned anywhere. This oversight could very easily scuttle the project at acceptance time.

I believe we have already determined that ignoring this lack of precision is a ticket to disaster, so what should the project manager do? Obviously, the solution is to clarify the terms and acceptance criteria. This can be done in association with the customer or unilaterally; that is, the project manager can document what he understands the acceptance criteria to be. Obviously getting the customer to clarify the terms and acceptance criteria is the best solution. It is sort of intuitive, is it not? What happens if the customer is cooperative but unresponsive? Suppose schedules conflict, the customer is not readily available, and time drags by. Suppose when the customer finally sits down to discuss the terms he is noncommittal, and nothing is really clarified.

This is actually a rather common occurrence. After all, every company has managers whose careers rest on their not being associated with a failure, just as every company has managers who cannot give a direct response as to the time of day. So it is very plausible that our project manager may find herself trying to determine what to do next. The options are all pretty grim once you eliminate the customer from the decision. Of course, the project manager can do nothing and escalates the problem to her superior. This is an excellent decision for those not interested in having a career. The project manager can suspend the project and keep working to get the customer to clarify the acceptance criteria. Hope does spring eternal, and that is about how long it would take, and it is unlikely the project can wait that long. Therefore, the project manager is really trapped into specifying the acceptance criteria, documenting it, and passing it onto the customer and moving forward with the project. Certainly this is a high-risk decision, not very elegant, and it will leave the project manager open to criticism from virtually every quarter. But, if she is successful, it is unlikely anyone will criticize her. In fact, if she is successful everyone will be congratulating themselves on how well *they* did. Of course, if she guessed wrong and fails, then she is in it by herself. After all, she did not follow procedure and get customer buy-in before proceeding with the project. Consequently, it is her failure alone. Does that sound familiar to anyone?

This situation is actually a composite scenario, but it is based on actual experiences. Certainly some of you will question this because you do not believe that vague and imprecise statements like these would be found in a contract written and reviewed by seasoned professionals. Unfortunately statements of this type are found in contracts and project plans written by some very seasoned managers. Well, perhaps like fine French cuisine— lightly seasoned, but the fact remains that contracts are written every day that are so vague and imprecise as to be meaningless.

For those of you who are skeptical and do not believe for an instant that anyone not using crayons regularly would write such imprecise statements, read on. These are some of my favorite quotes extracted from real contracts and provided to me by colleagues who were stunned by what their companies had willingly agreed to do.

- Enable (company name deleted to protect the guilty) knowledge workers to:
  1. Access global information quickly
  2. Reduce time to market for new products and services
  3. Satisfy complex customer requirements
- (Company name) will be the industry leader with creative products and services for its customers
- (Vendor) will manage all servers
- Significantly reduce the number of software virus problems
- Improve the flow of product information throughout the supply chain
- Transform people and processes within the organization
- Develop, document, deliver, maintain, and manage a site administration manual with procedures for administering the systems environment.

This is only a small sample of what can be found in contracts. Understand that these contracts followed all of the review processes to be found in most companies. This means the contract and terms were reviewed by the legal department, the sales team, the sales executives, and an assortment of other managers as well. These managers were not incompetent nitwits, but well meaning and capable executives. When placed in the context of a multi-page (and boring) contract, these kinds of statements are virtually invisible. Even when they are pointed out, they usually remain because all of the parties involved "understand" what is meant. Of course, the executives with the "understanding" are rarely there at the conclusion when all of the new players offer their own new and colorful interpretations of these clauses.

In the composite example, we were expected to expand the functionality of a system. In the actual example we were expected to make the customer an industry leader with creative products and services. Is this more precise? Do you have any idea of how we can determine in an objective way what is creative or who is an industry leader? True, you may have some ideas, but as your customer, I think you are wrong. What about "significantly" reducing the virus problems? Does this differ very much from improving response times? Of course, there is improving the flow of communications in the supply chain versus improving communications. The former is really no more specific than the latter. Besides, communications can include everything from smoke signals to Internet access. How about satisfying a customer's *complex requirements*? How complex are the requirements, and, for that matter, what are the requirements? What about *transforming* the people in the organization? Transform them to what? This could include everything from zombies to sex change operations.

The last point in this weird list appears to be very descriptive and complete. It describes precisely what is to be done, but it lacks the all-important *when*. When are these things to be done? Tomorrow? Next week? Next year? Without a clear definition of precisely when something is to occur, it is almost a foregone conclusion there will be a dispute between the parties with each claiming a different time frame for completion. But this opens the door to the next question regarding time frame because this appears to be an ongoing activity. Therefore, what constitutes completion? When the site administration manual is written and delivered, is that completed? If this is an ongoing activity, how do you know when it is completed? What event, milestone, or time frame must occur for this activity to be considered as having fulfilled the contract?

So, I believe the point is made—truth is worse than fiction, and our pretend manager is certainly no better or worse than her real counterparts. The point of this discussion on contracts is that virtually all companies have a process to review contracts. This process is usually rigorously adhered to because of the potential financial impact if the contract is carelessly written or commits the company to something that cannot be done. Yet, these review processes, which are carefully defined and rigorously followed, still do not filter out these landmines of interpretation. In these cases, the process is intended to review the contractual obligations from a legal perspective rather than the product or service perspective. However, even when a technical or content review is conducted, these imprecise terms frequently remain. Therefore, it is important that processes are established for change control, customer acceptance, and progress reviews; otherwise problems will arise. This simple scenario is an example of how a defined process and enforced procedure do not necessarily accomplish the objective, which in this case was to protect the company from unprofitable or impossible obligations.

We started this as a discussion of processes and procedures. Somehow the repeatable process has become the Holy Grail of management. There seems to be some sort of mystical belief among contemporary managers that if they can just get a standard repeatable process, then they can dispense with people and start using chimpanzees. We are bombarded daily with ISO 9000, Malcolm Baldridge, and the virtue of doing it right the first time and every time. This, of, course raises several questions, but most importantly, what is it you are trying to repeat? If you are in a manufacturing environment producing a tangible product then consistency is very important. This is especially true in high tech, biochemicals, toys, clothing, explosives, food, consumer products in general, or similar manufacturing activities. In these cases a standard process and procedure are crucial, and there are two ways to achieve this objective.

The first is to use robots. Robots are wonderful. They do not take time off, they hardly ever get sick, and, if one does, it can always be tossed out onto the scrap heap and replaced by another one that is just as good. In fact, the newer one might even be better. Robots can be relied on to work around the clock, never ask for overtime, and most importantly, will perform the same task the same way every time. Malcolm Baldridge is their god, and ISO 9000 their mantra. As if these were not enough reasons to dash out and hire Robby to replace your workers, there is an even more compelling reason. Robots do not belong to the union. They do not go on strike and complain about benefits and working conditions or ask for higher wages. In fact, oh joy oh rapture, every hour of production reduces their cost per unit! Therefore, for those managers who require consistent and repeatable processes, robotics are really the way to go. As computers become smaller and more sophisticated, this scenario becomes possible in more and more activities. The ubiquitous Voice Response Unit is a good example of this spread of robotics. When you call a business today you rarely get a person on the first try, and in some cases you never talk to a person. Instead, you are routed into a never-ending series of touch-tone menus. In extreme cases, the computer decides you are indecisive and terminates the call. This is an example of a fully automated process.

Unfortunately, no matter how small or efficient robots become, not all activities can be accomplished by a robot. This is where the drive for standard, repeatable processes enters the picture. Clearly if we cannot use robots, then we are reduced to using people. But as we know, people, unlike robots, are unpredictable. Therefore, it seems obvious that the next best thing is to convert our employees to robots. We dress them in uniforms (á la the Japanese and Theory Z), train them in a standard rote process, and provide them with standard phrases (Welcome to …), scripted responses, and pasted smiles (Hi. I'm Matthew, and I'll be your server tonight). The objective is to provide standard service in association with a standard product or output. Predictability is the objective and cultural homogenization is the result.

Personally, I do not believe these standard, repeatable processes work especially well. They certainly do not work well for that new breed of worker—the knowledge worker. Our society is increasingly filled with workers who hold the key to production and wealth creation in their heads. Unlike the assembly line worker, who served the machine and was dominated by the bosses, this knowledge worker is independent. Today, the machines are as generic as the workers used to be, and now it is the worker's knowledge and creativity that represent the means to create wealth. Consequently, the knowledge worker is independent of the bosses, the machines, and, like it or not, the processes.

These new knowledge workers are accustomed to using individual judgment and applying their critical review to processes and procedures. And, as we have seen in the examples, people (unlike robots) will communicate and interact outside of the procedural meetings and reviews. If knowledge workers decide a process is cumbersome or unproductive, they may modify it or ignore it entirely. This independent approach to processes can have a direct (and not always positive) effect on decisions, actions, and output.

THE SERVICE DELIVERY PROCESS

As more and more companies refocus their efforts on their core competencies, the door for small niche players has been opened. That is, the companies now *outsource* many of the services they formerly provided internally. Initially these outsourced services tended to be the mundane operations such as security, food service, janitorial services, trucking, and the like. However, as companies have become comfortable with outsourcing, they have begun to outsource many of their more sophisticated service requirements as well. Now companies are outsourcing purchasing, customer service, computer operations, voice communications, and laboratory analysis. Although outsourcing these services has enabled most companies to reduce their operating costs, it has introduced a very significant problem that they have not previously encountered, and that is, how do you manage all of these vendors? This was the problem facing the ABC Supply Company.

Although the ABC Supply company was considered a *large* company, it simply did not have enough people to provide all of their services in every nook and cranny in North America. Therefore, they outsourced many of their services but found they could not control these outsiders. This lack of control was affecting their customer satisfaction and profit margins. (Dissatisfied customers frequently want their money back or, at the very least, a discount.) The various outsourced service providers did not talk to one another, dependencies among vendors were unidentified due to misinterpretations or poor communications, and things in general were chaotic. After considerable pain, the company developed a standard set of management processes based on experience. These standard (repeatable) processes called for some very defined steps to be performed and reported in some very defined ways. This standard process was successfully piloted in the field, and, after some small changes, the standard process was released to the field managers for use with their customers. (The ABC company was essentially brokering some of these services.) And, quite unexpectedly, nothing happened. The process was ignored and directives from headquarters forced compliances, but the process was only halfheartedly followed. The results fell far short of what the process produced in the pilot, and all attempts to produce similar results using the field management team failed. So what was the problem?

There are actually several problems here, but the primary one is that old dependable, *The Human Variable*. The various vendors providing the services are represented by different people, who are being managed by different people, supporting different customers. The customers are not only different, their requirements vary, and the way things work varies from location to location. This lends credence to the regional managers' resistance to the standard process when they point out the process does not work here in Widespace, Montana. This leads to the creation of *flexible processes*.

A flexible process is one that can be modified to fit the circumstances, so it is mostly standard and mostly repeatable. Now this is not necessarily bad because the standard hamburger was replaced by the made-to-order hamburger, even though the majority of hamburgers are still standard. It is the flexibility to be different that is important. However, when flexibility was added to the standard process at ABC, the regional managers still performed the process in a perfunctory way. An outside consultant was called in to discover what the problem was. Why did the standard process not work in the regions as it did in the pilot? The consultant immediately recognized the problem, but in keeping with the secret rules of consultants, he scratched his head, furrowed his brow, and interviewed the local managers in Las Vegas (gambling), San Francisco (food), Orlando (Disney World), and Cincinnati (Mom). Following these in-depth interviews, the consultant pondered mightily, and then wrote a 30-page report, which concluded that none of the field managers were trained and that there was no enforcement process in place. In effect, there was a lack of training and discipline.

Processes and procedures, standard or otherwise, are necessary, and discipline is required for virtually all organizations. Organizations, no matter how democratic, must have structure or they sink into anarchy. Some disciplines are forced on the enterprise by external forces; for example, government bureaus, scientific processes, the law, and so on. Others are commonly accepted practices for example, segregated lavatories, standard office hours, authority hierarchy, and so on. The remainder may be unique to the company and its culture and so may be standard, but not universal. It is in this category where we find addressing superiors as Mr. or Ms., expense report processing, progress reporting, and the like. To a large extent these standard procedures create the corporate culture, but they also reflect it. The challenge for management is to provide this discipline and structure without smothering the creativity and flexibility of the organization.

This means that our scenarios pointed out some of the weaknesses of not having processes or having them and not following them, but they highlighted another point as well. Processes and procedures can exist and must exist, but they cannot be substituted for judgment and leadership. In the real world of management, if processes and procedures become too rigid and are slavishly followed, they do not necessarily produce the desired result or quality. Certainly there are some that must be followed absolutely, and if they are ignored then the risks dramatically increase and can lead to failure.

The conclusion is that standard processes and procedures are much like the Magic Bullets of management theory. They are aimed at creating or discovering the ultimate with a minimum of thought, leadership, or management involvement. Unfortunately, we must deal with uncontrolled variables, consequently, standard processes will not produce success by themselves. To be effective, processes must always be cognizant of the influencing variables. It is the human variable that causes standard, repeatable processes to be almost standard and almost repeatable. Therefore, although management theories are important and processes are necessary and valuable, managing people is even more crucial to the success of the enterprise. But, of course, we knew all along that the people are the problem.

5

MANAGING PEOPLE
The People Are the Problem

Leaders are people oriented, whereas managers are task oriented. Leaders inspire, whereas managers organize. Given that this dichotomy is accurate, why is this chapter titled "Managing People" and not "Leading People"? A logical question, but the earlier conclusion was that management and leadership are different sides of the same coin. However, that observation is from an external perspective and not from the trenches. Sometimes it is difficult to distinguish when you are leading and when you are managing. All of us have objectives and tasks to perform, and this requires planning, organizing, and directing; but the overwhelming task is the people. They must be found, hired, trained, organized, and applied to the task, which is what managing is all about. Certainly, people are a resource that must be applied in a planned and organized way, but they must also be inspired and motivated. This is leading people.

People represent a very large variable in all situations because they can be completely unpredictable. Some will resign to go surfing, others will demand unscheduled time off, quarrels will develop, and unfortunately health issues can impact the situation. The job of managing people is a combination of an opera impresario, a counselor, and a drill sergeant. The manager today is constantly attempting to balance the expectations of the company with those of the employee. The employees want more money, more time off, better working conditions, new equipment, free coffee, free pop, improved fringe benefits, and the list goes on and on. More recently, employees expect the company to be sensitive to their "quality of life." This term has many interpretations, but for the moment let us assume its meaning does not bode well for the company management. On the other hand, the company expects maximum return on its investment in people and equipment. The company expects the manager to control costs, improve productivity, and meet objectives in addition to motivating the workers. When you add competitors, external economic factors, and the omnipresent government to these expectations, you begin to understand why management, which has always had its downside, is now, in fact, a thankless job. So thankless that you begin to question why anyone would want to take on the aggravation. It makes you question the mental competence of the incumbents.

The essence of managing people is communication. Frequently personnel issues are traceable to poor communication. Every situation has an obvious set of actions, but sometimes the obvious and easy solution escapes the reactive manager who does not observe, question, and seek out more information than is initially at hand. When you are dealing with people you are dealing with emotions, cultures, government regulations, personalities, and a host of other quirky variables. The workplace does not always lend itself to open communication, so people frequently keep their thoughts in check for fear of showing weakness, fear of reprisals, or simply not wanting to display their total ignorance of the topic. Sometimes all of these things combine and leave the manager frustrated, exasperated, and longing for the good old days of the aristocracy when he could have flogged the dullards, hanged the rebellious, and started over with new people. This was certainly the case with "Jason."

Like all really bad problems, this one started innocently enough. The plant needed a computer programmer. They advertised, interviewed, and eventually settled on Jason, a recent college graduate in Computer Science. Jason was young, rather handsome, with the broad shoulders and narrow waist that is often associated with young athletes. His winning smile, sense of humor, and "can do" attitude made him very popular with the employees and his management. He sailed through his probationary period and became a valued member of the programming team. He received excellent performance appraisals and a promotion after his first year, but shortly after this the bomb was dropped.

The Director of Information Services arrived at work one Monday morning and found a very beautiful, tall, leggy brunette waiting for him. Her mini-skirt left little to the imagination, so the Director was definitely interested in pursuing a discussion, and he invited her into his office. She introduced herself as "Janice," formerly known as "Jason." She realized this was a shock, but she wanted the Director to be the first to know of her "transformation." She went on to say she had always felt she was a "woman," and these feelings had finally become so strong that she had decided to become a woman in fact. Unfortunately, there had been some impediments, including the realization that there were certain "physical alterations" involved and their exorbitant cost. Her original plan had been to save her money and have a sex change operation, but raising the money was taking too long and she felt the operation was really unnecessary because she was already a woman in spirit. Therefore, Jason had decided Janice would immediately begin her life as a woman but would continue saving her money for the operation just in case she changed her mind in the future. In the meantime Jason wished to be called Janice and henceforth, she would dress as a woman. Janice also told the Director that she expected to be treated like any other female employee from this point on.

Well, that certainly started the Director's day off with a bang! The good news was that no one, including the Director, had recognized Janice as Jason in disguise. The bad news was that because no one had recognized the good-looking woman waiting for the Director as Jason, the parade of young men up and down the hall had already started. To let Janice return to work was unthinkable, because it was only a matter of time before the young-bloods realized the truth, and the Director shuddered at the consequences of that revelation. On the other hand, what could he do? Jason was a highly skilled and very valuable employee. He was working on an important project, and firing him would seriously impact the schedule. While struggling to remember that those legs belonged to "Jason" rather than "Janice," our intrepid Director of Information Services gave Jason the day off to reflect on the impact "Janice" was likely to have on his future. Once Janice was safely off the premises, the Director acted in that time-honored method of handling difficult decisions—he bucked it upstairs to the Plant Manager.

As luck would have it, the Plant Manager was a former Israeli Army Officer and not one to either mince words or shrink from decisive action. The situation was described to him, and he summoned Jason to his office. Naturally, Janice arrived in place of Jason, and in very short order, Janice found herself and Jason in the unemployment line. Problem solved from the perspective of the Plant Manager.

As we all know, "Hell hath no fury like a woman scorned," and apparently that includes transvestites. Janice felt she had been abused and mistreated by the Plant Manager, who did not understand that she was really a woman hidden in a man's body and would not listen to her explanations. He called her names and then actually *fired* her. How dare he! She was determined she would show him he could not treat a lady like that and get away with it, and there certainly were not going to be any unemployment lines in her future. Janice went straight to the state unemployment bureau and stated her case, which in her eyes represented unfair treatment and sexual discrimination. The very kind people at the unemployment office agreed with her and could not understand how anyone could treat such a pretty young woman in such a mean way. With a dispatch uncommon in most state agencies, the unemployment bureau informed the Plant Manager that he not only had to return Janice to her rightful employment, but he had better mend his oppressive treatment of his employees. Janice triumphantly swept back into the plant, complete with mini-skirt, make-up, and a flirtatious coyness that would make a Jane Austen heroine wince. Total elapsed time: less than a week. But the story does not end there.

Janice resumed her duties, and, outside of the whispers and gossip, things returned to normal—or as normal as things could be under the circumstances. The usual grapevine informed most of the men that the "good-looking" programmer had some interesting characteristics. And Janice even developed some girlfriends among the female employees. It was not long, though, before a delegation of women arrived on the Plant Manager's doorstep. It seemed that Janice was using the "Women's" restroom, and, in their opinion, neither the restroom nor "Janice" were . . . aaahhh . . . *properly equipped*. In their view "Janice" was in reality "Jason," and no amount of make-up was ever going to change that. They demanded that Jason use the men's restroom beginning immediately.

The Plant Manager was incensed. The women were absolutely correct. Jason was Jason and not Janice, and even a cursory examination would verify that fact and that he should be using the appropriate facility. Forthwith, he summoned Janice/Jason to his office and explained that Jason could dress as a woman, act like a woman, and flirt with all of the boys like a woman, but he could NOT use the women's restroom. Jason/Janice was very understanding, and, in the spirit of cooperation, eagerly agreed to go back to using the men's restroom.

Within days a delegation of men arrived in the Plant Manager's office, and by this time the Plant Manager was wishing he had never heard of Jason, Janice, the state authorities, or most of the employees. It seems that Janice was now using the men's restroom as directed. The men did not object to "Jason" using the restroom, but "Janice" could not. It seems some of the male employees found it difficult to . . . aaahhh . . . *take advantage of the facilities* when "Janice" was there. The male delegation demanded that either Jason return to work or that Janice be forbidden from using the men's room. From this point on the situation became a bureaucratic and diplomatic nightmare as the Plant Manager attempted to satisfy the state, the employees, and Janice née Jason. Eventually they reached a compromise by allocating a bathroom for the exclusive use of Jason (or Janice).

This is actually more of an anecdote than an illustration of a serious management challenge. Certainly there are some management lessons here, but most of them are rather obvious. The Plant Manager was a former Army Officer and was thus accustomed to the command-and-control management model usually associated with Theory X. Predictably, this training overcame his judgment, which led him to dismiss Jason without thinking of the ramifications of that decision. He should never have acted so peremptorily. There was no attempt to determine the laws governing such a situation, no counseling for anyone, no attempt at compromise, and in general the whole situation became a comic opera as a result of appalling communications from the outset.

The point of the anecdote is that human beings are absolutely unpredictable. Who could have known that Jason was really "a woman inside"? This was not a question posed in the hiring interview, indeed even had it occurred to the manager to ask the question, he could not have done so without violating the law. Obviously, Jason either did not regard this aspect of his personality to be relevant, or he elected to keep it private until he could reveal it with impunity. On the other hand, the Plant Manager did not take the time to consider how the staff might react to this situation—he simply reacted. And who could have predicted that the Plant Manager would react so emotionally and in such a dramatic way? The human variable always lurks just beneath the surface of all management problems waiting to trip up the unwary. The fact is that the manager can never know everything about a situation and in many cases does not know crucial facts. The challenge for the manager is to question and probe until enough facts are available for a decision. However, this search for information must be balanced with the need for speed in decision-making. This is where most formal training programs fail because they are built on theories and predictable outcomes. In most actual operating situations outcomes are rarely predictable, and some information is almost always missing. As an example, take the "Window Cube." Virtually every manager who supervises employees working in cubicles must deal at some point with who gets the *Window Cube*. To those of you unaccustomed to working in cubicles, this must seem like a "tempest in a teapot," but to those of us in the corporate trenches, this is a very real and very serious matter. A poor decision regarding cubicle occupancy can have a far-reaching impact, as we shall see.

THE WINDOW CUBE

This situation always begins with the sudden availability of a prime cube, usually one with a view. As we all know, in the trenches these cubes have the same status as the carpets, office location, or artwork has in the executive suite, and, for the same reasons, the occupant is viewed as slightly superior or in greater favor than are the other denizens of cubicle row. Therefore, when one of these prime cubes becomes available, it is always the signal for internal struggles for status or dominance.

Perhaps the best place to start is by identifying the cast of characters, and, as is normal in most of these situations, *characters* is a very apt description. First, we have the manager and, in this case, a new manager only casually familiar with the other players. Being in transition from her previous assignment, the manager was not present when the cube became available and was unaware there was even an issue until John confronted her.

John is the most senior person on the team, having joined the company several years ago. He is familiar with the company, the products, and the procedures. Because of his depth of experience, the new manager relies on his knowledge. It is clear that John is an important, if uninspired, team member whose knowledge and experience are of great value to the overall success of the team.

Next we have Tiffany. She is young and inexperienced, but intuitive with tremendous drive, and is a very quick study. Tiffany is new to the team but is already an accepted and valued team member. Because she is new to the team, very little is known about her background or personal life. She is a willing worker with strong leadership skills and an excellent sense of humor, which makes her popular with the team.

Lastly, we have the Director. He is a longtime employee with a Theory X management style that he has been trying to correct. He has a tendency toward arbitrary decisions although he is making an effort toward "relating" and "understanding"; he is not Mr. Warm Fuzzy. This is our *Personae Dramatis*—so let our play begin.

One of the senior staff has recently been promoted and moved into an office, leaving his window cube enticingly vacant. Although there is no formal policy regarding cube assignments, the custom has been that the most senior staff members get the largest and most desirable cubes, but from time to time prime cubes have gone to the next person to arrive regardless of position. Essentially there is no policy and only a rough precedent governing cube assignment. As usual, the lack of formal procedure forms the basis for this problem.

Our new Manager arrived on Monday morning to find John waiting to see her. Although he is not exactly frothing at the mouth, it is clear John is very upset. Once the Manager has him calm enough to be articulate, the problem becomes clear. It seems when he arrived this morning he discovered that over the weekend Tiffany had moved into the vacant window cube. *His* window cube. John states that as the senior person on the team and the strongest contributor, that cube belonged to him. He was waiting until the manager returned to make his request. Even though he felt the request was pro forma, he played by the rules and was waiting for her return. In the meantime, Tiffany acted in a high-handed and sneaky manner, ignored the rules, and simply moved into the window cube over the weekend. When John confronted her and told her she had moved into his cube, Tiffany told him this was not his cube, it was hers, and she refused to discuss it any further. John decided to wait until the Manager returned so he could bring the situation to her attention, and she could rectify it. John states that he expects the Manager to immediately order Tiffany from the window cube and assign it to him. So now what does the manager do?

THE CHOICES

Our first question is what are the alternatives? Obviously this is the first step in any decision process and in this situation there may be many possible decisions or actions, but these seem like the most obvious ones.

1. The always popular: Do nothing. Accept the fact that Tiffany acted quickly and decisively in exercising the oldest rule of leadership, which is "it is always better to ask forgiveness than ask for permission." Go, Tiffany!

2. Summarily order Tiffany out of the cube and assign it to John: thus rewarding seniority and contribution. Shame on you, Tiffany!

3. Order Tiffany out of the cube and assign it to someone else, thereby depriving both John and Tiffany of the Window Cube. A pox on both your houses!

4. Call Tiffany in and demand to know why she moved into the cube in the first place without asking for permission. So who put you in charge, Tiffany?

5. Throw up your hands in despair and send the whole mess up to your boss, saving yourself from having to anger either Tiffany or John. May the Force be with you, Tiffany!

Ramifications—Option 1: *Do Nothing*

As we all have learned, some the hard way, no action is a form of action and no decision is in reality a decision. Even though this passive approach is noted for its unpredictable results, it is still a popular decision, especially with the corporate managers who are afraid of making a mistake. In this situation, there does not really seem to be any good answer because any decision will be challenged by someone. Therefore, the temptation is to do nothing, but as we know, this is, in fact, a decision. There are some managers who see aggressive and decisive action as a desirable trait and passive by-the-book behavior as uncreative, unimaginative, and thus less desirable. For these managers letting Tiffany keep the cube may be the proper course of action. After all, she saw an opportunity and acted swiftly and decisively while John dithered about waiting to be rewarded. Even though Tiffany is fairly new, her decisiveness may make her a stronger player than John in the long run. Therefore, for this manager, making no decision is really a conscious decision. By letting Tiffany stay in the cube while the manager "investigates," "rationalizes," or "prays for divine guidance," she is actually stalling John, hoping he will drop the matter and take no rash action. This is a risk decision because John could resign, escalate the matter to the Director, or simply become disgruntled. In the latter case, the extreme would be that John would "go ballistic" and shoot the place up, but this is an extreme. The reality is, by doing nothing; the manager has selected Tiffany as the employee to keep, consciously or unconsciously.

Ramifications—Option 2:
Order Tiffany out of the Cube

For the more traditional, hierarchically oriented manager, the decision to this situation is very obvious. John is a loyal, dedicated employee, who has contributed to the success of the enterprise over several years and is senior in rank to Tiffany. Therefore, Tiffany has no legitimate claim to the cube, and John is absolutely correct. She acted in a high-handed and arrogant manner. The facts are clear, the decision is obvious, and Tiffany must vacate the cube immediately. Furthermore, she must learn that arrogant behavior does not generate rewards or instill team spirit.

With this decision the manager has come down squarely on the side of John. She has decided that John is a more valuable employee than Tiffany. There is a risk, of course, that Tiffany will resign or take her case to the Director, but with this decision the manager clearly feels comfortable with these risks. It would be unfortunate if she resigned, but she is young, inexperienced, and replaceable—at least in the eyes of the manager she is replaceable. The risk of her escalating the problem to the Director is really a low-risk possibility. For all of his pretense otherwise, the Director is still an old-fashioned, authoritarian manager who can be relied on to support his subordinates even if he disagrees with them. Therefore, appealing the decision to the Director would be an exercise in futility for Tiffany. Of course, Tiffany could "go ballistic," but have you ever heard of a mass murderer named "Tiffany"? Naw, Tiffany loses.

Ramifications—Option 3:
Give the Cube to Someone Else

While the decision is obvious to the authoritarian Theory X manager, the new Theory Y managers may have to struggle with this decision. This situation requires the manager to pick one employee over another, and some managers hate picking and choosing between employees. They want to keep everyone happy, and they want everyone to like them. In this situation, it does not matter which employee you decide is correct because the other *will not like you*. For the manager who has been taught that every situation must be a "win-win" (don't you just love these quick solutions?), the only real solution may be to deny the cube to either one. Of course, both employees will hate you, but for some managers, this is preferable to having to choose between them.

To some managers, forcing Tiffany out of the cube and assigning it to someone other than John might be seen as a "lose-lose." But under the circumstances and for those managers who must have a win-win, this alternative may be better than selecting one employee over the other and creating the hated "win-lose" scenario. At least giving the cube to someone else shows the manager is fair and does not play favorites. In effect, this is punishing everyone for the infraction of one. It is unlikely that Dr. Suess or Mr. Rogers would approve of this management decision.

With this decision, the manager has created a situation that can take on a life of its own. Tiffany and John could bury the hatchet, join forces, and take action. Who knows what action because no one knows what evil lurks in the minds of men (do I say persons here?), but it is possible that they could appeal the decision to the Director, they could both resign, or they could hatch some plot to subvert the manager. In any case, by awarding the cube to a third party, the manager has created a situation that could be very unstable and result in a variety of outcomes.

Ramifications—Option 4:
Refer the Decision to Upper Management

Another popular decision is actually a variation of option one. In this case the manager cannot create a win-lose scenario, cannot stomach a lose-lose, and cannot see a win-win solution. Therefore, the obvious answer is to move the decision to a higher and presumably wiser level (stop laughing, this is a serious option). By getting the boss to do the dirty work, the manager has avoided choosing sides, but most importantly he/she is no longer responsible for any negative repercussions. For this manager it really does not matter who gets to keep the cube because he/she gets to be sympathetic to the loser while maintaining good relations with the boss. This requires two faces (Well, Tiffany/John, you know how he is, I'm sorry but . . .). At the same time we can sympathize with the boss (Can you imagine the nerve of John/Tiffany?). For the "I have never failed" fast-tracker, putting on the second face is usually not much of a stretch.

As a solution, this option has a lot of attraction. Certainly either John or Tiffany will be disappointed and can react in any of the ways already mentioned. The beauty of this decision is that it allows the manager to maintain good rapport with both Tiffany and John because, after all, the decision was the Director's. Furthermore, the manager can now attempt to mollify the loser by promising money, the next cube, a transfer, or whatever is necessary to retain the employee and keep morale up. It is possible that this harmony may have been purchased at the expense of respect. Both the Director and the employees may see the manager as weak, ineffectual, and indecisive. Why bring a problem to the manager if all he/she does is pass it on to the

Director? The Director may see the problem the same way, so this solution has some attraction but carries some risk as well.

Ramifications—Option 5:
Ask Tiffany Why She Moved into the Cube

This may or may not be an option by itself, because within any one of the previous options, the manager might have raised the all-important question of why she moved into the cube in the first place without asking for permission—a reasonable and not overly threatening question. There are many possible answers to this question, but they can be grouped into two categories: (a) because I wanted to, and (b) because I had permission. Certainly, if the response is basically: I moved into the cube because I wanted it, then the already described options apply. What if Tiffany had permission?

This scenario is very common, and rarely does the offender act unilaterally. Almost always someone somewhere has given permission. The problem then pivots on who gave permission, why did they give permission, and did they have the authority? Although there may be several sources of authority, the most probable are "real estate," the team leader, or the Director. The Real Estate people really do not care who occupies the cube; they are only concerned that the group paying the bill has possession. They really do not have the authority to assign the cube to individuals, so, if this was the source of Tiffany's authority, then it can be reversed. The team leader may have given Tiffany permission, thinking that the previous occupant was on his team, and therefore, the cube belonged to him and he had the authority to assign it. This is a plausible scenario and requires policy decisions for an eventual resolution. The Director may have given permission, and, in that case, it is difficult to reverse the decision—difficult, but not impossible. In these circumstances, the manager must have a very good case to move Tiffany and may opt for option 4 (ask her why she moved without permission).

This scenario is actually a composite of several events that have been compressed into this general situation. The actual results from the decision alternatives were in reality a mixed bag, but few of them good. In one of the actual situations, Tiffany had a doctor's request that she be seated near natural light because the fluorescent lights were a health problem for her. In another, the team leader had given permission even though it was a violation of policy. Because the policy was vague and unwritten, the team leader felt it was informal, and he was free to act as he chose.

We could continue this scenario and explore some of the other alternatives or options, but I believe the point has been made that things are not always as they seem, and managers are frequently put into situations where they are expected to make decisions without all of the facts. This does not mean that facts are being deliberately withheld, just that the people involved may not have all of the necessary information. After all, John did not know why Tiffany moved into the cube; he was simply reacting to what he knew. We really do not know why Tiffany moved into the cube, but with a few questions we might find that she felt she acted in good faith and had permission. Perhaps the principle point is that for those managers who are willing to act solely on the information immediately at hand, disaster awaits. For the more experienced and cautious, they have an opportunity to make a better decision, but that requires asking the right questions of the right people. Quick decisions are good, but only if they are based on an understanding of the situation. On the other hand the situation may be fully understood and still lead the unwary into bad decisions. Consider the young man whose mother had a stroke.

MOTHER HAD A STROKE

As the workforce shifts from hourly to salary and management moves from authoritarian to humanitarian, managers are increasingly faced with decisions that transcend business issues. At one time it was unthinkable for a person to decline relocation or to take time off for family issues. For better or worse, this situation has changed, and now it is virtually unthinkable to not consider family issues. For the manager, the trick is in finding a way to provide the support that the employee needs without losing sight of the needs of the business. That is what this scenario is about. Again this scenario is a composite from a variety of events, but I am confident that you will recognize the situation. The problem, of course, is how do you deal with it effectively?

Matthew is a young, single man, who has been with the company since graduation from college. He is a loyal and competent, if undistinguished, member of the accounting department. He recently returned from a two-week vacation, which he used to take a bicycle tour of New England with some college friends. Matthew was only back from vacation for a week when his widowed mother had a stroke. She has been in the hospital for several days and is now ready to return home. However, there is no one at home to care for her because she is a widow, and Matthew is an only child. Her sister lives in another state, but is not in good health, so it is up to Matthew to care for his mother until he can make permanent arrangements. Therefore, Matthew comes to his manager and requests some time off so he can bring his mother home and arrange for her ongoing care. He explains that he has discussed the situation with his colleagues, and they are willing to cover his duties while he makes arrangements. As Matthew's manager, what should you do?

The options here seem rather clear-cut. As Matthew's manager, you either give him the time off or you do not. The first fact to consider is that Matthew has already taken all of his annual vacation, so any time off is, in effect, unearned vacation. Furthermore, the manager must consider that Matthew has just been gone for two weeks, and during this time his colleagues had to put in extra time to fulfill his duties. To give Matthew more time off means that the other members of the department must continue doing the work normally done by Matthew.

Although not giving Matthew the time off seems like an option, it really is not—at least not in today's environment. To refuse the time off today would be viewed as insensitive by everyone and could easily undermine morale. At the very least it would affect Matthew, and in all probability he would resign. Therefore, refusing to give Matthew the time off is really not an option.

This scenario is played out every day, and in, virtually all of the cases, Matthew is told to take the time off to care for his sick mother. Usually, this permission is granted along with sympathetic comments like "Of course you can take the time off. Take as much as your need"; or "Certainly you can have the time off. Family is very important"; "Is there anything we can do to help you?" These comments are sincere and well meant. Most of us are sensitive to our co-workers and would extend a helping hand to them when they need it. Therefore, granting time off to Matthew is a logical and common decision. There is really nothing wrong with this decision—or is there?

Matthew is gone for three weeks. During this period he has been taking care of his mother, assisted by some ladies from the church. Things are mostly under control, but he still has been unable to find permanent help. The ladies from the church are of tremendous assistance, but this cannot go on forever. Matthew has looked everywhere for permanent help but has been unable to find any. He explains all of this to his manager. He thanks him profusely and explains that he realizes his absence is an imposition but he is doing the best he can. He is confident that he will be able to solve the problem of a permanent caregiver very soon. He just needs some more time off. As Matthew's manager, what would you do?

At this point managers begin to differ on what should be done next, and there are several obvious choices.

1. Give Matthew the additional time off that he is requesting. (Theory Y)
2. Tell Matthew that he cannot have any more time off. (Theory X)
3. Tell Matthew that he can have some specified amount of additional time? (MBO)

Before exploring the last two options, suppose the manager is sympathetic to Matthew and gives him the additional time off. There are several possible conclusions but generally these can be grouped into: (a) Matthew gets his act together and returns to work. Case closed; or (b) Matthew does not get his act together and seeks further relief. At this point Matthew has been gone from work for over a month. Perhaps his colleagues are still willing to absorb his workload, but more probably they are getting a little weary and impatient with the additional workload. If they are not, as a manager you should ask yourself if you are not overstaffed for the workload. Assuming that Matthew is doing his best (at this point this is a real leap of faith), what do you do now? Matthew has requested that he be permitted to work part time or to work at home until he can make some permanent arrangement for his mother.

Clearly the situation with Matthew is out of control, and we can continue this scenario ad absurdum, but there is really no point because the cause and effect are relatively obvious. Instead let us return to the two unexplored options. After giving Matthew considerable time off to arrange his personal life, the manager can simply call a halt and say *enough!* There is some attraction to this decision, but the probability is Matthew will resign because he cannot return to work and abandon his mother. Essentially this decision represents an ultimatum and is tantamount to either firing Matthew or forcing him to resign. If the workers who have been covering for Matthew are not complaining then this may be a very good decision. It allows you to reduce your headcount, because you may have been overstaffed anyway. The opening created by Matthew's exit can now be filled when it becomes necessary. In effect, this decision leads to a painless headcount reduction (excluding Matthew of course).

For the manager determined to arrive at a win-win solution regardless of the cost, Matthew can be given some specified period of time to resolve his problem. What is usually not said is the "or else" that goes along with this specified period of time off. This decision is only good if the manager is willing to enforce the implied "or else." Otherwise Matthew may be back looking for more time-off or some other relief.

Of course the fundamental question is what could have been done to control this situation at the outset? Before moving on to that point, remember that it is always easier to critique the manager on the ground after the problem has become obvious than to make the correct decision in the midst of battle. Matthew was a good and loyal employee. He was well liked, and he was a contributing member of the team. Like all of us, he suffered some unforeseen personal problems and needed some help. Any one of us would have given the help he requested—well, most of us at any rate; you may be the exception. Nevertheless, that does not mean that this situation should be allowed to spin out of control as it obviously has. What the manager should have done at the outset when Matthew asked for some time off was to say, "Certainly. Take a few (days, weeks, months, years)."

Situations spin out of control when they are left unbounded. By authorizing the additional time off and specifying the amount, the manager bounded the problem. At that point both Matthew and the rest of the team know that there is a forecasted endpoint. Even if the endpoint is extended, everyone including Matthew knows that an extension has been granted. By giving boundaries, the manager has remained in control of the situation. Certainly the scenario may end the same way as it did in the unbounded version, but the manager retains control and guides the events to a conclusion that he/she selects rather than allowing the situation to end in some random fashion. However, for the new manager there are times when events acquire a momentum of their own, and unless new managers are very alert they may find themselves in a position they never intended. This was certainly the case with Frank's birthday.

THE BIRTHDAY LUNCH

Birthdays are one of those workplace activities whose very triviality makes them treacherous. For some, their birthday is a significant event that they enjoy sharing with others, especially because it places them in the spotlight and usually includes cake. For others, their birthday is simply another year marked off in their inexorable march to the biblical three score and ten and not a time for celebration. On the one hand, to ignore a birthday is risking a morale problem, but on the other, acknowledging a birthday might cause offense. This is the tightrope the manager walks in every organization, and every organization approaches this problem differently. Although this is dangerous ground at any time, it is especially dangerous for the new manager, who must decide between public recognition and individual privacy.

In this situation, we have Tom, a newly appointed manager replacing a very popular leader. Tom had only been on the job for a week when he received the following e-mail from one of his team members.

Tom:

My birthday is Friday and I would like to take that day off as a vacation day. Is this OK with you? Also, as you undoubtedly know already, your predecessor had a policy of taking team members to lunch on their birthday. However, I expect to be on vacation that day so could we schedule my birthday lunch for next Thursday? If Thursday is inconvenient, perhaps we can schedule the lunch for another day.

Frank

It is this type of trivial request that can determine the long-term success or failure of the new manager, yet the request is so routine it would receive little attention in most cases. This is especially true if it were buried among other more important items. The new manager has several decision alternatives:

1. Grant the request
2. Reject the request
3. Establish a new policy
4. Ignore the whole thing.

Grant the Request

The most obvious decision is to grant the request for the vacation day and schedule the lunch at the most convenient time. This is a simple, direct, "don't rock the boat" response. This is the way things were done before, everybody expects to have lunch with the boss, and by continuing the policy, the new boss is maintaining the momentum and harmony of the group. But there may be more here than meets the eye.

With this seemingly inconsequential decision, the new manager has accepted the policies of the former manager as his own. The first policy deals with vacations. Tom has now established (accepted) that vacations can be scheduled a day at a time and with less than a week's notice. This policy was already in place, and it may or may not be a good policy, but the new manager simply accepted it without thought or investigation. Did his peers and subordinates agree with the policy? Suppose this policy had been responsible for ill feelings and slipped schedules? Suppose the new manager's peers had objected to the policy because it conflicted with their policies? By simply accepting the request without some reflection, the new manager may have put himself into a difficult situation. He has reaffirmed the existing vacation policy as his own.

With this decision the new manager has also accepted the custom of taking each person to lunch on his or her birthday. Is that a good decision? How many employees are involved? Is it a productive use of the manager's time? How do the employees feel about having an obligatory lunch with the boss? Certainly we know that Frank likes the policy, but for all the new manager knows, Frank is the only one that likes it. In fact, Frank may have dreamed up the whole scheme in the first place and manipulated the previous manager into establishing the custom. Suppose the previous manager was an entertaining raconteur and a charming luncheon companion, whereas Tom is as dull as dirt and his conversational spectrum is limited to current work, undone work, and work to be done, sprinkled with bons mots about garden fertilizer. Would that change everyone's opinion about the birthday lunches?

Reject the Request

The new manager can simply reject the request out-of-hand. Frank does not get the day off, and he certainly does not get a free lunch just because he has been able to survive a year since his last natal milestone. Naturally this is a decision more likely to cast Tom in the role of Ebenezer Scrooge than Bob Cratchit. Although this decision has some attraction, it probably is not the best one. This decision rejects the previous vacation policy as well as the birthday policy. Rejecting these is not really the issue; the problem is the style. By rejecting this request with no explanation, no investigation, and no consideration, the new manager has established the impression as a domineering and authoritative "boss."

Without doubt this decision will require only nanoseconds to spread throughout the team. Frank will repeat it as the abused employee, who not only did not get his lunch, but he did not get a *vacation day* that he earned— a day that he was planning on taking his sick mother to the doctor or volunteering at the soup kitchen for indigent waifs. No doubt about it, Tom will be the blackhearted villain in this scenario. This does not mean that Tom should seek popularity over good management, nor does it mean the decision was wrong, but again it is the style. This is a leadership issue so it must be handled as what it is . . . *a people issue.*

Establish a New Policy

This decision is probably the best decision but also a decision that does not immediately leap to mind, especially if the new manager is comfortable with the existing policies. There is a high probability that the new manager will see this situation as trivial and not worthy of much thought or reflection. The decision can be classified as "whatever," with about that much thought and effort. This is not necessarily a terrible decision or pivotal event in the manager's career, yet it may be a missed opportunity.

Establishing control of an organization is always difficult, especially if the manager wants to gain control while building rapport with the team. In this case, it really does not matter what the new policies are, only that they are clearly labeled as the new manager's policies. There are many ways this can be accomplished, such as, team meetings, written notification, and discussions. The technique is not especially relevant. What is important is that everyone affected is involved, and that the decision is clear. The best time to establish a policy is the first time the need arises, and the best policies are those that have the buy-in from all parties (Theory Z).

Ignore the Whole Thing

Actually, this may be the most common decision to this problem. Because of its incredible triviality, this is the kind of issue that gets a low priority and is put at the end of the list of things to be done. As more pressing matters absorb the manager's time, this request gradually evaporates from the manager's consciousness, but rest assured that it is at the forefront of Frank's consciousness. By failing to take action, the manager has failed to affirm an old policy or establish a new policy, thus leaving the issue in limbo. Worse, by not responding to Frank's request, the manager has sent a very strong message that Frank (and the employees in general) is not very important to him. Certainly this is not the message that Tom or any manager wants to send to the employees, but more often than not, it happens unintentionally.

In this situation, Tom is a new manager trying to make a positive impression. The question is: Who is he trying to make a positive impression on—his employees or his boss? Whether he means to or not, by prioritizing the work over the people Tom has demonstrated that the employees are not very important to him. As time drags on without any action being taken to schedule or cancel the birthday luncheon, Frank will begin to talk and complain about the new manager's insensitivity. It is imperative that any personnel or people issue be given a high priority no matter how trivial, because it is these small issues that can destroy a team as well as a reputation. Doing nothing is probably the worst decision possible in this situation.

This is a very trivial example of a very trivial problem. One that is usually associated with first- or second-tier managers rather than the senior executives of the company. But is this little problem over birthdays and vacation time really much different than the problems faced by incoming executives who are asked to make decisions regarding more complex policies? Suppose you are the new Executive Vice President of Manufacturing and you have just received the following e-mail from your Plant Manager in Mule Shoe.

Tom:

My HR guy just pointed out to me that the annual picnic is scheduled for next Friday, and you are scheduled to be in Europe that day. This picnic is very important to all of us here in Mule Shoe, and as you may know, traditionally the Executive Vice President has attended and recognized our Employee of the Year with a plaque. Therefore, I propose to shift the picnic to the first convenient Friday on your schedule.

Frank

This brief little message is filled with potential. It confirms the annual picnic, attendance by the EVP, and an "employee of the year." If you were the EVP of Worldwide Manufacturing, the probability is that you would not pay very much attention to this note; in fact, it is highly probable that it would have been handled by one of your aides. Nevertheless the same decisions are possible, with much the same probable outcomes. Is an annual picnic a good idea? How much does it cost? Do the employees attend or just view it as an extra holiday? Is this a good use of your time? Is an "employee of the year" award a good idea? How is this decided? Who has received it in the past?

Certainly there is nothing wrong with any of these policies, or at least obviously wrong, yet each carries a problem potential. This problem potential is magnified if the EVP is surrounded by aides who shield him from trivia. In that case, these policies might go unchallenged, because they are in place and probably part of the corporate culture.

The point is that incoming managers at all levels must be on their guard. Seemingly small decisions can have great influence on a department, a project, and especially the bottom line. No policy or procedure should be endorsed or perpetuated without examination. This does not mean that the new manager should throw out everything and start over. But it does mean that even if policies are to be continued, they should be continued only after review and the final decision establishes them as the policy.

THE QUALITY OF LIFE

It is the unpredictable human variable that we have covered in the scenarios, which generally centered on working conditions, including Jason and Janice. However, the Jason scenario introduced the issue of "lifestyle" rather than the "quality of life." Jason represented a facet of life that managers rarely had to deal with in the first half of this century. Obviously these things have always existed, but they were hidden or under the surface and not part of the workplace. But this has begun to change, and increasingly managers are confronted with problems dealing not only with "lifestyle" but "quality of life." Workers come from single-parent homes, dual-income homes, mixed-race homes, single-sex homes, are handicapped, minorities, or virtually any human variant you can imagine. The manager is inundated with sensitivity training and the "advantages" of cultural diversity (an interesting topic that we cannot explore here). The media focus on these issues like a starving man at a banquet to the point where sound business decisions are expected to be subordinate to life quality. Certainly this is not all bad, and leadership is closely tied to the happiness and well-being of the subordinates. However, as most managers know, this is the tip of the iceberg.

Consider the situation of Jack, a Product Manager for a large firm. Jack and his wife, Jeanine, decided with the birth of their first child that she would be a "stay at home" mom. This entailed some financial sacrifice on their part because Jeanine had a very promising career with an income about equal to Jack's. Nevertheless, they felt that the traditional family structure enabled Jack to focus on his career, spend more time with the children, and offer more stability to their family. They believed these advantages more than offset the reduction in income.

Most of Jack's peers were similar in age, education, and circumstance except that they had working spouses with all of the associated problems that come with dual-income families. These problems spanned the usual gamut of sick children, PTA meetings, spousal travel, and day care. These were the very problems that Jack and Jeanine decided to avoid with their decision to become a one-income family. That is, they thought they avoided them.

It started innocently enough when Sarah, another Product Manager, asked Jack if he could complete a report she was writing because her daughter was sick, and the school had asked her to come and get her. This was a personal favor, and Jack was happy to oblige. He did not mind working a little late to help Sarah, after all he was a parent and understood the situation.

It was not very long before Ted asked Jack to fill in for him at a crucial meeting, because his wife was out of town and he had to meet with the school counselor. In very short order, Jack became the designated department substitute. He found himself working late most nights so he could keep his schedules, because he was filling in for others during normal working hours. He was missing dinners with his family, missing school events, and, in general, missing most of the advantages he anticipated when he and Jeanine decided to become a one-income family.

Jack asked to see his superior and outlined his situation. Essentially he and his wife had made a decision that included financial sacrifice. They had made this decision because they felt it would improve their quality of life. Now his colleagues, who had not made that financial sacrifice, were expecting him to subsidize their decision by filling in for them. The rationale was that Jack had a wife at home so he did not have to be concerned about when he came to work or when he left. Therefore, it was not a problem for him to stay late or come in early. Jack felt the others were taking advantage of his situation. He wanted his manager to either fix the problem or pay him for the extra work.

This is the type of problem that managers are increasingly being asked to resolve. Jack and Jeanine made a decision regarding their quality of life. Other department members had made decisions regarding their lifestyle, and these are now in conflict. Historically, this problem would not have occurred, and issues involving families and life choices rarely became workplace issues. This is no longer true, and Jack's manager is faced with a problem dealing with private matters that affect the workplace. So what are his options? They appear to be:

1. Take no action.
2. Pay Jack.
3. Forbid substitutions.
4. Establish a policy.

Take No Action

Sometimes taking no action is a good decision, but in this case it is equivalent to telling Jack to stop whining and get back to work. In many cases ignoring a problem buys time for reflection, and in others it can be a form of passive resistance. However, this is not one of those times, and refusing to take any action will eventually create a larger problem. Certainly Jack will be unhappy and eventually might resign if the situation is not corrected. Of course, losing Jack may or may not be a problem, depending on his abilities, past performance, future career plans, or impact on the organization as a whole. But Jack really is not the problem, is he? If the others are taking so much time off that it is affecting Jack's work, how effective are they? Is the company getting a day's work for a day's pay? What constitutes a day's work? At some companies the employees are expected to put in more than the normal eight hours, especially for those aspiring to higher position. If Jack leaves, would this cause the performance of the entire group to decline due to missed schedules, reduced quality, and incomplete work? In effect, taking no action is tantamount to whistling past a graveyard.

Pay Jack

In most cases this is not only ludicrous, it is not even an option. If Jack were an hourly employee, the problem would not have occurred in the first place. As he is a salaried employee the extra pay would sound alarm bells in the chain of command, which no manager wants. Of course, the manager could give Jack bonuses, but this is really sidestepping the problem. Besides, if you listened to Jack, you would realize money is not the issue—it is the time. Jack wants what he sacrificed for and that is the time necessary to improve his quality of life. Therefore, extra pay for Jack would not necessarily resolve the problem in the long term.

Forbid Substitutions

This requires the manager to tell the entire team that they cannot support each other by picking up the slack. In effect, this policy would dissolve the team and substitute a group of individuals each responsible for individual performance. The manager who would opt for this as a solution is probably not destined for stardom. Besides, because the manager was unaware of Jack's situation, how would he know if the policy forbidding substitutions was working? He would have to rely on someone filing a complaint, and that is not very likely. This is really not a very realistic option.

Establish a Policy

And what policy do you suggest the manager establish? Should the policy govern starting and quitting times? Perhaps it should limit the amount of time a person can take off for personal business. What about family emergencies. Are they exempt? Should the policy address the number of working hours expected of each employee? How would these be measured? Establishing a policy seems like a glib answer to a very complex problem, and the probability is there is really no easy answer to this problem.

In the actual situation, Jack filed a complaint, the manager dithered, and ultimately Jack simply refused to take on the extra work. The immediate reaction is that this was the obvious solution from the outset and that Jack should never have taken the problem to his manager in the first place. In effect, this attitude says he created the problem by his spineless acquiescence to unreasonable demands by his co-workers. In reality, Jack was attempting to be a team player and to maintain harmony within the group, but the team decided his position was "designated substitute," which was not a position that Jack wanted to play on a permanent basis. When he finally did refuse to be the patsy, his popularity declined, and he was viewed as not being a team player. However, it did allow him and Jeanine to enjoy the benefits of their personal sacrifice.

While this resolution satisfied Jack and Jeanine, it did not really address the fundamental issue, which was the conflict between one employee's quality of life and another employee's lifestyle. Although it can be argued that this was a tempest in a teapot brought on by Jack, the fact remains that this is a very commonplace problem today, and most managers are not prepared to cope with the decisions required. And you probably noticed that I did not offer any good solution either. That is because I do not know of any. This is a good example of a "least worst decision," which is why the manager dithered and could not make a decision.

In this chapter we explored people and some of the management problems associated with them. Managing people is always challenging, because the human variable puts risk into every situation and decision. This means that circumstances are never exactly the same (Chaos Management) because the people involved are not the same. It also means that as circumstances change, plans must change, and organizations must be flexible enough to accommodate those changes. Some of these changes are internal, and they concern some of the problems we addressed with Jason and Janice and Jack and Jeanine. Managers must be prepared to cope with employees like Jason and to resolve issues dealing with lifestyles and quality-of-life issues. Not too many years ago managers did not have to consider the quality-of-life issues, but this is no longer true. Employees are no longer willing to uproot their families and move to new cities for new opportunities, even when these opportunities come with promotions and increases in compensation. Managers must now contend with expectations for family time, challenging work assignments, working hours, working environment, and many similar issues, which is driving how we organize our people resources. Frequently, in lieu of physically moving an employee, we allow them to work remotely thus creating a virtual organization. Virtual organizations not only require new management techniques, they require new structures as well. Therefore, managers must be prepared to organize these employees more creatively and to modify their personal management style to accommodate these new organizational structures.

6

MANAGING THE ORGANIZATION

From Bullets to Bubbles

When we left our friends Og and Nog, the latter had just assumed the mantle of power. And like all new managers, Mr. Nog was immediately faced with two issues. First priority was to ensure that he got the lion's share of the mammoth steaks, and the second was to organize his team into a more effective force. In the millennia since this first transition of power, things have changed very little. New managers are always faced with the question of how to organize *their* people. Of course, the operative word here is *their,* and therein lies the problem. Inherent in the statement is the presumed hierarchical organizational structure that has been utilized since Og organized the first hunting party. The organization and reorganization always starts with the question "are my people organized effectively?" and the answer always begins with the top box labeled "Me" or some variation thereof. Regardless of what happens next, the resulting structure is the classic pyramid, which has stood the test of time. However, as anyone who has seen the Sphinx knows, time takes its toll, and the organizational pyramid is no exception. Just as sand, wind, and rain have eroded the Sphinx, so has technology eroded the effectiveness of the organizational pyramid.

The original purpose of the pyramidal organization was not to elevate an individual above his fellows, rather the intent was to capitalize on the knowledge and expertise of the most effective hunter (Og) and to transfer these skills to the group. Thus, the underlying success of the organization was dependent on communications. By making Og chief and dividing the others into expert groups (e.g., scouting, tracking, skinning, and so on), the structure provided for the most effective use of the resources, but it also permitted more rapid and thus more effective communications (I realize that primitive man did not organize for mass production, but work with me here). However, the primary objective, which was to capitalize on the knowledge and expertise of Og was short lived as Nog exercised brawn over brains to seize power, with power being his objective. This primordial organizational struggle between power (Nog) and expertise (Og) has been with us ever since. The secondary objective of rapid and effective communications remains intact and continues to be an organizational objective even today. From Og to Nog to you this objective of communications has depended on technology, ranging from hand signals, to smoke signals, to satellites and from crude signs, to writing, to e-mail. The objective has always remained the same—to pass orders and information from the top to the bottom and to report results from the bottom to the top.

However, as power over others became consolidated at the top of the pyramid, some members ascertained that they were more likely to get a larger share of the mammoth if they pleased the chief and manipulated the information flow, meaning "no news is good news." Thus was introduced by the layers of vice chiefs and buffers that provided an information screen that ensured only selected (read positive) information reached the top. Because the chief was shielded from the real facts (read negative), situations rarely appeared as grim as they were in reality. Therefore, directives from the top appeared to be unresponsive, slow, or beside the point. Consequently, the leaders in the trenches either implemented the directives from the top slowly and in piecemeal, or just ignored them entirely. Thus organizational impedance was created.

Organizations have always resisted change, because people generally resist change, so the impact of a directive from the CEO, even when it made sense, has always dissipated as it flowed downward in the organization, and the larger the organization, the more this can be observed. As many senior executives can tell you, the higher you go in the organization, the more power you gain, but your ability to impact things seems to decline proportionately. I had first-hand experience with this several years ago, when a major manufacturer engaged me as consultant. Our objective was to effect some procedural changes between the various factories and suppliers. Once we had defined a solution, the problem was getting it implemented, and the representatives from the client were very concerned about the resistance they felt that they would encounter. I suggested to the Vice President that he ask the CEO to simply issue a directive that these changes were to be made. When I made this suggestion the Vice President looked at me as if I had a deranged mind. As patiently as he could, he revealed one of the great corporate secrets. He said, "You don't understand. Two levels down from the CEO no one knows what he wants, and three levels down, no one cares." This is an excellent example of how influence can (and does) dissipate as you move down in the organization. This normal resistance to change has now been joined by other factors, which are creating additional problems that are also driving the decline in the effectiveness of the pyramidal organization. Among these new factors we find a change in the expertise and expectations of the employee, the rapid availability of information through technology, and the globalization of business.

THE WORKFORCE

Perhaps the most significant change in the work environment has been the shift from a general direct labor force to a service based specialized workforce. The labor pool of interchangeable (and frequently unionized) workers who performed simple repetitive tasks is both aging and shrinking. These workers were loyal and dependable and frequently spent their entire working life with one company. However, as we already know these workers and this form of the workplace are disappearing, even in the low-cost labor markets overseas. A new form of worker is taking their place. These new workers are highly trained and have specialized knowledge. It is this knowledge, which gives them a level of independence, that workers have not had since the beginning of the industrial revolution. Unlike the traditional workers, the knowledge worker is not easily replaced and in some cases may be irreplaceable. If not technologists themselves, they are familiar with technology and how to utilize it to deliver their service. They are specialists with a high degree of training and a drive toward professional improvement. Their first loyalty is to themselves and their discipline.

For example, a neurosurgeon wants to become a better neurosurgeon, not a better employee or another struggling minion climbing the corporate ladder to become the hospital administrator. This is a very important distinction, because it highlights how specialization shifts the organizational structure from a control to a support orientation. The hospital administrator and the organization he/she directs is expected to provide the environment necessary for the staff of knowledge workers to deliver their service. Essentially the organization becomes an infrastructure responsible for providing the state-of-the-art tools necessary to enhance the knowledge workers' skill level. If the organization fails to fulfill this expectation, then the employee must and will seek this elsewhere.

This new type of independent worker has little loyalty to the company and has little fear of the management. Because, unlike the old days when jobs were in demand and the supply of workers was large, the knowledge worker of today is in demand, and the need for their specialized skills is great. However, for many of these knowledge workers, the technology advances so rapidly that their skill set is in constant need of renewal. So these highly trained workers are increasingly like athletes in that they have a limited shelf life unless they can refresh their skills. Therefore, these highly skilled technicians are receiving (and expect to receive) star treatment. Furthermore, they do not expect to stay with a company longer than it takes to improve their marketability and increase their income. Some managers have found that challenging work, that is, work that expands and enhances the knowledge and skills of the worker, can be used as a method of retaining these workers. Nevertheless, it is difficult for a manager today to know precisely how many people are available on any given day. The labor force has become very unstable and unpredictable, and this is affecting the way managers manage. This is especially true for those managers whose companies need these esoteric skills but cannot offer new and exciting growth opportunities.

Perhaps the most significant change has been the subtle change in the organizational philosophy from control to support. This is a change that is well under way yet has gone unrecognized by managers at all levels. The familiar organizational pyramid with its hierarchical tiers with rank and power determined by position or level is still there, but the control it was intended to provide is eroding. The control objective has quietly declined because the professionals are not comfortable taking direction from individuals whom they regard as having no knowledge or understanding of their discipline. The hospital administrator cannot instruct the neurosurgeon nor advise him on proper procedure. Attempts to do so will be met with silence, if not outright derision, and, in the worst case, might result in the neurosurgeon going to another hospital. The result is the hospital administrator has moved into a supporting role as a service provider. This does not mean that the manager of these knowledge workers is reduced to the position of administrative nonentity. But it does mean that he/she must develop a new style that accommodates these workers and their expectations. To the manager this means recognition of professional excellence and establishing guidelines and direction rather than "bossing" people about. Managers who attempt to apply authoritarian methods in managing these workers may find themselves either without workers or with a second-string group. Essentially managers must relinquish control and provide inspiration. They must stop being called leaders and actually *become* leaders. This represents a major change in the way things work and how people are organized.

Leaders *must* have the respect of those they lead because their leadership is granted to them by those being led. It is true that many (perhaps most) organizations have shifted from managers to leaders, but few have shifted from management to leadership. The fact is the old authoritarian (Theory X) management style is becoming extinct. But just as the dinosaurs did not all die at once, the authoritarian management model is still present to a greater or lesser degree in most companies. Much of the confusion present in organizations today is a result of managers attempting to retain control and the hierarchical model even though it is evident this is not working.

This does not mean that control is bad or should disappear nor does it mean that hierarchical structures should be abandoned. It does mean that the command-and-control model based solely on authority must be replaced by one based on leadership and respect. A symphony orchestra is led by a maestro, but as everyone knows not all maestros are created equal. Although many maestros can play multiple instruments virtually none play every instrument, and those that do play instruments rarely play as well as the artists. Yet the artists respect the skill of the maestro because they recognize the value the orchestra conductor brings. This is the form of leadership that is required today. This new maestro manager must be able to utilize the abilities of the professional team without having their level of skill or knowledge. He/she must be capable of selecting and retaining the best workers to ensure the highest-quality result. Thus the maestro manager is more of a focal point, an organizer, a mentor, and a planner rather than a commander. Peter Drucker makes this point very effectively.[1]

In the symphony orchestra, several hundred highly skilled musicians play together; but there is only one "executive," the conductor, with no intermediate layers between him (or her) and the orchestra members. This will be the organization model for the new, information-based organization. We will thus see a radical shift from the tradition in which performance was primarily rewarded by advancement into command positions, that is, into management ranks. Organizations will have very few such command positions. We will increasingly see organizations operating like the jazz combo, in which leadership within the team shifts with the specific assignment and is independent of the "rank" of each member. In fact, the word "rank" should disappear totally from the vocabulary of knowledge work and the knowledge worker. It should be replaced by "assignment."

The reality is that the means of creating wealth is passing from the hands of the capitalist and into the hands of the workers (Marxists, take note). In the old paradigm the capitalist owned the specialized machines that produced the wealth, and the workers merely operated them. The skill involved was minimal and largely restricted to watching the machine work. Although the capitalist today may still own the machines, they are of little value without the knowledge carried by the worker. When the knowledge worker leaves the company, he carries with him the means of creating wealth. For example, it is not the machine that makes the electrocardiogram that creates the wealth, it is the doctor's interpretation based on knowledge and experience that is the basis for the fee. The same is true for the ubiquitous desktop computer, which is in reality a general purpose tool. It is the worker who applies this tool that generates the wealth. Certainly this worker can be replaced, but not as easily as in the past and quite probably without the equivalent skill. Therefore, this worker must be cared for and nurtured, otherwise he/she may leave and go to a competitor (non-compete clause be damned).

This trend toward support-oriented organizations led by leaders who guide and influence is already evident. For those managers unable to understand or accept these changes, the future looks grim, especially for those managers who have climbed the ladder of success, only to find the skills that brought them that success are obsolete and may no longer be relevant or yield success. The manager, who started on the plant floor and climbed the ladder from foreman, to supervisor, to manager and is now a department manager, may now have difficulty adjusting to the new environment. Instead of the employees he was previously accustomed to, today his workforce is composed of hired contractors, outside suppliers, and a handful of employees. Not only are new management skills needed, but a mastery of technology is required as well. Because it is the technology that is driving the changes and their survival depends upon their ability to master it.

TECHNOLOGY

The second factor affecting management and organizations is the spread of technology. Technology has made information available to everyone at any time. No one is ever out of touch with their boss or subordinates no matter where they are on the planet. Pagers have become fashion accessories, and virtually everyone has a cell phone, voice mail, or at least access to the technology. Personal computers are ubiquitous, and many employees have multiples of this technology. Whether we like it or not and whether we are ready or not, this spread of technology is changing the way we live, the way we work, and how we organize ourselves to work. More and more workers are working at home while many others find themselves working in airports, customer sites, corporate apartments, and hotels. The sale of business attire is declining, and fewer and fewer workers want the corner office, especially if it means having to dress uncomfortably, drive to work everyday, and then be saddled with dull, unproductive administrative tasks.

At first the impact of technological changes was small and insignificant. The introduction of computers added technicians to the staff, and the organizational structure was modified to accommodate this group of arcane and eccentric experts. This simply required adding another box on the organizational chart, preferably FAR down on the chart. Gradually, but inexorably, companies began to rely on the technology and the technologists, who had information that was organized, useful, readily available, and crucial to the enterprise. Slowly their little organizational box began to rise on the charts like a star in the East. Then the personal computer burst on the scene, and, like a flash flood, the stream of information flowing from the technology went from a trickle to a torrent, and the lines of communication within the organizational pyramid were overwhelmed.

Traditionally the CEO of the classical organization made decisions that were passed downward through the multiple layers of management until they reached some one who actually knew how to implement the directive. This communication chain was simple and effective, but slow, labor intensive, and prone to error. The managers that made up the information chain-of-command were necessary due to the lack of technology. There was simply no faster way to communicate, but with the growth of technology much of this communications structure has crumbled, because executives found that the tiers of subordinates manning the bucket brigade of information could not keep up. Information was either lost along the way or arrived so late as to be valueless. The lines of communication were clogged with checks and balances, time delays, and outdated processes. This new and faster-moving competitive environment began to change the role of CEO from "Captain" to "Navigator." For the CEO, strategic planning and competitive and industry analysis became increasingly important over the day-to-day management issues as competition increased and the planning horizon shrank. The quality and speed of delivery of this information became crucial to the success of the enterprise. This became exceedingly difficult to accomplish because just as new technologies rose virtually overnight, so did new competitors. Consequently, the CEO could no longer command the enterprise. Instead, it became necessary that he/she establish a vision of the future and then plot a course to bring that vision to reality, leaving someone else to steer.

When people are sick they go to doctors but when a company is sick they turn to consultants. And just as the doctor has a dose of medicine for what ails you, the consultants had a diagnosis and a cure for the sluggish corporation, which was to reengineer the processes and downsize or de-layer the organization. The company processes were evaluated and compressed and hundreds, even thousands, of employees were fired, retired, or otherwise liberated from their drudgery. Downsizing or flattening the organization sometimes improved the flow of information, but just as often the loss of staff introduced delays that were not there before. Employees, who were fully engaged before, now found themselves overcommitted and working longer hours. Additionally, downsizing often caused the number of direct reports to increase, sometimes dramatically. Therefore, the elimination of management layers disrupted the classical concepts regarding the span of control and the relationship between managers and workers.

Just as Band-Aids and aspirin treat the symptom without addressing the root cause, these corrective actions made everyone feel better without actually correcting the basic problem and in many cases exacerbated the problem. This occurred primarily because there were some underlying assumptions that were not fully examined in the rush to fix the problem. The first assumption was that the processes were necessary and the second was that the "excess" employees were redundant. While these assumptions could easily be applied to the traditional organization, they did not necessarily apply to the emerging dynamic organization that was about to enter the world market.

GLOBALIZATION

Globalization is an overworked term, but it is certainly a major factor affecting business today. The fact is that the Internet is only a phone call away whether you are in Albuquerque or Zaire and for businesses this means that they have instant access to a global market. With the Internet the world market is available to even the smallest of companies. To some, this fact is not only old news—it might seem to be a downright *snoozer*. Perhaps that is because they have not yet been impacted by the realities of globalization and the organizational problems it brings. Globalization has had a very real impact on many of us, as our workday extends to include teleconferences with our European and Asian colleagues. Certainly many people still work an eight-hour day and a forty-hour week, but for global workers the workday is much longer. Furthermore, the weekends and weekdays are blending into one continuing blur of activity determined by time zones and availability of people. The reality of globalization is that business has become a 24-hour, 7-days-a-week activity and the workers as well as the managers are expected to be available when needed. Time off occurs between work events, and weekends are little more than suggested periods for relaxation.

At one time managing people on another floor was a challenge, then that became managing people in another building. Gradually we mastered managing and organizing people who were dispersed around the country. Now we must master how to organize and manage work spread around the world using workers with different cultures and different languages. Additionally managers may find themselves managing a global organization composed of people who are not direct employees, but contractors, outsourcers, and employees whom they may never actually see in person. For these managers, MBWA is simply out of the question.

Globalization and access to the world market brings a whole new set of problems for the classical organizational structure. For this structure to retain its effectiveness, operational decisions must be made at the lowest possible point, which means that the CEO must delegate operating authority to the organization that is on site and faced directly with the issues. To be agile and reactive the on-site manager must be able to take whatever action is necessary without having to build a business case, submit a long-range plan, prepare an impact statement, and then wait for the CEO to emerge from his retreat in Shangri La.

Global management requires delegation of authority and an "empowered" organization. The term "empowerment" is certainly overworked and is really just a trendy way of saying "effective delegation." But this level of delegation is absolutely mandatory for a global corporation if it is to be responsive and competitive.

However, with the empowered organization divisional managers becomes completely responsible for the success or failure of their operational divisions. Some would argue that they were fully responsible before, but that really was not the case. Power, the real power, was retained by the CEO, who continued to function as an operating manager with approval authority. Consequently, the divisional executives still had to keep a "weather eye" on the CEO and what he would approve. As change began to accelerate, increase in complexity, and span the globe, the CEO approval process (like MBWA) became impossible to implement.

The result was that the divisional managers still reported to senior managements and were accountable for the performance of their operation, but the day-to-day decisions and profit and loss responsibilities were now theirs alone. For many this was the first time they had to rely on themselves. They were definitely empowered, but the resources required for their success were not necessarily under their direct control. Regardless of the circumstances, the workers were often dispersed around the globe and may have had little loyalty to the company, the division, the manager, or his or her career within the company. Thus we see that empowerment and control are not synonymous terms in the global enterprise. It not only requires an understanding that business practices vary between countries and cultures, but that the local management must be given some autonomy in how the corporate business is conducted locally. Globalization of a company requires real delegation of authority and a willingness by senior management to trust the judgment of the local management. This is very difficult for managers accustomed to hands-on operational control as we can see in the case of International Petro-Chemical.

International Petro-Chemical

The International Petro-Chemical Corporation (IPC) is one of the largest petro-chemical companies in the world. It is headquartered in Badwater, Texas, where it was founded in the 1920s as a wildcat exploration firm. Today it employs over 100,000 people dispersed throughout dozens of countries around the world, with approximately 30,000 employees in the United States. It is organized as a global company with executive vice presidents for Asia-Pacific, North American Operations, Middle East-Africa, European Operations, and Latin America (this includes Mexico, which says a great deal about the role of geography in the American educational system). Each country within these regions has a country manager, who is responsible for operations within the country. The usual complement of headquarters functions such as marketing, sales, product development, human resources, and the like support each of the geographic regions. All in all, IPC has a relatively standard organization for a global company.

However, IPC has been under severe competitive pressure and has been losing market share slowly but steadily. At one time it held almost 40% of the world market, but that has now declined to slightly less than 30%. The corporate leadership has labored over this problem for some time and, with the aid of some very expensive consultants, has decided that the company should be "globalized." (The miracle of the English language is you can make a verb out of anything.) This decision meant that the number of expatriate Americans running the companies was reduced to the bare minimum and nationals were named in their place. It also meant that the corporate infrastructure had to be modified to recognize that the company was now "global." Therefore, a Business Standards Committee (BSC) was established at headquarters with the charter of standardizing operations worldwide. This would ensure a rapid transfer of information around the world, which would permit rapid reaction to changing conditions anywhere. After much debate and many field trips and demonstrations the BSC (Americans also love acronyms) decided on a standard set of software applications residing on a personal computer. This standard system was to be used worldwide and supported through a centralized support center. This concept and standard was presented to the CEO, Geographical Vice Presidents, and various home-office executives. The plan was soundly endorsed, and implementation began with North American Operations.

Things went very well, and within six months all of headquarters had the new software and computer systems. Not everything was working perfectly because only half of the systems had been installed, but that was to be expected. After careful review the decision was to forge ahead, and plans to install the system worldwide began while the remaining systems were installed in the United States (notice how Canada disappeared).

The first storm clouds appeared when it was determined that the primary system, manufactured by the Alpha Corporation was not available in Latin America, and the secondary system was available, but carried a very high tariff in Brazil, making it financially unattractive to the country manager of Brazil. In the spirit of corporate cooperation, the Executive Vice President for Latin America overrode the country manager for Brazil and ordered that the financial targets for Brazil be adjusted to reflect the more expensive equipment cost. Naturally, when the equipment finally arrived, the documentation was in English and Spanish (geography as we discovered earlier not being a strong point in the American educational system). Installation and training were delayed while everything was translated into Portuguese. Almost immediately problems also began to appear in Europe regarding the equipment and its "country content," meaning if it was not built there, it should be constructed of some components that were, otherwise there would be "difficulties." Fortunately, the secondary system passed muster so it became the primary system for Europe. Documentation was available in English, German, and French although the French felt it did not meet their language standards and would have to be "adjusted." Neither system was readily available in Africa other than South Africa although both systems were available in Israel. The result was that the Executive Vice President for Middle East/Africa was elected to deploy the standard system on a highly selective basis. And by this time, you realize that the international segment of this program was less than a resounding success and certainly cost a great deal more than initially forecasted. What went wrong?

When this situation is reduced to its essence as it is here, the problems seem so obvious that it is hard to believe that this is a very commonplace problem. However, in the defense of my fellow managers, situations like this are usually surrounded by a myriad of other problems. The issue is not really "globalization" or even "standardization." The original problem and objective, if you remember, were to recapture market share and to provide a more rapid response to shifting competitive moves in foreign markets. This is a much more complex problem that the corporate executives were addressing, and the standards issue was actually delegated. Furthermore, consultants were brought in to assist and at least some of this marvelous solution came from them.

Therefore, from our perspective here in the bleachers where we can watch the instant replay, the whole thing seems elementary. Furthermore, it seems obvious that there are two very fundamental problems in this scenario, and both problems are related. The first problem is that the executives in this company do not understand the distinction between internationalization and globalization. This is probably the same group that changed their managers to leaders by rewriting the job descriptions. Calling in a group of consultants and "standardizing" on a global basis is not "globalization" anymore than saying "uno mas cerveza, por favor" makes me bilingual in Spanish. Internationalization is when a company operates within a foreign country but retains its identity as a foreign company. Globalization is when an international company operates within a country but acts as if it were a local company. These are subtle but meaningful distinctions.

It is not my intent to beat on my colleagues, but the myopia that afflicts so many American executives is absolutely astonishing. It starts with "North American Operations," which almost always excludes Mexico. When Americans turn their attention southward they see Los Angeles, the Rio Grande, and the Panama Canal. Everything in between is either invisible or sort of lumped together into "Mexico City." Even when Mexico is included in Latin America the focus is almost always on Brazil and Argentina. Canada does not receive much better treatment. Canada is either invisible because it is seen as simply an extension of the United States (Gee, you don't LOOK Canadian!) or as a market too small for serious consideration. When we move out of the Western Hemisphere things do not improve. For the most part, American managers are at least cognizant of the geopolitical situation but many of the cultural and most of the legal subtleties escape us. There is a tendency to view the world as simply an extension to the United States, but with less sophisticated plumbing, and this is the attitude that was displayed in this scenario. The problem was identified in America at the corporate headquarters. The American team was called in to resolve the problem, which they did. They reviewed it with the Geographic Vice Presidents (and presumably their advisers), tested it in the United States, and then successfully deployed it in the United States. Because it worked here it should work anywhere, which it undoubtedly would if the conditions were the same (but they are not), because they never are, and that is the problem.

In this scenario there was no attempt to determine what problems, if any, existed in other countries. The country managers were not involved in either determining the problem or the solution. The standards committee was comprised of headquarters personnel, the vendors were essentially domestic, and, not surprisingly, so was the solution. The country managers were simply handed the solution wrapped in red, white, and blue with a note from corporate headquarters instructing them on how and when to implement it. This is what is meant by internationalization. Had IPC actually been a global company, this scenario would have played out much differently. First the problem, which truly is a strategic problem, would have been identified, then the country managers would have been polled to see if the problem was affecting them and, if so, how. Following that determination a strategy would have been formulated and agreed on by the country managers, possibly by country. Ultimately, a solution on how to increase market share and improve the information flow and decision process would have been determined, for each country, and then implemented.

It should be noted that in this alternate solution the roles of the various players were slightly altered. First, the country managers played a very decisive role. They not only were responsible for determining the scope of the problem within their country, they were asked to recommend solutions, review the strategy, and eventually to implement the solution that they helped to establish. Their role gave them much broader authority, it allowed corporate headquarters to ensure that a problem existed, and the solution was adjusted to fit the conditions within the country before implementation was attempted. The Geographic Regions and the Executive Vice Presidents responsible for them played a reduced role. At worst they were superfluous and at best they acted as an administrative entity, collecting and disbursing information. The corporate headquarters team defined the problem and recommended a strategy, but this was for the United States only. They acted as a focal point for the collection of the global information and facilitator for the formulation of the eventual strategy. This is a much more global approach.

The second obvious problem faced by IPC was the organizational structure itself. It was a classic pyramid with the CEO at the top making decisions and everyone else passing them down. I am reminded of the old comedy routine where the director yells "quiet on the set," and his minions one after the other simply repeat his commands verbatim. What is the added value of someone whose sole contribution is to say "yes" at the appropriate time, and repeat the boss's commands? Certainly this is an overstatement of the conditions that prevail in the classic organization, but not by much. At IPC the CEO was faced with a problem, which he identified as a declining market share brought about by the inability of the organization to quickly respond to changing market conditions. The CEO wanted a solution so he pointed the staff in what he felt was the right direction (picture Mr. Magoo here) and moved on to the next problem. When the staff returned with what they believed was a right decision the CEO reviewed it with his direct reports. These executives, assuming the low-risk position, determined what they believed the "boss" wanted to hear, then nodded their heads in agreement, and the decree was given. Through the miracle of modern technology this decree travels at the speed of light to the next level down to where it is reviewed (revered?) and couched in terms that would make a biblical prophet blanch. It is sent on its way at the speed of light to the next stop, eventually arriving at a point in the organization where it is either implemented or ignored depending on how garbled it got in the process or how relevant it is when it arrives. In any case it is clear that the technology allowing decisions to flow at the speed of light did not accelerate the decision process very much, because the number of stops was not reduced. The underlying assumption here is that the layers of managers, reviewers, and checkers that previously formed the information bucket brigade are still required because each one receives the bucket, inspects it, modifies it as necessary, and then passes it on. The technology actually allows decisions to be made at the executive level and almost immediately given to the implementation level, but this means converting to "hoses" and giving up the cherished and familiar buckets. This requires change, and change is very hard for most people to accept. Some CEOs recognize this and attempt to solve the problem by "delayering," which is undoubtedly necessary, but they usually start at layers somewhere below *their layer*. The fact that the typical CEO is no longer sufficiently aware of the day-to-day problems and conditions to act effectively eludes many.

NEW ORGANIZATIONAL FORMS

Managers have many tools available to them. The one most commonly used is perhaps the one least recognized as a tool. That is the organization. This tool like so many common tools has remained unchanged for so long that it is simply accepted in its current form, and few consider how it might be modified to increase the effectiveness of the company. The pyramidal organization is the way we organize, and that is that. However, technology, changing worker attitudes, the shift to knowledge work, demands for quick response, and even faster decision-making are undermining the effectiveness of this classic management tool. While the relationship between technology, management, the knowledge worker, and the global organization is generally recognized, few have attempted to tie these together into specific solutions and even fewer have experimented with new organizational forms.

The challenge for the traditional manager is to incorporate fewer management layers, efficiently use and incorporate new technologies, and empower the workforce while continuing to retain the existing hierarchical structure. These are clearly conflicting goals, which have led us to a state of chaos and organizational upheaval with varying impact on productivity and the competitive edge of our enterprises.

Everyone seems to intuitively recognize that the current organizational structure and possibly even our organizational philosophies are failing us. What to do about it is unclear, especially because we are really uncertain what the problem is. Consequently, most managers continue to struggle with what is known and familiar to them but with ever decreasing success. We know that for all practical purposes Theory X as a management technique has gone the way of the Dodo. There are still many Theory Y and Theory Z managers around who are convinced that the existing structures can be retained and made to work if only the workers are included in the decision-making process

Among the alternative organizations emerging from this desire to make the existing structure work while accommodating the need to include the workers in the decision process was one described by Russell Ackoff (1994) in his book *The Democratic Corporation*.[2] In this book he presents us with a circular organization that attributes authority to each worker both within his area of expertise and within the organization as a whole. Dialogue is exchanged through interlocking boards representing every level of the organization (see Figure 6.1).

Although the circular organization addresses the knowledge worker and opens the lines of communication, it does not account for technology nor does it limit the number of management layers. Even though the circular organization is called an empowered organization where decisions are pushed far down, the ultimate control still resides at the top. It is a purely cosmetic solution that is cumbersome and neither addresses the need for speed and agility nor the role of technology.

For those individuals for whom meetings are a way of life this is definitely the organization. It virtually guarantees that you will spend the bulk of your work week interfacing with virtually everyone in the organization because this organization emphasizes communications at the expense of the work itself. In effect it recognizes that it is more fun to talk about work than to actually do it. But remember, the purpose of changing the classical organi-

Figure 6.1
The Circular Organization[3]

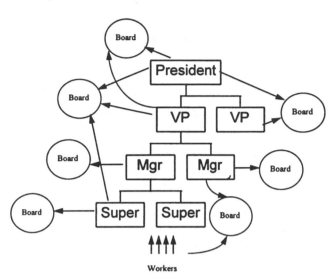

zational structure was not just to involve people in the decision-making process, it was to reduce the number of management layers, capitalize on the ability of technology to move information quickly, increase the speed of decisions, and empower the organization. This organizational structure really does not accomplish any of those objectives. In fact it might decrease the speed of decisions while increasing the number of people required to arrive at a decision.

However, the Theory Y and Theory Z managers are not the only ones attempting to meet the challenges of the changing workplace by revamping the organization. There are some who have recognized the strengths of MBO, MBWA, and, most of all, Chaos Management and are attempting to introduce these into a fresh, new organizational structure. Hesh Kestin in his book *21st Century Management*[4] presents another circular organization that can be described as a ring structure, which consists of an inner ring of executive management surrounded by an outer ring of their direct reports. This in turn is surrounded by a dynamic structure of rings and hierarchical pyramids (see figure 6.2).

This structure is very avant garde, and in my opinion its success relies on the unique corporate culture where it is currently employed. In this corporation, nepotism is part of the basic culture where large segments of these rings are composed of friends and relatives in various combinations. Virtually everyone is in some way personally connected to everyone else. The philosophy is that you can trust your friends and relatives but not someone who is not personally connected to you in some way. This belief is

Figure 6.2
The Kestine Ring Structure

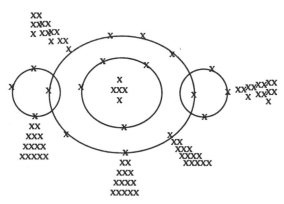

the cornerstone of this unique structure, which is very reminiscent of the political and organizational structure of Renaissance Italy, where the city states and principalities were ruled by various families allied through marriage and treaties. However, this unique blend of friends and relatives is rarely found in most corporations and, in fact, is usually discouraged. Even though this ring structure is in actual use, it is unlikely it would work anywhere else. But for the adventurous or those given to intrigue, this would certainly be an interesting structure.

Perhaps the more useful response to the needs of the global marketplace and the demand for organizational overhaul is the Multi-dimensional

Figure 6.3
The Multi-dimensional Organization

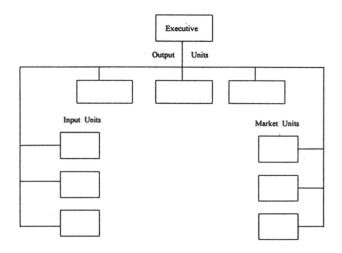

Model, which is implemented in an attempt to be flexible enough to allow reaction to changing circumstances without requiring significant structural change or major re-organization.

The multi-dimensional organization is an updated view of "Matrix Management." It is founded on the concept that an organization has three dimensions or functional groupings: Input Units, Output Units, and Market Units (see Figure 6.3).

1. Input Units
   - Are functionally defined units.
   - Produce goods and services used by other parts of the organization.
   - Include: Manufacturing, Transportation, Warehousing, Data Processing, Personnel, Legal, and Accounting.
2. Output Units
   - Are product or service defined units.
   - Are responsible for all activity required to make available and sell products and services to customers.
   - Include: Management, Research, Planning, Customer site operation, Production control, Telecommunications, and Personal computing services.
3. Market Units
   - Are units defined by the markets they serve.
   - Sell products and services generated by the organization to both internal and external customers.
   - Act as advocates for the users in the markets they serve.
   - Include: Market research, Marketing communications, Customer Assistance centers, and Customer Service centers.

In the multi-dimensional organization the members of one unit provide services to another as if they were an external customer. The workers have one manager (their service manager), and the person for whom they are working is their client manager. Thus the client manager's involvement with the worker may be entirely limited to the task at hand while the worker's service manager retains responsibility for long-term issues such as career planning, employee development, salary, and performance evaluation.

In the multi-dimensional organization the workers are selected for their specific knowledge and experience and are assigned to tasks as long as their knowledge is required and they are in demand. This requires the service manager to be concerned with customer satisfaction issues because the client manager can dismiss an unsatisfactory worker. The flip side of this is that the worker can refuse to serve an abusive or incompetent client.

Managers within the multi-dimensional organization may find it difficult to sustain an organization where workers come and go, duties vary daily, tasks come to an end, and there is an expectation of individual performance for everyone including the manager himself. These managers may view their employees as products that they are now required to market and in turn may find themselves being evaluated by their subordinates. Failure to successfully manage this dynamic organization can result in the inability to attract the best team of knowledge experts, who may now refuse to work for these managers.

Certainly the multi-dimensional organization represents an evolutionary step from the command-and-control model. It is more task-oriented, more fluid, and more cognizant of the many needs of the knowledge worker. However, the role of manager takes on new meaning and requires new skills to effectively cope with this fluid and transitory structure. If the manager does not have the skills of his workers, the question can then be asked—what value does the manager add beyond that of information gatekeeper? Therefore the manager must have a job that adds value beyond simple administration. The manager's role in the multi-dimensional organization is that of a leader able to inspire and lead through example while at the same time maintaining an outward focus. The cumulative effect of the multi-dimensional structure is the creation of an entrepreneurial-oriented enterprise staffed with knowledge workers, geographically dispersed on multiple sites, dynamic in nature, lead by creative and responsive managers able to attract assignments and retain workers.

Although the multi-dimensional organization is more task-oriented, more fluid, and recognizes many of the needs of the knowledge worker it retains most of the attributes of the hierarchical model with a central head controlling tiers of subordinates occupying various levels in the management pyramid. It perpetuates the inward focus that characterizes the traditional organizational thinking and structures. It does not recognize the effect of technology or provide for the empowerment of the worker at a level necessary for quick decisions. To achieve this we must turn to an organizational structure that is even more flexible and empowered. One that recognizes that managers may not control all of the resources and in fact may find themselves allied with competitors.

BULLETS TO BUBBLES

Just as "Glinda the Good Witch" arrived in a bubble, perhaps the solution to the need for a flexible organization lies in a transparent and temporary organizational bubble that coalesces to meet a specific need and then disperses. This new structure recognizes the core competencies of the enterprise and leverages both internal and external resources while reducing the number of managers. It must also eliminate the "checkers" and "delegators" altogether. This new structure must be fluid, with decision authority and profitability pushed as far down in the organization as possible. This new model represents an evolutionary step beyond the multi-dimensional model. Although the organizational structures may be similar, the roles and responsibilities of the people within them are quite different.

The most vivid difference is that the "Boxes and Bubbles" model has external focus with no single leader responsible for daily operations. Instead the senior leadership is focused on the future, predicting new markets, competitive moves, and customer needs. In the new structure, the CEO is not an autocrat but a member of the strategic leadership team responsible for setting goals and direction. The daily operation is delegated to Business Unit leaders who *do not* report to a single person, but are responsible to the strategic leadership team (MBO). This group of operational managers function within the framework established by the senior leadership, but they are virtually autonomous within that framework. These operating unit managers have responsibility for daily operations, profit and loss, and achieving the goals established by the CEO and senior staff.

The operating units are supported by an infrastructure of specialists. These resource centers consist of two types: administrative and services. The administrative centers are the necessary administrative functions such as legal, finance, and human resources, etc. The service centers are more highly specialized and would vary from company to company. Some examples would be programming, microbiology, cinematography, and materials planning. These specialists may be either incumbent within the organization or contracted from outside suppliers. In any case, the operating units use these resources on an ad hoc basis.

The "Boxes and Bubbles" model incorporates some fundamental changes to the organizational structure. One of the most significant ones is the incorporation of *strategic partners or alliances*. Another is the recognition of the transitory nature of the work through the creation of tasks or projects, which form the Bubbles in the model. These Bubbles coalesce around a leader and/or task with the resources being drawn from the specialty Boxes within the enterprise or external suppliers. In this way the enterprise becomes trimmer and more responsive to changing conditions. It also allows for tighter cost control because resources, both internal and external, are only used to the extent that is absolutely necessary. Furthermore, all internal support organizations (boxes) are put onto a competitive footing with external suppliers, which further reduces costs.

The cumulative effect of these differences is the creation of a *virtual enterprise* composed of multiple independent companies each allied with multiple internal and external activities. By definition the *virtual enterprise* is geographically dispersed with multiple sites and a dynamic staff. It consists of a constantly changing array of projects (Bubbles) staffed by a dynamic set of human resources composed of contractors, external suppliers, and specialists. The Bubbles vary in size just as the managers of each Bubble vary in "rank" and experience.

The Boxes and Bubbles organization is shown in Figure 6.4 and illustrates the flexibility and responsiveness of the organization. The need of knowledge workers to remain with their peers is recognized, and the focus is on the task rather than managers in the traditional sense.

This organizational structure operates with far fewer managers and employees. The less stable workforce and the egalitarian nature of that workforce are recognized. Although the Boxes and Bubbles model may not be the final structure used in the 21st Century, it represents a logical evolution from the traditional to nontraditional organization.

Well, that was certainly a torrent of facts. Sort of a cross between Uncle Bill's story about how he knocked over the chicken house with the tractor and the time Mom served brussels sprouts and broccoli in the same meal. You have heard the story so often you can repeat it in your sleep, and you know vitamins are good for you but you still hate brussels sprouts and broccoli. The point is, it really does not matter if any of the organizations discussed above are good, bad, or indifferent. The fact is they represent serious attempts to correct an organizational problem that is becoming more apparent every day. The classical hierarchical pyramid of authority simply is not responsive enough to maintain a competitive edge. Technology moves information very rapidly, but within the classical framework it is like a bullet

Figure 6.4
Boxes and Bubbles: A 21st-Century Organization Chart

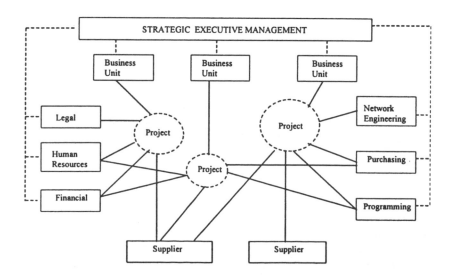

train that is forced to stop at every crossroads and hamlet. The potential for speed is unrealized. Companies strive for globalization, but the multi-national companies have a difficult time distinguishing between internation-alization and globalization. Unfortunately, the classical organization is structured along multi-national lines, which makes globalization difficult, if not impossible, without organizational change.

There is a natural tendency to continue doing what you know how to do and what has been successful for you in the past. This is true of everyone, including CEOs, so it is natural for them to assume that they are not the problem, or even part of the problem. Instead, the problem lies somewhere below the clouds of good news that usually separate them from the harsh reality of the trenches. The role of CEO must change and is, in fact, chang-ing. The days of the hands-on tough-as-nails CEO with a cigar clenched in his teeth and a finger in every pie are pretty much over. Today the CEO must focus on the future, where it is, and how the company is going to arrive there equipped and ready to compete. This cannot be done if the focus is on daily operations. It is necessary to move daily decisions to a level as close to the customer as possible, with decisions flowing up rather than down. To some this sounds like turning the asylum over to the inmates but that may be necessary in order to save the asylum. The trick, of course, is to pick good inmates.

NOTES

1. Peter Drucker, *Post Capitalist Society* (New York: Harper Business, 1993) p. 93.

2. Russell Ackoff, *The Democratic Corporation* (New York: Oxford University Press, 1994).

3. Not all of the lines are drawn between boards to avoid clutter.

4. Hesh Kestin, *21st Century Management* (New York: The Atlantic Monthly Press, 1992).

7

VIRTUAL MANAGEMENT
Welcome to Oz

Surrounded by giant technicolor flowers, an army of Munchkins, and a recently deceased witch, Dorothy reckons she is "not in Kansas anymore." This stunning observation is one of the great understatements of all time. This comment by Dorothy on her arrival in Oz could be made by me or you or many managers in today's workplace, because "things sure aren't like they used to be." Like many of you, I find myself in a very different sort of workplace, one that is as surreal as the flowers Dorothy found in Oz. One of the first of many differences I have observed is that titles are either invisible or have almost no meaning, and attempts to exercise authority or control on the basis of a title or position are met with indifference or even uncontrolled laughter. Another difference and significant challenge that I have encountered is that the employees may actually be someone else's employees and either contracted to you or assigned to you for the purpose of accomplishing a specific task. Consequently, in many cases the work has taken on a project orientation with defined boundaries and objectives, which has redefined the workplace as a series of decentralized locations where the workers have little, if any, supervision. Furthermore, the constant pressure to downsize and decrease the management layers has brought all levels of the management team into sharper focus.

The irony is that the closer the executives at the top come to the workers at the bottom, the more out of touch they seem to be with actual events and the more their control seems to ebb away. The fact is, things have changed and organizational control is shifting to the leaders in the organization. Specifically, what I see is control shifting to people with titles like *team leader* or *project leader* or even no title at all. In effect the traditional management structure and orientation that we were used to are being replaced by virtual enterprises run by virtual managers, managing virtual employees working in a virtual workplace.

From my personal observations, I believe that much of this unreality stems from a disconnect between what many of us are experiencing on a daily basis and what the senior corporate executives believe to be true. To a large extent the senior executives of most companies continue to work in a relatively stable organizational environment. They are accustomed to dynamic market conditions and competitive action and reaction, but they are also accustomed to the resources they rely on to be relatively constant and available when needed. But as you move downward in the organization, out of necessity the working environment becomes less stable, the organization more fluid, and the resources available less dependable. This organizational instability, although necessary, is often viewed as a lack of discipline, unresponsiveness to corporate directives, and a general lack of focus by upper management. Furthermore, this organizational instability seems to be exacerbated by management attempts to stabilize the situation, because the underlying assumption is that the old management techniques, processes, and structures can still be used. I do not think this is realistic.

As the upper-level management team becomes more involved with the daily operations, they also become more visible. This visibility, in association with their attempts to establish control using the traditional command-and-control techniques, increasingly triggers a negative response with the employees. This is primarily because the employees do not see these managers as being qualified either to give direction or to establish processes in areas where they have no experience. The initial reaction from the employees is to ignore the directives, processes, or policies they feel are unnecessary, irrelevant, or counterproductive. Any subsequent attempts to enforce these frequently lead to active resistance or employee turnover as the employees move on to other projects or companies. Even when these processes or directives are sound they may still fail, not only because the employees may be virtual, but also because the leaders needed to enforce them may not be in the formal chain of command. That is, these leaders may be team leaders with no official standing in the hierarchy, and therefore they are unaware of the directives or policies, which tend to be passed down through formal management channels and may bypass or ignore the actual leaders.

Certainly these virtual leaders report to someone, but that manager may be removed emotionally, geographically, or even organizationally from the actual leader. This disconnect between the daily operation and the actual leadership appears to be where the problem begins. The management team thinks they are in control and providing direction, when, in fact, the people actually doing the work may either be unaware of the directives or aware of them but disregard them as irrelevant. This leads the management team to additional (and perhaps stronger) efforts at establishing control.

These attempts to establish control bring many managers into contact with employees who are openly critical of their compensation, perks, and performance, and skeptical of their abilities and right to govern. As we shall shortly see in one of the following scenarios, this changing attitude toward management is difficult for some to understand, much less accept. As if this shift in attitudes toward the management team weren't bad enough, there is another trend that is beginning to rear its ugly head. Many of these employees are expecting to be paid in accordance with their contribution and skill level, just like actors, doctors, and athletes. There is a growing attitude among knowledge workers that it is they, not the executives, who create the wealth of the enterprise and that they should have a larger share of that wealth. This attitude first appeared among the entertainment community, then spread to the entertainment infrastructure (writers, directors, and other professionals), and then to professional sports. Now this attitude that those who create the wealth deserve to share in it is spreading into the community of knowledge workers.

The common manifestation of this new attitude can be seen with the growing inclination of top-quality professionals to function as "contractors" or virtual employees. At one time these employees would have jumped from company to company to increase their salary, but as the demand for their skills increased, it just seemed easier to become an independent contractor. And like actors, as the demand for their talent increases, their salaries increase as well. They hire out to do a job, then take their money and leave. They have no loyalty to the company, the management, or the CEO. Like the true mercenaries they are, they work for the highest pay and will leave a project in the middle if a competitor offers more money. It is not just that loyalty between companies and employees is eroding, if it has not already gone, but that the organizational structure is taking on a strange look as functions are outsourced.

Please understand that this assessment is based on observations and discussions with other managers and consultants and is not necessarily shared by the executives of most large companies. In fact, the efforts by some of these executives to regain control over their organizations parallel attempts by King George to curb the rebellious American colonists. The British government, in an effort to regain the initiative and restore the status quo, hired mercenaries with the intent to capture and hang the rebels. The result was a huge expense with no improvement in the situation and, as we all know in retrospect, this decision actually inflamed the situation. The approach used by the British government is still attractive today, because it shifts responsibility for a solution away from those normally responsible. Consequently, modern executives hire consultants who, in the time-honored fashion, recommend the very latest solutions (process reengineering, best practices, delayering, off-with-their-heads, etc.) intended to restore the status quo. Proving yet again that those who refuse to learn the lessons of history are doomed to repeat them.

Corporations have done everything that they have been led to believe would restore the status quo. They have right-sized, down-sized, reengineered, delayered, and adopted best practices. Therefore, decisions should be faster and crisper, margins should be larger, productivity greater, and the enterprise more nimble (whatever that means). However, most of these things have either not happened at all or have not met expectations. Furthermore, the original objective, which was to restore the organization to a "normal" state, has not happened either, and, if anything, the situation continues to deteriorate, just as it did for poor King George.

The reality is that today there are two different views of the organization. On the one hand the leaders and workers view the organization as an administrative convenience and the managers as *enablers*. On the other hand, the managers continue to view their role as the directors and commanders of the organization, responsible for setting the direction, establishing solutions, and then implementing them. They see the workers as a resource, as they always have. When these differing points of view come into conflict, the workers see the managers as a meddling, irrelevant group who do not understand either the problem or the solution. But the managers see the workers as a disloyal, mercenary, and rebellious group who must be brought back under control and stuffed back into the hierarchical box from which they somehow escaped. I think putting toothpaste back into the tube would be a simpler task.

Before we move on to managing the virtual organization, let us stop for a moment and review some situations wherein the executives were functioning in the old command and control paradigm and were unaware that the employees were no longer part of that paradigm, at least psychologically.

THE EMANCIPATED WORKER I

In the following example the company had a team of midlevel managers scattered across the country. Each was highly experienced and functioned with a high level of autonomy. This was a tight-knit team that answered to a Vice President who had the respect and loyalty of these managers. Without notice, this Vice President was summarily replaced by a crony of the President. This replacement was widely viewed as an *executive-lite*, with limited experience, limited ability, and no concept of what his new job entailed. Within minutes of the announcement of his appointment to the management team, each manager, acting individually, submitted his resignation. The loss of any one of these highly skilled and experienced managers would have been a blow to the organization, but the loss of all of them would be devastating. The President was horrified, but he was accustomed to the command-and-control school of management, so he saw this as a direct challenge to his authority and was prepared to accept the resignations. After all, if he allowed this revolt to succeed what would be next? It was best (for him) to rid the organization of these troublemakers, otherwise he would be their puppet just as King John was a puppet of the Barons after the Magna Carta. However, other members of the executive staff recognized the impact of losing these managers. Without them the entire field operation would collapse and replacing them before that happened was a practical impossibility. Attempts were made by various executives to reason with these managers individually and collectively. The merits and accomplishments of the new Vice President were explained to no avail, and then money was offered, but the managers remained adamant. They would accept one of their number being promoted over the others, they would accept the old Vice President, or they would even accept someone else whom they respected, but not the one selected by the President.

Furthermore, as the rumor spread that the management team was about to leave, many of their subordinates came forward to say that once these managers left the company, they would leave as well. This made the possible departure of the managers even more of a catastrophe. Faced with a disaster, the President yielded under pressure to the inevitable and named a candidate acceptable to the team of managers; and this time they were consulted on whom they would accept. Consequently, the management team remained but the circumstances and overall environment had irrevocably changed. The new and acceptable manager understood very clearly that she was the leader because the team she was leading *allowed* her to lead. Therefore, the team became the source of her power and not the President who had appointed her as the new Vice President.

Furthermore, from this point on, the President was viewed as a figurehead by his subordinates, just as he had feared. His opinions and directives were acknowledged but largely ignored by the people reporting to him. Just as King John remained King, so too did he remain President, but he had lost credibility with the workers and with the midlevel managers. But more importantly, his ability to influence events or direction was sharply reduced.

This is an example of how things have changed. For years we have been told that the company is a team and each person is an important part of that team. The reality is that knowledge workers, especially those with unique skills, will no longer tolerate being placed under the direction of a corporate *fast-tracker* whose only accomplishment is graduation from a prestigious university or some similar achievement. Because of their market demand, the skilled specialists that represent the backbone of the enterprise expect to decide to whom they report, and any effort to do otherwise will be met with resistance and, if necessary, resignation. Replacing an unskilled worker is one thing, but replacing a first violin player or database administrator is quite another.

This is not the only example of a senior executive publicly demonstrating how out of touch he is with the workers. Many managers still view the employees as *theirs*. These are the managers who talk about people *working for me*, or worse, as *my people* without recognizing that not everyone would agree, and some would consider the phraseology to be arrogant. (I know we are all guilty of this, but just as we learned to be politically correct in other areas, we must learn this one as well.) In a team the members of the team are equal and do not work for an individual but work together as a team. Even though it is commonplace for managers to say "we are a team," not all of them understand exactly how that translates to the workers. From their perspective, everyone, including the managers and executives, works *for* the corporation and *with* each other. This may seem like splitting hairs, but this new breed of workers do not feel they work *for* anyone and are quite particular about whom they work *with*, as we shall see.

THE EMANCIPATED WORKER II

In another example of the treetop not knowing what is going on with the squirrels at ground level, the executive of a Strategic Business Unit found himself without a technical assistant. After searching through the Business Unit roster, he located what was reported to be the best technical person in the organization. In the spirit of noblesse oblige, he personally called on the young technical genius and found him hard at work in his cubicle. As if calling on him in person were not honor enough, he thought he would add to the honor by publicly complimenting the young genius and asking if he would like to *work for him* as his technical aide. This inquiry was made with pride and loud enough for everyone nearby to hear. After all, the objective was to honor the young genius with a public promotion. Without even a microsecond of hesitation or even acknowledging the presence of the executive, the young man said, "No! I won't work for you." The executive could not believe his ears and was completely nonplussed. He spluttered for a moment and then pointed out that the young man already worked for him and he was offering him a significant promotion. The young man turned to face the executive and explained that he *did not work for him*. He worked *for* Betty. She was the one that hired him. He came to the company to work *for* her, and when she left he would leave as well. He spun around in his chair, in effect dismissing the dumbfounded President and went back to work, leaving the President to retire with as much dignity as he could salvage.

Betty was a team leader roughly four management tiers beneath the executive, so the executive was completely nonplussed and embarrassed by this rebuff. He could not understand the attitude or the entire situation. He had been treated with disdain and publicly humiliated by some *lowly technician* whom he had offered to promote into a position reporting directly to him with exposure to *powerful* executives—a situation he believed everyone would view as a huge career opportunity. Instead of accepting this signal honor, this *technician* rejected the offer in favor of working on some dinky little project run by a team leader no one had ever heard of before. The executive never did comprehend this attitude because it was so foreign to his own experience, motivation, and value system.

This is another case where the executive reacted within the old command-and-control model where titles, office size, and hierarchical position were important. At least they were important to him. He was unprepared (and is probably still unprepared) for a value system where these things are unimportant and are replaced by respect for the leader, a master/apprentice relationship, and the work itself; an environment where management titles are virtually meaningless, and where the accouterments of power once so sought after are viewed as valueless and, in extreme examples, as impediments to professional growth. In this example, the executive viewed himself as superior to the technician because of his position within the hierarchy and was surprised when the technician did not see it the same way.

From the technician's perspective, the executive had no technical credentials, had nothing to teach him, and was expecting to exploit him by using him as a *dancing bear* capable of speaking technical jargon on command. This was not a job the technician was interested in because it did not provide him any professional growth and would probably earn him the contempt of his professional colleagues. The team leader, on the other hand, had the technical credentials, understood the technology, and was capable of extending the knowledge of the technician. This represents the fundamental shift in attitudes that can be observed in virtually every environment that uses knowledge workers to create wealth. The hierarchical executive equates career growth as a climb up the corporate ladder of power and position, whereas the knowledge worker sees career growth as an enhancement of his/her knowledge and expertise. After all, these are the skills that have brought him success so far. He is not marketing his management, people, or political skills, which he may view as unnecessary or of minor importance.

This is an attitude or viewpoint that is shared by many workers today. Their first loyalty is to themselves and their discipline, and their drive is to improve their knowledge and expertise, not to climb the corporate management ladder. In fact, they may view many of the occupants of the corporate hierarchy with skepticism and suspicion, especially if these individuals have little operational experience. These knowledge workers view themselves as specialists and expect to be treated as if they were individual contractors even though they are actually employees. For example, a very large company recently needed a Project Manager. The group responsible for providing project managers contacted one of the team who was currently awaiting assignment. She listened to the details of the assignment and then submitted a list of conditions and information she would need *before accepting the assignment.* The idea that she might not have had a choice in accepting this assignment never occurred to her or to her manager. They both simply accepted the idea that she had the right to accept or reject the assignment. This is an attitudinal about-change that is changing the way we manage and the techniques we use to function in this new laissez faire working environment. At the very least it requires a level of leadership skill that was formerly required only at the middle to upper levels of management. But this is not all that is changing. In fact, these changes in attitude are not only driving changes in management and leadership techniques, they are affecting the organizational structure and redefining the workplace itself.

THE VIRTUAL WORKPLACE

From the moment that Og stepped outside of his cave to begin the daily hunt, people have been *going to* work. That is, the work was centrally located somewhere, even if it were just outside of the cave or the shop downstairs. In fact, the work was usually located nearby, simply because the technology did not exist to allow the work to be further away than a man might walk in a relatively short time. With the industrial revolution came the technology that allowed the worker to live further from his work, and as technology has grown so has the distance the worker might live from his work. Today it is not uncommon for a worker to live many miles away and to spend as much as two hours commuting to and from his work, and in some extreme cases, people actually live on one coast and work on another. The important point is that until recently the worker was *still going to work* and the improvement in technology simply allowed him to live further away. However, the recent advances in computer and communications technology is now changing the workplace, so the work for many workers comes to them. Still others go to places to work, but these places vary and include places not ordinarily seen as work locations. It is now common for people to work at home, in hotels, in corporate apartments, customer sites, and anywhere the work demands. These workers are working in a virtual workplace, and you see them everywhere—talking on cell phones on the beach, in their cars, and in restaurants. You see them and their ubiquitous computer cases on airplanes, in hotels, in conference rooms, and anywhere they can stop for a moment. In effect, the workplace for these workers has become anywhere and everywhere.

This redefinition of the workplace is a huge change for me and, I think, most managers. Instead of having an established workplace, defined by cubicles, offices, and a telephone, the new workers define *their workplace.*

This means they work whenever and wherever they choose and to a growing extent, as we have already seen, for whom they choose. Consequently, the change to a virtual workplace is forcing me, and I believe many of you, to shift to a new management style, one based on leadership and more suited to this new working environment.

The first and perhaps the most difficult change for many managers to accept in the virtual workplace is that the worker is now invisible. To an extent, this has always been true for some professions, such as sales, postal, and trucking, but only recently has this spread to jobs traditionally performed in a central and supervised environment. Obviously, the workers are not *invisible* in the true sense of the word, but the "boss" cannot see them because they are working somewhere else. That somewhere might be their *home office*, a temporary office rented by the day, a hotel room, a customer site, or even a campsite. For those managers who need to watch the workers or require daily interaction, this becomes a very significant psychological hurdle. After all, if you cannot *see* the work being done, how do you know it is getting done or that the worker is not overworked? Or perhaps the worker is only working a couple of hours a day and goofing off the rest of the time? Or worse, how does the manager know that the worker is not holding down two jobs, one with a competitor? Of course, the answer is you do not. Any or all of these things could be going on, and that brings us to one of the fundamental requirements of the virtual environment and virtual management—*trust* (Theory Z). This new environment requires that the manager has trust in the workers, and without that trust it is unlikely the virtual enterprise will work. And unlike the Ring Organizational Structure, where trust is based on personal relationships among the workers, trust in the virtual organization must be developed through action.

As important as trust is for the manager to be effective, there are other fundamentals that must be considered before this is an issue. The first question is, who should work in the virtual workplace, and, specifically, who should work in a home office? None of us are naive enough to believe we can trust everyone we meet so it logically follows that not everyone is suited for working in an undisciplined and unsupervised environment. It is probably too early to establish firm criteria for selecting workers to work in the decentralized and distributed workplace, but at the very least, they must be self-disciplined and self-motivated. Obviously these personality traits are not easily determined in a normal interview or through casual contact. Therefore, I suggest that, except in unusual circumstances, new hires should not be selected for working at home or working without supervision. Of course, an employee whose existing workspace is cluttered with papers stacked willy nilly and a sign proclaiming that "A cluttered desk is the sign of a brilliant mind" is not someone you would immediately describe as "disciplined." Still, you never know, which is why workers selected to work at home or work in virtual workplaces should be employees who have established a solid record as productive self-starters, which brings us to managing in this virtual environment.

Virtual Management

At one time the Boss would sweep down the hallway, flanked by assistants carrying papers and briefcases, intimidating some and striking awe into others by his mere presence. The management team was in place, and the workers were right there where you could see them. Managing was largely a combination of observation and conversation. But when workers are dispersed, new management techniques are required. Some workers will be at customer sites, some will be co-located with other employees, others may be in foreign countries, and still others stay at home and telecommute. This is the reality of the virtual workplace, and the challenge is how to effectively manage, lead, guide, and direct a group of people whom you may not see, who are in different time zones, and more importantly, who will *allow* you to be leader.

Perhaps the first technique we can abandon is that staple of the authoritarian manager, MBWA. Watching others work is not one of the techniques we can employ in an environment where the workers are dispersed. In fact, this type of manager, the kind that has to look out and see everyone with their heads down working away, may find it impossible to function in this new environment. This is especially true if the manager sees his role and that of the overseer on a slave ship as being roughly the same, except in the one case there is tongue lashing and in the other just plain lashing. This probably explains why some managers long for the good old days when "shape up or you are fired" carried some weight.

Today the threat of "shape up or ship out" more than likely would be viewed as a joke, because it would be an empty threat. The employees may not even administratively report to the manager, and that brings us to the nub of the problem. How do you *virtually* manage employees, whom you cannot see, cannot fire, possibly cannot replace, and who may view you and your superiors as irrelevant bureaucrats? This is not a very pretty picture for the traditional manager, but for me and many others, it is what we face every day. How do you evaluate the performance of these employees? How do you supervise them? How do you determine who works and who shirks? These are difficult questions but ones the virtual manager must be able to answer. However, that is easier said than done because the fact is that the manager cannot observe the worker, so any evaluations carry some subjectivity, and that is where the issue of trust comes in. In the final analysis, the manager must trust the worker, and that brings us to a real situation involving trust and performance.

ARE YOU SLEEPING?

A new manager assumed responsibility for a team of technical management consultants for a large firm. These consultants were scattered across several states, some working out of their homes and others working in local offices. Among those working out of home offices was a project manager named Jim Bob, who had several years of experience but only recently had joined the consulting team. His manager, who was headquartered in Chicago, had never actually met Jim Bob. Jim Bob's first assignment was at the Electric Company of Delaware, where he was charged with overseeing the installation of new equipment. This was a relatively simple task, even though the previous project manager had been unable to bring the project under control. At this point the customer was tired of the delays and false starts that had characterized the project management and resulted in Jim Bob's replacing the previous project manager.

Jim Bob was based in Denver, and it was agreed that he would work partially at home and partially at the customer's site in Delaware. Immediately after being assigned to the project, Jim Bob flew to Delaware where he met with the customer, presented his credentials, made a very polished presentation of his assessment of the situation, and generally impressed the client and his virtual boss. Although he appeared to be the man for the job, weeks went by and Jim Bob had yet to produce a basic plan. Furthermore, he was not always on site when expected and was spending more time in his home office in Denver than was anticipated. As concerns grew, Jim Bob's manager flew to Delaware to review the progress on the project and to clarify everyone's expectations. The meeting went fairly well and Jim Bob presented the plans and estimates that had been lacking. These were very professionally done, complete with colored graphs and handsome bindery. Everyone seemed satisfied that the project was on track. Jim Bob did take this opportunity to meet privately with his manager to explain that he could not spend so much time at the customer site because it distracted him from his work. When he was on-site, he was dragged into meetings dealing with issues outside of the scope of his project. Jim Bob also noted that his girlfriend did not like him gone so much, and it was putting a strain on his relationship. His manager took this opportunity to reiterate that the policy was to be at the customer site when required by the customer or as necessary to complete the project. Jim Bob indicated he understood the policy, but felt the managing consultant did not understand it.

Shortly after this event, the managing consultant called to complain that Jim Bob was *rarely* on site, even when needed. Efforts to contact him by pager, telephone, or voice mail were usually unsuccessful, and when he did respond to these attempts to contact him, it was usually hours or even days later. He ignored requests for information and copies of documents, and invitations to meetings. After listening to this list of Jim Bob's failings, his manager spent several days attempting to reach Jim Bob and had the same experience as the managing consultant. When Jim Bob's manager finally contacted him, he asked why he was not on site when requested and why was he so difficult to reach. Jim Bob explained that his pager was out of batteries and the telephone rolled over to voice mail when he was on the phone. Logically then, why did he not answer the voice mail? Jim Bob felt that he was very attentive to his voice mail, but frequently there was no message or the caller did not leave a name or number. As the complaints from the managing consultant grew, these telephone conversations gradually grew in complexity, acrimony, and incredulity. Jim Bob explained that he was unresponsive because of the poor quality communications equipment, improperly installed software, incompatible software, dead batteries, sunspots, and magnetic orientation. Essentially *the dog ate my homework* was the final explanation.

Gradually Jim Bob's manager obtained new pagers, a new computer for him, and had new Internet connections installed. The customer's e-mail software was upgraded, and Jim Bob was given access to the customer's network. Additionally, all of the other paraphernalia that he blamed for his unresponsiveness was replaced or upgraded, except the sunspots, which were someone else's province. Essentially there was no longer any reason for a failure in communications.

The subject of not being on site was quite another matter. It seems Jim Bob felt that he and the managing consultant did not have good *chemistry*. Specifically, the managing consultant was not allowing him to run his project as he wanted to and was giving him direction that he felt was incorrect. After several teleconferences between all of the parties, this issue was, more or less, resolved, and Jim Bob spent more time on site. However, when he was not on site he continued to be elusive and difficult to reach, and the complaints continued to pour in. Furthermore, the quality of the work was becoming an issue. Although everything was very flashy, it did not appear to be original, and certainly lacked the expected detail. This initiated another series of complaints by the managing consultant regarding the superficiality of Jim Bob's work.

As Jim Bob's manager tried to correct this situation, he found Jim Bob virtually impossible to reach by any means, in spite of the new equipment and upgrades. It seemed that any cell phone, telephone, or pager did not work properly until well after 10 A.M. and all attempts to use these prior to that time were garbled, distorted, or never received. Generally the communications infrastructure seemed to sustain miraculous improvements the higher the sun was in the sky (presumably mitigating the effect of the sunspots). Jim Bob's manager smelled a rat. Probably the same rat that you smelled, but this incident has several aspects that should be discussed beyond the obvious rat.

Perhaps the first question is how would you have handled this situation? Whom would you believe, Jim Bob or the managing consultant? Of course some of you may take the position that this situation would never have occurred in the first place if Jim Bob had simply been sent to the customer site until the job was done. That way he would have been under supervision, and this uncertainty regarding his performance would either not have occurred or would have been resolved much earlier. Although that may have been the solution once upon a time, it fails to recognize the realities of today's environment or to address the basic question. People like Jim Bob are hard to find, hard to keep, and frequently do not want to be away from home for extended periods. In fact, many do not even want to drive across town to work. Therefore, to assume that the manager could simply have dispatched Jim Bob to Delaware for the duration of the project is both simplistic and naive. The fact is, the events described are what happened, and the question remains: What would you have done if you had been Jim Bob's manager?

Once placing Jim Bob on site is eliminated as a solution, the remaining alternatives are relatively few, and all pivot on the most fundamental requirement for an effective virtual manager—*trust*. How much trust do you have in Jim Bob? Is he sleeping late? Is he working a normal workday in his home office? Do you care what hours he is working? Is he getting the job done? Is he living in a mysterious magnetic power center that wrecks electronic communications as he claims, or is he just a victim of circumstances or coincidences? In short, do you trust him?

We have always expected the worker to trust the manager but until recently it was not necessary for the manager to *trust* the worker. In fact, it could be argued that managers exist because the owners of the business do not trust the workers. After all, in the old paradigm the manager could see who was working and who was not, who was tardy and who was on time. Trusting the worker was not a significant issue. However, the manager managing in an activity scattered across the country must *trust* the worker because direct supervision and observation of work habits are not possible. This means the virtual manager must select people who are self-disciplined, self-directed, and capable of working independently. In short, the virtual manager must select people whom he can trust, but trust to do what? This raises another fundamental issue regarding work habits.

In a traditional office environment, with the boss sitting right across the hall, a great deal of time is wasted. This time is lost not only in driving to and from work, but in trotting down the hall to the bathroom, going out to lunch, making copies, getting coffee, drinking coffee, and chitchatting with fellow workers. Consequently, the typical workday in terms of actual work is a great deal shorter than it appears. Most home workers report they are more productive at home because they do not have these interruptions. They do not have the commute time, extended lunch hours, or other distractions. In fact, a common complaint from people who work from home is that the proximity of the work causes them to work longer hours than they did in a traditional environment, and this has been my personal experience as well. Therefore, the question is: Should the manager care what hours Jim Bob is working? Does it matter?

Suppose Jim Bob was sleeping until noon every day, should that be an issue? The concept of a "day's work for a day's pay" was predicated on the hourly wage, but is that a realistic concept for the salaried knowledge worker working at home in the middle of the night? Does sitting at a desk blankly staring out of the office window differ from Jim Bob lying in his bed staring at the ceiling? Does observing a worker in thought or casual conversation have greater value than not knowing precisely what a worker is doing at any given moment?

The answer to this question may distinguish the traditional manager from the virtual manager, who really has no way of determining the hours worked by the worker and may not see that as especially relevant. Based on personal experience and anecdotal reports, the probability is that the home worker is working more hours than he/she would in the traditional environment. Therefore, the manager for a geographically dispersed team must accept the fact that the worker cannot be observed and must assign work on the basis of objectives (MBO again), time frames, and expected results. The performance of the worker is then evaluated based on achieving these goals and objectives with supervision coming from regular status reports and reviews. On this basis, it probably does not matter if Jim Bob is sleeping, working, or mowing the lawn, as long as he accomplishes his objectives on schedule. However, that seems to be the problem with Jim Bob, He is not meeting schedules, objectives, or expectations.

What about *availability*? After all, this was a major issue with the managing consultant, and it is a fundamental requirement for success of any team, especially for anyone working in a remote location. Also, the constant demand for availability is the basis for the claim of long hours by many of these decentralized and dispersed workers. The reason is that the workers are globally dispersed across time zones so that teleconferences may be scheduled at odd times. In this example, Jim Bob lived in the Mountain Time Zone, his manager was in the Central Time Zone, but he was working in the Eastern Time Zone. Because the workday for everyone involved was extended, so was each person's anticipated availability. So the issue with Jim Bob was not if he was sleeping until noon or the number of hours being worked, but his *availability* was the problem. Whenever the team needed him, they could not reach him, and, in their opinion, he made little effort to maintain contact with them. However, Jim Bob maintained from the outset that he was working long hours and was always available but was not receiving the pages or phone calls. When he received these, he felt he was prompt in responding and was always available to the team. So what or whom do you believe?

The next issue is the work itself. Managing workers in a virtual environment means the manager only sees the work at points in time or as a completed piece. With Jim Bob the results were presented in a very flashy way, but, on scrutiny, the plans and results were high level and lacking in details or specifics. When pressed for results, Jim Bob produced what was expected, but not in the time frame or the quality level expected. This is a major problem for managers managing in a nontraditional organization. Regular reviews and teleconferences can be conducted just as they are in a traditional environment, but if the worker cannot be reached, then no review can be conducted. In these circumstances, what can the manager do? How far do you allow things to go before you take action?

Actually, there are very few options. Counseling and coaching are the obvious choices, and these are the ones used by Jim Bob's manager, with little success. Formal objectives and regularly scheduled meetings can also be used, but as we saw with Jim Bob, these are not always completely effective due to extenuating circumstances. In the actual situation Jim Bob's manager terminated him on the basis that the work itself was not of the quality required. His unavailability to the team was a factor, but not the only reason. However, before terminating him, Jim Bob's manager gave him the option of relocating to the site and working in a traditional (supervised) environment, but he declined.

Although performance and availability were the basis for the termination, the underlying issue was *trust*. In effect, Jim Bob's manager no longer trusted him. None of Jim Bob's colleagues in Denver suffered from the same communications problems, which Jim Bob insisted were localized. Although this may have been true, there were simply too many problems and coincidences to be ignored. When these were taken into account with the poor quality of work, there was a loss of credibility, and the conclusion was another project leader was required.

This scenario highlights not just some of the problems encountered in the virtual workplace but the changes in management style as well. The manager of dispersed employees does not relinquish control, but must rely on methods other than observation. Regular communications and an effective communication infrastructure are imperative. Selecting people capable of working in a remote environment and with minimum supervision is fundamental to the success of the virtual manager, but suppose you cannot select the people. Suppose the employees work for another company but are key to the success of the project. This adds another dimension to virtual management when the manager is managing contract workers, working in a dispersed environment, as part of a virtual enterprise.

THE VIRTUAL ENTERPRISE

In the traditional organization, power flowed down from the top and provided managers with control over the workers. There were generals, colonels, lieutenants, and privates, and everyone knew their position in the hierarchy. Challenges to authority were rare because the outcome was pre-determined. Mutineers were always shot (or hung from the yardarm for those of the naval persuasion), but the traditional view of power, authority, and mutiny is changing. Certainly the organizational charts still have a hier-archical flavor to them, but it is harder to distinguish any correlation between position, rank, and authority. As we saw in Figure 6.3, contempo-rary organizational charts include such new elements as strategic partners, outsourcers, and employees from other groups. Managers may control large numbers of people but have little administrative control over them, which results in a fuzzy chain of command. Furthermore, in these new organiza-tional forms there may be multiple chains of command, which results in uncertainty regarding who has what authority. The career path for the employees in the virtual enterprise may have as many lateral moves as verti-cal and may not include the corner office as a career objective. Career paths are becoming blurred as career objectives shift from climbing the corporate ladder to professional development and quality-of-life issues. Functional departments are becoming *service areas* that compete with external suppliers of similar services.

Remember *Chaos Management* that we discussed earlier? Well here it is, right in the middle of the virtual enterprise where managers are supervising employees working in an organization that is constantly shifting and chang-ing as people, contractors, and alliances come and go. Of course, as we saw earlier, the problem with virtual *realities* is there are no rules. To read about managing chaos is one thing, but to actually attempt to do it is quite another, because most of us have little experience in managing people who come and go and over whom we have little control. On the other hand, there is nothing new under the sun. Therefore, to learn how to manage remotely, we can turn to the history books to find lessons in managing decentralized organizations that are geographically dispersed, using virtual employees. There we will find that we are not the first to create and operate virtual enterprises. Perhaps the most well-known example of one is the Roman Empire.

In case the similarities between the Roman Empire and the Virtual Enterprise are not self-evident, observe these similarities. The Roman Empire had a central authority, but day-to-day operations were in the hands of the Provincial Governors. The Virtual Enterprise has a central authority with daily operations controlled by empowered business unit executives. The Roman Empire was made up of provinces, strategic alliances, and client states. A virtual enterprise is made up of a company supported by strategic partners and suppliers—not so very different. The management structure of the Roman Empire consisted of the central imperial bureau-cracy in Rome, military leaders in the field, the provincial judiciary, tax col-lectors, and so on. These imperial administrators were scattered throughout the provinces and were not centrally located. The Virtual Enterprise has corporate management, line management, service area managers, managers from outside resources, contractors, and possibly managers from the customer as well. These administrators and resources are geographically dispersed. In the Virtual Enterprise the corporate management (like the Roman Senate) establishes objectives, profit targets, and policy. Beyond that, the managers of the various business units make all of the decisions in association with their various supporting services, just as the Roman Governors made the daily decisions regarding diplomacy, finance, and military affairs. The central management of the Virtual Enterprise receives periodic reports and performs regular reviews, but other than that, the business unit managers are on their own, just like the Roman Governors who reported periodically to the Roman Senate. Obviously there are differences because the Romans used a command and control management technique in addition to their virtual style, but it is their virtual technique that bears examination.

The Romans had excellent administrative methods that allowed them to control most of the civilized world without fax machines, telephones, computers, or more than elementary cost accounting, and all of this using Roman numerals for everything requiring computation. (If that doesn't boggle your mind, consider filling out your income tax using Roman numerals.) Roman communications were primitive compared to what is available today, nevertheless they could communicate with the farthest parts of the empire within days. They were able to administer this terribly complex society due to their virtual management techniques (certainly not due to their arithmetic).

Naturally the Romans did not call their management style "virtual." In fact, they probably did not call it management, because that is a fairly recent concept. But the fact is they developed and employed some very advanced administrative techniques. First, the prerequisites for Roman Governors were very strict because they held absolute power over the province and all of its inhabitants. These governors were military veterans, held other public offices, and had proven administrative skills (demonstrated qualifications and experience). The Roman Senate established their objectives, defined the scope of their activity, and held them accountable for the results (set standards, defined measurable objectives, established critical success factors). Once they left Rome, these Governors were free to act as necessary within the broad parameters of their commission (delegation). This meant they could hire mercenaries, make treaties, collect taxes, and even fight wars (empowerment). However, all of these things had to be conducted within what we would call *guiding principles*. For instance, there was complete religious freedom, local customs were accepted and honored, taxation was established by law, and local laws were observed to the extent possible. Violations of these guiding principles could be (and were) prosecuted in the law courts in Rome (regular reviews, audits, and reassignment). The success of these Roman techniques is demonstrated by the longevity of the Roman Empire. This doesn't mean that a virtual enterprise can (or should) endure for a thousand years, but it does provide some lessons for how a virtual enterprise should be managed. The key parts are:

- Select managers with broad experience and a demonstrated record of success.
- Expect operating managers to work well with suppliers, strategic partners, customers, and contractors. This means respecting their methods and culture.
- Provide clear objectives, critical success factors, and guiding principles.
- Delegate responsibility and empower (in the true sense of the word) the operating managers to act within the framework of the guiding principles.
- Conduct regular reviews and audits of activities (not second guessing).

Like all analogies, the lessons from the Roman Empire only go so far. In the final analysis, they did have a command-and-control model, and failures were dealt with quite harshly, with terminations being quite literal. Nevertheless, there are similarities, and the basic techniques can be applied. Just like the Roman Empire the virtual enterprise consists of some combination of employees, strategic allies, contractors, customers, suppliers, and consultants. Each of these groups has their own management structure and internal career path. They may report to a virtual manager in charge of a project but that manager may not be able to fire them. Frequently the virtual manager may only have the ability to *recommend* the removal of an individual. For example the managing consultant could not fire or remove Jim Bob from the project, unlike a Roman Governor who could have had him tortured and executed, a scope of authority that probably would have appealed to the managing consultant.

To effectively manage a virtual enterprise requires diplomatic skill, leadership, and empowerment. Experience indicates that empowerment is frequently just a buzzword used by managers to delegate correct decisions (decisions they would have made) while retaining authority to reverse "bad" (your) decisions. True empowerment requires executives to establish the boundaries (just as the Romans did) for decisions and authority and then live with the results of the decisions made by the empowered leaders. This requires the managers within the Virtual Enterprise to establish directions, set objectives, establish procedures, and generally build a framework for the empowered leaders to work within. However, as important as these things are, and at the risk of starting uncontrolled laughter, the fact is the most important item for success in the Virtual Enterprise is the people.

PEOPLE VERSUS RESOURCES

The old cliché that *people are our most important asset* has achieved epic comedic proportions in the face of massive reductions-in-force, but for the manager of a nontraditional organization, this is a reality. In the virtual world, nothing gets done without people, so the manager's success is directly dependent on the availability and skill level of people. However, the employees are not hers to hire, fire, or promote and in many cases, even to select. Therefore she determines what she needs in the way of resources and then orders them from the appropriate group. (I'll have two project leaders, a microbiologist, and a side of fries, please.) When they arrive she may accept or reject them for any reason. On the other hand, the people resources may recognize her from previous projects and refuse to work with her again. It is very much like buying cantaloupes at the market, except the cantaloupes cannot refuse to go home with you.

Once the people resources have been identified, the next challenge for the virtual manager is to stop being a manager and to become a leader. To be a leader you must have a vision that you can articulate clearly enough to inspire others to help you achieve it. This means that instead of instructing people on what to do, you must first explain what you want to accomplish, why it is necessary, how you intend to achieve it, and then *ask* them to help you attain it. In many cases the leader may be expected to explain what their contribution will be. In effect, the manager is expected to be a leader and to lead by example. That sounds simple, doesn't it?

WHERE ARE MY MINIONS?

Leading by example is easily said but not so easily done, especially in a virtual environment. Back in Kansas when the resources were identified, they were assigned tasks and were generally located in some proximity to their colleagues and manager. If the manager could inspire others and act as a leader, that was a bonus, but in the final analysis, it was not necessary. After all, everyone was present every day and under some level of control. For the leader of a geographically dispersed team, leadership is a great deal more challenging. How does she organize and lead this team of geographically dispersed people whom she may never have met and who may not directly report to her?

For the purposes of our discussion, let us assume that she begins by establishing an organization and that attaining her objectives requires four projects. The people necessary to complete these projects will come from internal service groups, one external manpower firm, and one strategic partner. The first challenge is organizing these resources into some sort of logical group, which is essentially basic management. Because there are four projects, we logically have four project managers. However, the challenge is to determine who the project managers are and whether they are employees of the strategic partner or the manpower provider, or if they are from one of our internal service groups. This is a very fundamental question because it establishes the level of *control* that the overall manager will have. Project Managers from an external manpower provider may provide the tightest control, but the level of expertise, experience, and subject knowledge is unknown. Therefore, selecting a project manager from this source becomes a roll of the dice. Are you feeling lucky? Selecting a project manager from a strategic partner may provide a high level of knowledge and expertise, but it also provides the least control, because the project manager is an employee of another company. Even if you are able to establish a high level of control over this project manager, the scope and flexibility of the project may be restricted by the core competence of the strategic partner. Therefore, let us assume that the project managers are from our internal service providers, which means we now have a virtual manager, managing four projects each headed by a project manager and staffed by a mix of real and virtual employees.

Control is the basis for the second challenge, which is to decide where the work is to be done. In the centralized workplace this was never a problem. The work was in a fixed location, and the workers came to it. In the virtual workplace the location of the work is flexible and the manager may have an option of determining where the work is to be done and whether it is to be centralized or decentralized. In this case the virtual manager is located in Denver, the project leaders are located in Phoenix, Toledo, Houston, and Chicago. The manpower provider is located in Denver, and the strategic partner is headquartered in Houston. The manager can bring all of the team together at one central location (e.g., Denver), bring some of the team and their project to a central location, or leave them wherever they are and manage the project managers remotely.

Centralize

For the traditional thinking manager, this sounds like the best and most efficient way to lead a project. Everybody is gathered in a central location where the communications are simplified, supervision is available, and the manager has maximum control. This means that the project leaders must either relocate (expensive) or spend an extended period away from home (not desirable). However, there are still the employees of the strategic partner to consider, and they may not want to go to Denver for extended periods. These extended stays away from home are "quality of life" issues that are increasingly becoming pivotal issues in resource planning. Although this is probably the easiest way to manage this project, in reality it is probably not viable for a virtual team.

Here and There

Locating the project leaders and their teams around the country in locations convenient for the team members is a very attractive option. However, this structure presupposes that all of the team members and the project leader are local. If this is not the case, and some (or all) of the team members must travel or relocate, then nothing has been gained. Possibly a small reduction in travel costs can be attained, but the greater quality-of-life issues and leadership challenges remain. Of course, if the team members are local, then this arrangement gives the project/program manager tighter control and greater supervision potential than a fully decentralized environment.

And Everywhere

Leaving everyone where they are and working in a completely decentralized environment is the most challenging for the leader and manager. It minimizes the quality-of-life issues while maximizing the control issues. The team members and project leaders are scattered. There is little face-to-face contact or direct supervision. For this structure to be successful, the project manager must be experienced, self-motivated, and above all, a good communicator. The team members must be knowledgeable and capable of accomplishing their objectives with a minimum of supervision. Managing in this environment requires excellent and frequent communications as well as clearly defined tasks and objectives. If the projects are not carefully defined and formally tracked, this type of dispersed structure can quickly lead to disaster.

As awkward and complicated as this decentralized project structure may seem, it is a growing trend. And as we have seen, technology allows these decentralized structures to exist. Virtual organizations will become more and more prevalent, allowing people to work remotely and to live in places attractive to them. Many are drawn to the country, to the mountains, or to families. Some are even drawn to cities and this brings us back to Kansas. When we left Kansas everyone was sharply dressed in their corporate uniforms and joined the lemming-like throng of commuters every morning. Suddenly, we found we were in Oz, where nothing was quite like it used to be. Most of us are still adjusting to this new environment, and of course the environment itself continues to change. Is it good or bad? Only time will tell, but it is highly unlikely that things will ever be like they were. In the meantime, those of us here in the trenches must learn to deal with these new challenges. Even the decisions associated with the organizational structure of a virtual enterprise are critical and as we have seen carry some risk. But all decisions have risk and this brings us to what is perhaps the single most difficult aspect of management, which is decisions and risk assessment.

8

DECISIONS AND RISK

To Be or Not to Be?

"To be or not to be?" is the famous question Hamlet asks himself as he contemplates the decision he must make. Should he accept the situation as it is (to suffer the slings and arrows) or to take corrective action (to take up arms against a sea of troubles)? However, like all decisions, Hamlet's carries an element of risk, and it is the assessment of that risk that drives the indecision and vacillation that characterize the Prince of Denmark. But Hamlet is not alone in the box of indecision and "what if's." All of us at one time or another have been gripped by indecision, and many of us have worked for managers whose entire style is characterized by indecision and vacillation. Yet decisions are what we do as managers. We set the direction, develop the strategy, decide who goes where and how much money to spend. But, as we all know, these tend to be the easy decisions. Indecision creeps in when there is no obvious solution to the problem or, worse, every solution seems to lead to disaster and the only decision left open is deciding which is the "least worst" decision. Almost always the indecision and vacillation associated with these types of decisions rest on determining the risk. And this brings us to risk assessment and decision making, the basic elements of management.

Everyone recognizes that doctors make life and death decisions, but not every decision falls into that category. The same is true of managers. Many of our decisions involve people, their livelihood, vast sums of money, or even the future of the enterprise, but rarely do our decisions fall into the "do or die" category where a poor decision would bring destruction of the enterprise. Furthermore, just like doctors, when we are confronted with one of these decisions, we usually recognize it and proceed carefully. We seek other opinions, bring in specialists, and review the alternatives before making a decision. But it is the other decisions, the small ones that we often put less thought into, ignore, or fail to recognize the associated risks, and it is these that seem to create the most problems. Of course, that leads to the obvious question of "How do I spot a trivial decision that carries a hidden risk factor?" As hard as it is for me to say, the fact is I do not know. Furthermore, I am not sure anyone knows (well maybe Madam Garboni, our secret psychic adviser, might know). As we discussed in the introduction, the failure to give an employee a company jacket ultimately led to his resignation and an undetermined loss in dollars, time, and prestige. Perhaps the conclusion is to recognize that every decision carries some risk and that it is not possible to explore every conceivable risk. Instead it is better to consider any obvious risks and then to react as quickly and decisively as possible. But it is important to recognize that even the smallest decision has some associated risk. I am sure that some people will disagree with the statement that it is better to act quickly and decisively because it seems imprudent, but it is *pragmatic*, and that is what life is like in the trenches.

On the other hand, decisions are tricky things. Some people make decisions on-the-spot with or without information. Others cannot seem to make any decision until they have collected every possible scrap of information, examined every nuance, and then they delegate the actual decision to a committee. Neither of these types of decision-making is good. The manager who reacts to every stimulus is volatile and undependable. Making a poor decision quickly is still a poor decision, and this fact will not be wasted on the other managers and employees involved. There is nothing wrong with asking a few questions and gathering a few facts before opening that nifty little box labeled "Pandora." That brings us to the other style of decision-making commonly known as *paralysis by analysis*. These are the managers who, when told to open the box, become glassy eyed with fright. They cannot decide to take action on their own because they might make a mistake. It would also spoil their unblemished record for never having made a wrong decision (or possibly any decision), so they quickly call in the experts. A committee is formed, which leads to a task force, which leads to a consensus, which leads to the question of what is in the box. This investigation and analysis will go on until it is no longer possible to establish who is responsible for what. Generally, the need for a decision regarding the box has become moot because the box disappeared and the investigation has shifted to an analysis of what might have been in the box had it not gotten lost.

The fact is, every decision should be timely. For some decisions the right time is now, for some it is never, and for others the right time is later, with later being established by circumstance. Obviously the trick is to determine which situation you are in when the demand for the decision arises. This is hard to determine, but the first question should always be: What happens if I do nothing right now but decide in an hour, two hours, a day, or next week? It is imperative for the manager to remain calm and focused during an emergency. This is especially important when the staff is running around waving their arms in the air and pressing for immediate action. This is the point where the manager must decide when the right time to decide is. Decisions should not be postponed indefinitely anymore than they should be made prematurely but they should be made at the right time. Perhaps this point of when to make a decision is most easily addressed through some simple examples.

THE CASE FOR IMMEDIATE DECISIONS

Suppose you are a manager standing on a sidewalk, and a passerby yells for you to run because there is a safe about to fall on your head. Clearly, the immediate response for some managers would be to run, but for some the warning merely raises a whole series of questions. Whose safe is it? How do you know it is falling? How fast is it falling? Where will it land? How do you know it will land there? How much time do I have before I must decide to step aside? Splat!!! The only thing remaining of our inquisitive manager is a lump of flesh clearly imprinted with *Amalgamated Safe Company*. In this instance, as in so many in real life, the time ran out for a timely decision before all of the pertinent information could be collected. In this case the risk assessment resulted in a default decision of "do nothing," which in turn proved fatal. Some of the questions asked before the fatal moment could be construed as being relevant whereas others were irrelevant under the circumstances. In fact, the most relevant questions were "Where will it land?" and "How do you know it will land there?" These two questions acknowledge the threat and are pertinent to a decision regarding what to do. The answer to the first question tells you whether you should move or stand fast. The answer to the second question allows you to assess the accuracy of the first answer so you may determine the probability of making a good decision on whether to move or stay. Interesting questions, but they required too much time.

Of course, when the warning came you might have quickly jumped aside on the assumption that the warning was valid and that you must take immediate action. However without sufficient information, you are unwilling to commit to a complete response, so you jump one or two paces aside with the idea that you have bought enough time to fully evaluate the situation. Believing you have safely moved out of harm's way, you

begin a complete evaluation by asking the passerby the questions you feel
are required to fully evaluate the situation and take further action. Again,
this is the mixed bag of relevant and irrelevant questions such as: Whose
safe is it? How do you know it is falling? How fast is it falling? Where will
it land? How do you know it will land there? As so often is the case with
cautious incremental decisions, you were overtaken by the events, and
before the data gathering is complete, the safe lands squarely on your
head. Splat!!! The Amalgamated Safe Company's careless handling of their
equipment has claimed another victim with poor decision-making skills.
The essential problem here was not the timeliness of the decision but the
manager's commitment to a solution with the least risk and least con-
sumption of energy (resources).

And, we have the third possible situation: when the warning came, we
immediately ran to the side of the passerby who is wildly gesturing to warn
us of impending doom. There is a resounding crash, and the Amalgamated
Safe has crashed harmlessly into the sidewalk. Of course, we ran much farther than was needed and we only found out where the safe was going to
land after the fact, but we have avoided a disaster that our more conserva-
tive friends did not. In this case we overcommitted resources (energy) by
running farther than was required, but the decision was a "good" decision
because we survived. This decision recognized the risk, determined the
safest position under the circumstances (the passerby wasn't running for
HIS life), and immediately committed to that solution.

In the first instance there were simply too many questions and many were
irrelevant. After all, who cares whose safe it is at this particular moment.
This may be relevant later when the decision of whom to sue must be made,
but it becomes relevant only after you have saved yourself. Otherwise the
subsequent lawsuit is relevant only to your heirs. Asking the passerby how
he knows the safe is falling and how fast is an example of a high-risk decision. These questions are intended to ensure that no action is taken until
absolutely necessary. By attempting to minimize risk, the decision-maker
has actually made a high-risk decision, because he may be overtaken by
events before the necessary information is gathered. In general, this effort
to collect and examine what could be self-evident facts prior to jumping
aside is a vivid example of a manager who must have every single fact before
deciding anything. If any question is relevant in these circumstances, it is
probably "where will it land?" because that determines where we do not
want to be. But even this question has obvious answers. The first is "I do
not know where it is going to land" and the second is "it is going to land
where you are standing." This question and the obvious answers are an
example of how some managers insist on gathering facts to corroborate
what is either common knowledge or self-evident. Timid and insecure managers often fall into this trap and frustrate their colleagues in the process. In
fact it might have been the colleagues of this indecisive manager who

dropped the safe knowing in advance the victim would never be able to decide how to save himself before being "amalgamated."

Asking how much time is available before making the decision is a more interesting question. The circumstances are very dangerous, but the question is indicative of a manager who is willing to make a decision but only at the "right" time. Naturally, the question is when is the "right" time, and the answer varies by circumstance. Certainly if someone is yelling "a safe is falling on your head, run" the probability is that you do not have much time, and asking how much time you have before acting could be fatal (as it was in our example). On the other hand, in less dire circumstances, this is a valid question because things change, and the decision might be different at a later point in time. After all, by waiting we might be able to discern precisely where the safe will land and discover we are safer by not moving. The action-oriented manager simply reacted to the threat and ran to the obvious point of safety, which was next to the passerby. Because he did not yell that the safe was falling on him, the obvious presumption is he is standing in a safe spot. Of course, in management terms the manager overreacted and expended more resources than were necessary. Hasty decisions frequently are more costly, but in times of great danger the primary objective must be to survive, and in this simple example, the only manager to survive was the decisive one.

Very few managers are put into such extreme life or death situations as described in the example, but many are placed in situations where quick, decisive action is needed. Sometimes these situations are obvious, sometimes less obvious, but their common point is that a decision must be made even when none of the alternatives are desirable. That is, each entails risk and the manager must decide which is the greater risk, even when there is no time to assess the risk. Consider this manager who found himself in a situation regarding a super computer that worked, one that did not, and two customers.

THE SUPER COMPUTER

Super computers are very expensive and normally used by very large companies with highly specialized needs. These computers are usually built to order and on a very defined schedule. They are also very delicate and have rigorous environmental requirements. The ABC company had built and then installed a super computer at a highly secret government installation. Unfortunately, since its installation two months previously, this computer had been very unstable. It was prone to crashes and had not run more than 24 hours without a crash since its installation. The company had some of its best troubleshooters on site attempting to find the problem and repair it if possible. In the meantime the head of the government agency was calling the CEO of the company demanding that the system be fixed immediately. However none of his demands offered any solutions, so they were of limited value to the engineers attempting to stabilize the computer. Then things got worse. The system suffered a major short circuit that damaged the system to the extent that it could not be repaired on site.

One of the unvarying laws of the universe is that disasters strike on Friday evenings, usually before a holiday, which, of course, is the situation here. They had hardly extinguished the flames before the head of the government agency was demanding service, his money back, fixes, and important body parts from the engineer in charge. Once the on-site team got the agency head calmed down, they called the only manager they could locate at that hour, the Director of Product Marketing. They quickly explained the past history and the gravity of the current situation. The computer would have to be de-installed and shipped back to the factory, because, in their estimation, it was so badly damaged they could not repair it on site. Furthermore, the head of the agency told them if they removed it they could keep it. Important tests were scheduled on Monday morning, and if these tests were delayed, millions of dollars would be wasted. It was absolutely mandatory that the computer be up and operational by Monday.

The engineers told the Director of Product Marketing that they would need at least two days to repair and test the computer once they got it back to the factory, but it would take at least one day to prepare the computer for shipment. Once the Director of Product Marketing understood the scope of the problem, he began calling the managers responsible for solving the problem. None were available, but he did succeed in locating the Plant Manager who ran the factory where the computers were built. There were no computers available at the plant. They were built to order and none were scheduled for completion for at least a week. However, they had one sitting on their shipping dock waiting to go to a customer in Atlanta. The Director then called corporate aviation and told them to send a jet to Wichita where the computer would be waiting for them. By Saturday morning the damaged computer was moved aside and the new computer was on site. The engineers managed to get the new system installed and tested in time for the customer test on Monday morning.

As in our earlier simple illustration, this situation required immediate and decisive action. Time was of the essence, and any hesitation would have had serious consequences. The responsibility for the decision did not belong to the Director of Product Marketing. He just happened to be working late and there was no one else available to take the call, to assume the responsibility, or to make the decision. Under the circumstances he could have side-stepped the problem with little to no risk. All he had to do was to pass the problem back to the engineer on site and tell him to call his boss. Instead he asked a few questions, got the essentials of the problem, and recognized that the company was at risk. He then diverted the shipment of a million-dollar computer from one customer to another on his own nonexistent authority.   *

Again acting outside of his scope of authority, he ordered the corporate jet to function as a freight carrier and pick up the new computer and fly it to Washington D.C. He then arranged to have the engineers install and test the new equipment prior to the customer's Monday morning deadline.

For some this may appear that the Director of Product Marketing overreacted. It is possible that the head of the government agency was just blustering and the test on Monday was not that important. It is possible that more experienced engineers might have been able to repair the system on site. It is possible that the customer who was expecting the new equipment might be at greater risk than the government agency. All of those things are possible, and had any of the responsible corporate executives been available they might have used that information to make a different decision. But none of these people were available and none of this information was available to the Director of Product Marketing. He had to act immediately and on the basis of what data he had to work with. Instead of waiting to gather all of the facts and risk having the safe fall on his head, he evaluated the risks and took the actions he felt were in the best interest of the corporation. What would you have done? Would you have attempted to get all of the information, to line up all of the right executives, and try to make the right decision? That is certainly the decision with the least personal risk, but under the circumstances the one with the greatest risk to the company. But isn't that an example of what our managers did while the safe was falling?

Certainly, every manager encounters situations that require rapid decisions with a high-risk potential, but these are not the everyday fare of most managers. The decisions most of us face require reflection and consideration and usually allow us enough time to analyze the situation before deciding on a course of action. Of course, some of us consider and reflect longer than others, but ultimately we must arrive at a decision that balances result with risk. Whether to exceed the speed limit or not is perhaps the most common decision of this type. Does the excitement or time saved warrant the risk of a speeding ticket? A simple but common question and from observation it seems that a great many people feel the risk is worth the reward. But there are other common examples of risk versus reward decisions.

All of us, at one time or another have either witnessed or experienced the headstrong three-year-old in the toy store who is demanding that the parent purchase a toy. The parent bends over to the child and patiently explains the Freudian concepts of child development and the Jungian counterpoints. The child begins to scream and insist that the toy is the only thing that will ever make him (or her) happy. The patient parent moves on to explain how child psychologists have determined this type of toy leads to violent behavior and will harm the developing personality. Of course, the parent is talking to a three-year-old who only understood blah, blah, blah, NO, blah, blah, blah, NO. At this point the child throws himself onto the floor screaming, kicking his feet, and threatening to hold his breath until he is dead. Naturally the parent knows that this is impossible but the child does not. Therefore, the parent is faced with the decision of buying the toy in order to reduce their embarrassment (reward) or to persist in their denial. The analysis pivots on the risks involved. Of course, the possibility of the child holding his breath until he is dead is nil. However, the risk of further embarrassment to the parent is great and some parents will give in and buy the toy for the child just to avoid any further embarrassment. Other parents will stand fast and let the little brute turn blue, thereby accepting the risk of embarrassment in exchange for teaching the child a lesson. In business, these risk/reward situations usually revolve around taking an unpopular stand, with the risk being loss of profit or reduced customer satisfaction and the reward being more business or a happy customer like Farmer Jones.

THE BARN BURNER PROJECT

Farmer Jones has hired the Barn Raising & Stable Cleansing Corporation to build a series of new high-tech state-of-the-art barns for his agricultural enterprise. This is an enormous project with a multimillion-dollar budget and a "cast of thousands" (well certainly a cast of tens) planned over the next two years. At the conclusion of the planning phase and after the project was launched, Farmer Jones approached the Program Manager (Johnny) and asked if he had heard about the newly released computer-driven barn-heating system being sold under the name "Barn Burner." "Certainly," the Program Manager replied with enthusiasm, "we are the world's leading Barn Raising and Stable Cleaning concern, and we are up-to-date on all new barn technology." "Excellent," Farmer Jones replied, "because I think I want that system installed in all of my barns. Since you are going to install a heating system in all of my barns anyway, would you evaluate the "Barn Burner" system as an alternative and let me know how effective it is relative to its cost?"

As we can see, Johnny is now faced with a decision that he must make on the spot while Farmer Jones chews on his piece of straw. Of course, the very first thing Johnny must think about is schedule and resource impact. Who would he assign to this evaluation and what effect would that have on the project? How long will this evaluation take? Has someone else at BR&SC already evaluated the "Barn Burner"? Of course, there are many other factors that Johnny must consider as well, but the immediate question is: What should he say or do right now? Johnny can stall and make no decision *at this time*, or he could decide to either do the evaluation or not.

The Risk of Saying No

In spite of the popularity of the simplistic "just say no" approach to decision-making, the reality is that this position is usually espoused by those who do not have to say "no." Suppose Johnny quickly runs through in his mind the ramifications of saying "yes" and realizes that the risks outweigh the advantages, so he "just says no." How do you think Farmer Jones will react to that response? After all, he is spending millions with BR&SC and he asks for a simple favor and gets turned down. Undoubtedly, Farmer Jones will be upset and has several courses of action open to him. He can go over Johnny's head and demand the evaluation be done; he can forget the whole thing and stick to the original plan; or he could terminate the existing contract.

What is missing here is any discussion of cost or payment. Johnny has *assumed* that Farmer Jones asked for the evaluation to be done as a favor, meaning at no additional charge. On the other hand, Farmer Jones did not volunteer to pay for the additional work, so perhaps he did mean that the evaluation should be absorbed into the cost of the existing project.

The Risk of Saying Yes at No Charge

Our Program Manager Johnny could just say yes, but to what is he agreeing? As we all know, the devil is in the detail and "evaluation" is one of those wonderfully unspecific terms that sounds so precise. Therefore, Johnny really has two ways of saying yes. He can say, "Yes, I will do the evaluation" and not mention or discuss any additional costs or he can say, "Yes," followed by "I will have an estimated cost by tomorrow."

Certainly the way to mitigate this risk is to view the evaluation as an expansion in scope and indicate there will be a charge. I am confident that many of you have your eyebrows raised at the mere suggestion that there was even a question about additional charges in the first place, and I can hear "OF COURSE, this is an expansion in scope and should be billed." But as you know, more often than not, the answer will be a "yes" with no discussion regarding expanded scope or additional cost. So why would Johnny "just say yes" to this (outrageous) or at least costly request? Certainly the two obvious (and relatively common) reasons are a lack of courage and/or experience or the more common motive—the desire for more profit. But there are other reasons as well. For example, Johnny may feel that the real cost of the evaluation is below the profit potential from the expanded scope represented by the installation of the "Barn Burner." In essence, Johnny thinks that by giving a little he can gain a lot. Therefore, the answer is "yes." Another possibility is that BR&SC is interested in evaluating the new "Barn Burner" product anyway, and this represents a chance to do it at a low cost and please a customer at the same time.

The Risk of Saying Yes with a Charge

If Johnny does not charge for the "evaluation," he is assuming some risk. But risks remain even if the project is viewed as add-on work. The basic risk is that even with a relatively firm idea of the cost and impact of the added work, the estimate is based on Johnny's interpretation of what is included in the evaluation. Without a firm (and preferably written) interpretation of what is included in the evaluation, any output could be disputed later by Farmer Jones. More than likely, Farmer Jones will dispute that there should even BE a charge. After all, from his perspective the project calls for a heating system to be installed anyway and all he is asking is for Johnny to consider the new "Barn Burner." Therefore, the cost of this evaluation is already in the project and Johnny should simply evaluate the "Barn Burner" instead of the heating system originally planned. The fact that BR&SC did not include an evaluation of the heating system in the original deal may be denied by Farmer Jones on the basis that he did not understand that and it certainly was not spelled out in the contract. If Johnny and his company persist on the basis that no evaluation was needed for a standard, the dispute is on, because Farmer Jones is appalled that BR&SC would install any heating system without first testing it.

The Risk of Saying Yes Phase II

For the sake of our discussion, let us assume that Johnny sees the evaluation as an opportunity to expand the scope of the project and enhance the profitability of the project and agrees to do the evaluation. Clearly Johnny has decided that the profit potential is great enough to assume the risk. Johnny and Farmer Jones shake hands, and the new project is named JANUS after the Roman god of beginnings and endings. And if you believe this is the end of anything, you should go immediately to the rear of the class, because as any manager knows NOTHING ever goes according to plan. The resources to do JANUS had to come from somewhere, and that was from the original project. Consequently, the Barn Raising begins to fall behind schedule so Johnny must move the JANUS resources back to the original project, which causes JANUS to slow to a stop. This delay leads to complaints from Farmer Jones that JANUS is behind schedule because Johnny does not care, cannot manage, put the wrong people on the project, or whatever. Take your pick. Of course through some heroic sleight-of-hand, Johnny may have been able to keep both projects on schedule, but is this an outstanding achievement? Absolutely not. All that proves is that the original project was padded to start with and BR&SC overcharged Farmer Jones from the outset. If it proved anything at all it was Farmer Jones was right to insist that they do this evaluation for nothing. Furthermore, the next time the issue of scope creep is raised, there will be no negotiation based on how JANUS was absorbed.

This discussion of alternatives and what if's could go on indefinitely. The point of the discussion is risk assessment, and, as I said at the beginning, there are no hard and fast rules for assessing risk. Certainly every project manager includes a contingency factor in the project estimates because precise estimates are not possible. How much of a contingency is included varies, because every situation is unique (human variability) and the risks associated with any given decision are unique to that set of circumstances. Because the project manager knows that there is some ability to absorb some extra work, the temptation to use this for scope increases is great, but as we saw it is very risky as well. However, studying some typical everyday situations that we all encounter may give some additional insight into risk assessment and what might result from some of the more obvious alternatives to seemingly simple decisions.

Of course, the use of the word "simple" might be interpreted as referring to those decisions made by lower-level managers and leaders, but every tier in the organization has simple decisions. Unfortunately, the higher you go in the organization, the wider the impact of those simple decisions, and executives are not immune from making decisions for the best of reasons that turn out to be less than brilliant. Take for example the Wizard, which looked so good on the outside. Of course, this was the same observation made by the Trojans only moments before bringing that magnificent wooden horse inside the city walls.

THE WIZARD

From time to time products are proposed that are such technical advances that they seem too good to be true. This was certainly the case of the Wizard, which was a simple-to-program computer (ignore that vision of a VCR flashing a perpetual 12:00) targeted at the small business. When the prototype of this product was demonstrated to the CEO and his team of senior executives, they were virtually jumping for joy. This was an incredible new product whose functionality could be modified by a few simple keystrokes. It required little technical knowledge, but promised improved productivity through customization. This product was so good and held such promise for profit that the executive team immediately committed it to production, bypassing the usual market studies and focus groups. The Sales Vice President submitted a monster forecast after a brief meeting with his staff who was equally enthusiastic about the Wizard. Normally the sales forecasts were submitted after a careful analysis of competition, trends, impact on existing products, and the usual marketing steps, but in this case the process was ignored, because it seemed redundant. Armed with the monster sales forecast the factory began manufacturing Wizards. Normally products were built on the basis of orders to avoid the cost of inventory, but the forecast was so large that this process could not be followed and still meet the monthly demand forecasted. Therefore, the Vice President of Manufacturing decided to start manufacturing without orders to build a backlog of Wizards. That way when the orders came in he would be able to ship immediately and keep ahead of the orders. The

Wizard was then introduced to the world with a great deal of hoopla and enough pre-release orders to meet the first month's forecast. The Wizard was off to a great start, but then so was the Trojan War.

Even though Wizard sales got off to a good start, they still fell below forecast. The second warning came when the sales figures for the existing products dipped below previous levels. But the Wizard sales offset the dip in revenues, and therefore, this change in sales pattern was viewed as what is normal when a product like the Wizard is introduced. By this time some of the normal staff work was completed, and it was left to a midlevel manager to point out that the sales forecast for the Wizard was so large that it would require 125% of the entire sales team to sell nothing else. Furthermore, the sales analysis showed the experienced sales people were not selling the Wizard because the commissions were too small. The less experienced sales people were not selling at the level forecasted because they had difficulty demonstrating the Wizard and explaining how it worked. This analysis was not well received by the executive team because it indicated there might be a problem with the Wizard program. The executives knew the Wizard was a fantastic product and if the sales were not meeting forecast it had to be because the sales force was not trying hard enough or did not have the proper sales materials. In their eyes what the sales team needed was some motivation because they were not trying hard enough. Essentially, this was the classic "keep flogging the troops until morale improves" management approach. In addition to the motivational speeches, the marketing program was revamped, the product was enhanced with new features, and the Wizard became the Wizard II.

Of course, you know the rest of the story. Sales never reached the forecasted levels and gradually declined. The sales of the existing products also declined due to efforts to bolster Wizard sales. This caused a decline in revenues and profits because the Wizard sales were not great enough to offset the lost sales from the other products. Inventories grew at an alarming rate, so manufacturing was halted temporarily. When this was reported in the trade press it was viewed as a signal that the Wizard had failed. Efforts by the company to point out that more Wizards had been sold than any other product in the history of the company fell on deaf ears. If the product was so successful, why was there an inventory and why had manufacturing stopped and revenues dropped? Also there were growing rumors that the product was difficult to program, and many customers were demanding that the company pre-program the Wizards prior to delivery, which would consume most of the profit in the product. After more than a year of struggling, the Wizard was withdrawn from the product line. In the meantime the company had sustained a huge financial loss from lost revenues as well as the costs associated with the Wizard.

There were many questionable decisions in this scenario, but they began with the initial commitment and unconscious, or at least unspoken, decision to ignore the processes set up to minimize risk. Generally, risk/reward decisions tend to focus more on the risk, but in the case of the Wizard, the potential reward was so great that it overshadowed the risks, which were hardly considered. The Wizard was a great new product that promised improved productivity, ease of use, and a competitive price. This was so obvious to the team of seasoned and experienced executives that they bypassed their own processes to rush it into production. The productivity improvement and competitive price were tied to the ease of use, which was established by the executives, not by the usual focus group. This was a risk recognized by the executives, but one they were willing to take on the basis of the potential reward. The sales vice president enthusiastically presented the product to his staff who shared his enthusiasm for the new product. The risk that this enthusiasm was a result of his own enthusiasm (or worse, simply a reflection of what the boss wanted to hear) was ignored altogether. The result was an unusually large sales forecast that was viewed as corroboration of the initial evaluation of the Wizard as a terrific new product. No one thought to question the forecast.

Because everyone was enthusiastic about the Wizard and the sales forecast was huge, the Manufacturing executive elected to make a risk decision. Instead of following the normal procedure and building the product on the basis of sales, he decided to build to inventory. The risk of excessive inventory seemed less than the risk of having unfilled orders backlogged. Again the potential rewards outweighed the potential risks.

When it became apparent that the Wizard was not selling as well as expected, the executive team made a second series of risk decisions, except these were based on even less reflection and analysis than the first series. Perhaps the most disastrous decision of this series was not really a decision at all. It was simply a denial of facts. When the analysis showed that 125% of the sales force was required to meet the forecast, the executive team either could not believe it or did not believe it, but it does not matter because they ignored the analysis. Instead, they retained the sales forecast, enhanced the product (meaning more investment), revamped the marketing plan, and redoubled their efforts. The impact on the existing product revenues was ignored in their efforts to prove the original decision was sound. But these decisions represented huge risks without any improvement in the potential for reward. When the end came it was a direct result of a series of ill-considered or unevaluated risk decisions.

Certainly in this example everyone will have a different view of what went on and what was intended by each of the players. A straight reading of the scenario indicates a group of executives overwhelmed by enthusiasm (and perhaps greed) made a series of business decisions that led to a disaster. But suppose there were other agendas that motivated the business decisions. None of us can really know what people's motives are, and even if the players in this situation were to tell us, there is no way short of a lie detector to determine the truth of it. But suppose the disaster resulted in the CEO replacing the Vice President of Sales? Perhaps the enthusiasm expressed by the CEO was actually part of a plan to establish a basis for replacing the Vice President of Sales? Or more probably, suppose the Vice President of Sales submitted the monster forecast knowing it could not be met and that the Board of Directors would probably react to this disaster by replacing the CEO. In that case the risk/reward equation is suddenly changed. On the one hand the reward becomes the opportunity to succeed the CEO or on the other hand for the CEO to replace an executive who may have become a burden. The risk, of course, is having the hidden agenda discovered. If this were the situation then the financial risks would have become anticipated and part of the "reward" and sales success would have been one of the "risks." By changing the motive and objective behind the decisions, they take on a completely new dimension, even though the decisions remained unchanged. Suddenly, the urging by the CEO for immediate action takes on sinister overtones. The monster sales forecast becomes bait in an executive trap. The Wizard itself ceases to be a high-potential new product and becomes a weapon in an executive competition. But these are risks taken between executives who more or less know each other. Consider the risks that you take as an outsider when you join the company as an executive.

THE AMALGAMATED SAFE COMPANY—REVISITED

The tag line to the earlier reference about the Trojan Horse was "to beware of Greeks bearing gifts." This is especially good advice when you suddenly receive an unexpected benefit or unanticipated support. This does not mean that you should look your gift horse in mouth, but it does mean that you ought to keep a good eye on the horse, because for all you know he may have eaten the last owner into bankruptcy. To clarify my point, let us revisit the situation where the Amalgamated Safe inexplicably leapt to its death, jeopardizing our manager. As you recall, the manager was ambling down the street minding his own business, when a passerby yelled that a safe was about to fall on his head. The manager was faced with a situation requiring a rapid risk assessment and quick decision. At that time our analysis focused on the safe, the manager, and his reaction to the shouted warning rather than on the passerby, who we presumed was a total stranger. But suppose that the manager was the newly appointed boss of the passerby. Would that change anything? How would the passerby benefit from a simple warning? This is a question that frequently goes unasked, because it presupposes that things are not as they seem, and it introduces the concept of the hidden agenda. It is quite possible that the passerby did not shout his warning as a simple reaction to a dangerous situation but gave the warning with an ulterior motive.

We really did not determine how the Amalgamated Safe got dropped in the first place. But there are a great many possibilities. Certainly it could have been accidentally dropped but just as easily it might have been deliberately dropped. The employee might have arranged for the safe to be dropped so he could save the manager's life. This presents us with the dichotomy of: (a) Did he shout the warning just to save a life? or (b) Did he shout the warning in order to ingratiate himself with the new manager? After all, it was through his quick-thinking behavior that the manager is even around to be grateful, but perhaps he arranged to have the safe dropped on his new manager just so he could save him. Of course, the risk to this strategy is that he might not have known that the manager was indecisive thus shifting his timely warning from heroic to "oops."

Naturally, these speculations only become relevant, if the manager was decisive enough to have avoided the falling safe. In that case, we will find the manager standing safely by the side of the passerby, profusely thanking him for the timely warning. Once the manager has thanked his savior and determined that he is actually one of his employees, the manager then has several possible reactions. The most trusting, if not the most logical, would be for the manager to simply accept that the safe was dropped by accident and the employee passerby was coincidentally there to warn him and thus save his life. In this case, the most important point is that, although never discussed and in spite of any tangible reward, the manager has become obligated to the employee. This obligation may not amount to very much, but it could easily place the employee last on the layoff list or place him in the forefront of the manager's consciousness when the time comes for promotion. This view is the most trusting because it accepts everything at face value. But what if there are other unseen factors?

After thanking the passerby for saving him and then discovering that his savior is actually an employee, a more discerning manager might have asked why the employee was there at that particular moment. Given that the employee had a plausible answer, the next question might address how the safe got dropped to begin with and by whom. If it turned out to be a company safe being moved by other employees, then the manager might suspect that this was more than coincidence. In any case, it really does not matter for the purposes of our discussion, which centers on risk assessment and decisions.

This anecdote illustrated a situation that is more common than most people realize, which is the employee with the hidden agenda. The problem for the manager is determining that a hidden agenda even exists. In our anecdote the manager was saved from disaster by a timely warning from an employee. However, an actual situation would not only be less dramatic, but much more subtle. Consider the new manager who has been brought in from the outside. She does not know any of her new subordinates and has little idea of how they will receive her. While our new manager is trying to adjust to the new environment, a serious problem arises. This problem requires some insight into the corporate culture and knowledge of internal processes. She is unsure of how to proceed and really does not know whom to turn to for advice. Before she can decide what to do, one of her new subordinates approaches her offering some advice (obviously he did not come running into her office yelling watch out for the safe, but you get my point). This advice offered by this person seemed sound but also included subtle but distinct warnings regarding another one of her subordinate managers.

Suppose this subordinate manager is cold and aloof, not rude and unfriendly, but distant, while the one giving her the warning is warm and friendly. Human nature being what it is, the natural inclination is for her to trust the warm and friendly subordinate, who assures her the problem was not the result of his plan, but the failure of the other manager to execute it properly. At this point our new manager has been warned that the safe is falling and has also been informed by a supporter regarding who dropped the safe (the cold and aloof manager). For some, no additional information is needed before taking action. However, if you recall in our risk assessment, there were some other questions that were asked, specifically: Whose safe was it, and how did it get dropped? Therefore, our new manager, in her effort to resolve her crisis, might ask what prompted the crisis in the first place (identify the owner of the safe). Her self-appointed adviser has assured her that his plan was not at fault, but that the failure was the result of a faulty execution of his plan—meaning that he actually owned the safe and was responsible for its precarious positioning, but someone else dropped it because they failed to follow the plan. What the new manager must now do is determine if the safe was dropped through poor execution of the plan or because of a poor plan.

An examination of the plan and an in-depth discussion with the aloof manager might uncover that the plan was poorly conceived but well executed up to the point of failure (watch out for the safe!). Once this is determined, the hidden agenda of the warm and friendly manager begins to emerge. His warnings were intended to deflect criticism and responsibility from himself and onto a competitor. This analysis (and a very labored analogy) could go on through a variety of possibilities, but the basic point is that risk assessment must be thorough even when that assessment comes after the fact. This investigation is usually termed "going on a witch hunt" and is widely viewed as being counterproductive and politically incorrect. However, there is a big difference between identifying a witch and burning a witch at the stake. What is being advocated here is identifying who is responsible for a failure. The fact is that we cannot live in a blameless society, and those responsible must be held accountable for failure. This does not necessarily mean punishment, but it provides the basis for improvements in performance. By driving to the root cause of the problem, the manager can determine what to address in future appraisals, evaluation of future advice from the individual, or deciding whom to trust and rely on and whom to view with suspicion.

Some of you, perhaps most of you, may not consciously consider ulterior motives or hidden agendas when making a decision. Generally, we tend to think that what we are told is the truth and the facts presented are all of the facts available. This is probably true most of the time. Nevertheless, the types of corporate competition described here are neither fictional nor unrealistic. Every company has its share of individuals who view the company as a game board and their colleagues as pieces to be manipulated for their personal benefit. Because these individuals view the company as a game they usually do not see anything wrong with withholding information, imparting partial information, or in some cases downright lying. After all, deception is the very basis of athletic competition, is it not? So why should business competition be any different? Are not bluffing, deception, and psychological intimidation part of our competitive games? Of course, this leads to the question of what is legal, what is ethical, and where does that boundary lie when business issues are involved?

9

ETHICS AND MORALITY

I Cannot Tell a Lie

Everyone knows the story of how George Washington cut down the cherry tree, and when confronted by his father he admitted to the dastardly deed by stating "I cannot tell a lie. I cut down the cherry tree." Of course, as any of us with small children knows, George was probably caught with the hatchet still in his hand, fresh cherry juice all over his face, and the response was probably more along the lines of "What cherry tree?" Nevertheless, there was a moral decision in this case, and a moral boundary was drawn, which is the point. Everyone in life, at one time or another, must make a moral choice. Little George drew the line at lying, others will draw the line at stealing, and still others cannot draw the line at all. These are known as criminals, or in George's case, juvenile delinquents. In reality moral decisions faced by most managers rarely involve what is legal and, when they do, most people take the lawful course. Contrary to what the typical Hollywood producer thinks, very few members of the business community embezzle funds, produce shoddy products, or take kickbacks (or have $30,000 in office furniture either, but I digress). The vast majority of businesspeople are ethical and refuse to violate their moral principles even for personal advantage. Nevertheless, business is very competitive, and successful managers are frequently fierce competitors. With this competitive spirit comes the decision of how far will I go to win? For some, winning is so important that nothing else matters, but for most of us a win outside of the rules is hollow. However, when winning is the only objective, this single-minded focus often brings us to the edge of ethical behavior and sometimes legality. But breaking the law or even "winning" is not really the issue. The issue is what does the manager do when the decision alternatives to a problem are perfectly legal, but may push the moral boundary. This brings competitive managers face-to-face with the necessity of establishing precisely what they are willing to do to obtain a competitive advantage for themselves or their company. As we all know, some companies skate along the boundary of legality and may expect their employees to adhere to practices that are legal but could be viewed as unethical. The person who needs the job may be put into a nearly impossible situation by the company's moral laxity. They must choose between what they feel is ethical and what the company expects. However, the decision to adhere to a personal morality or ethical standard rather than the ambiguous standard of others is still an individual choice. In fact, this ability to know oneself, have a clearly defined moral and ethical code, and act accordingly may constitute the major criteria that separate today's leaders from the managers of yesterday—managers who acted in disregard to the environment, well-being of their employees, or the public. One of the great advantages of the command-and-control model is that it requires very little thinking, and it rarely puts employees into an undefined ethical situation because these are predetermined. Of course, the moral boundaries in these circumstances usually reflect those of the executive who established them, and the employees are expected to conform. Certainly, the code of honor established and practiced in the military rests on this principle.

The atrocities committed by the military are legendary and span all eras and all countries. Because of this bloody history, members of the military are commonly viewed as human robots willing to follow any order issued by a superior. This attitude is so prevalent that it is the source of the cliché or classic oxymoron "military intelligence." Yet, as any student of military history knows, a code of honor lies at the very heart of the military, and the most daring and creative leaders have sprung from the military. In fact, the military has probably spent more time in studying leadership and developing associated training programs than any other organization in the world. The result is a tightly organized, highly motivated, and disciplined organization founded on rigid rules governing integrity, ethics, morality, and honor and more often than not led by leaders who embody those principles. Some of the rules and customs are documented, many are not, but every person in the military is acutely aware of all of them and the penalties for violating any one of them. And as we have recently seen, more than one has been court-martialed for violating the moral and ethical code. For our purposes, it is enough to know that a person lacking in these moral and ethical qualities may command others but will rarely command their respect, and without respect success is often elusive. Therefore, one could say that the core of leadership is respect, which is gained through moral and ethical behavior. But how does a manager gain respect and move from the ranks of managers to that of leaders?

The comedian Rodney Dangerfield made a career of not getting respect, but it is unlikely that very many of us can duplicate that, including Mr. Dangerfield. Not only was Rodney in great demand as an entertainer, many erstwhile comedians attempted to copy him, and *that* is a sign of respect. So, in the final analysis, even Mr. Dangerfield had respect. When you have become worthy of emulation, you have respect, and that is a direct result of your reputation and conduct.

How you conduct yourself in difficult circumstances is crucial to your effectiveness as a leader. I am reminded of a comment once made to me by my platoon sergeant. He had suffered great hardship as a POW. As a prisoner he was literally starving, so food meant survival, and how you got food was much less important than what food could be obtained. Hoarding and stealing became survival techniques, which led to numerous moral decisions regarding when and what to share with others who were starving as well. Although there were some residual guilt feelings, he made a very cogent observation which was: "It is easy to be generous on a full stomach." The same might be said for honesty and integrity. They are easy to maintain if they are never tested. However, all managers eventually will have their honesty and integrity tested, and when this test comes they must establish their own moral boundary. Unfortunately for some, this test comes suddenly and requires an immediate decision, but for others the test is over before they are even aware there was a test. However, most leaders have defined moral and ethical boundaries, so that when these tests come, they react instinctively and in predictable ways.

Sometimes you blunder into these moral and ethical tests, other times they are forced upon you, and then sometimes, through a series of seemingly unrelated decisions, you find yourself and perhaps your company squarely in the middle of a problem involving morality, good business, and honor. For outsiders, using the terms "business" and "honor" in the same sentence might seem like an oxymoron, but to those of us who are grouped under the heading of "businessman" (and I include both sexes in this generic term) our honor and ethics are very real issues. Many of us have been accused of having "situational ethics," which is a term that can be interpreted in many ways. For some, especially those not directly involved in making business decisions, this usually means stretching your moral boundary to encompass any act, no matter how base, if it yields personal advantage. In my opinion "situational ethics" addresses the many ethical nuances surrounding decisions that businesspeople must make on a regular basis. Each of these situations is unique and each requires some soul searching regarding what is "right." The following situation is a vivid example of this dilemma.

THE CONVERSION

Large computers, sometimes known as "big iron," are very expensive, even hideously expensive and have a technical lifespan roughly equivalent to a fruit fly. For this reason they are frequently leased from the manufacturer. These massive computing machines also have approximately the same maintenance requirements as the average teenager's car; therefore, the lease agreement usually includes maintenance. In this case, the lease and maintenance payments were separated. Additionally, the lease agreements commonly have clauses that allow the lessee to convert the agreement from a lease to a purchase. This is all very garden-variety stuff and certainly not the sort of thing that would require much scrutiny once it was in place. Consequently when the phone call came, it was handled by a low-level clerk in accounts receivable who really did not understand the problem. Therefore, it took some time before the research was completed and the problem reached a management level high enough to recognize the magnitude and ramifications of the problem.

The vice president of computer marketing was enjoying his Saturday morning breakfast al fresco when the call came summoning him to an emergency meeting of the executive staff. When he got there, the conference room was already filled with the vice presidents for legal, field service, sales, and finance, plus the executive vice president for North American Operations. The meeting started immediately, and the vice president of finance wasted no time in getting straight to the point. It seems a customer (one of the Fortune 100) had called regarding an invoice for field service on their computer. Ordinarily they would have paid the invoice, but they had sold the computer over a year before. When they investigated, they found that they had been paying for service on this nonexistent computer for a year, and they were requesting a refund. Their money had been refunded immediately and a letter of apology written, but this was not the problem. The problem was how many more like this were there?

It seems when a company converted their lease to a purchase, the lease contract was terminated. Unfortunately, the converted equipment was dropped as an asset, and the new maintenance contract was given to field services. When the company subsequently disposed of the converted equipment, field services continued to invoice for maintenance because they had no way to know the equipment was sold. Many companies were unaware that their lease agreement had been rolled over to a maintenance contract. Consequently, field services continued to issue invoices and some (and no one knew how many) companies continued to pay for an unneeded service. Because no records were kept, the company no longer knew how many computers had been converted to purchase, who had them, where they were, if they had canceled their maintenance contract, or if it was still in force. Therefore, the executives had no way of knowing how many other customer companies had disposed of their equipment, but were still being billed. Worse, no one had any idea of how much money had been erroneously collected, but it could be (and probably was) millions of dollars. On the other hand, until this call came in there had never been any complaint, and it was entirely possible that this was the only one. The question posed to the team of executives was: What should we do now?

The vice president of field services pointed out that he had no way of telling what actual equipment was on site without visiting every site and taking an inventory. The maintenance contracts covered everything from terminals to printers to computers, and the rates varied. His system was predicated on the assumption that no one would pay for a service they did not need, and it was incumbent upon the customer to cancel support on a piece of equipment. Unless his team physically visited every site, he would have no way of determining if his fees reflected what was actually there. Furthermore, his invoice addresses did not correspond to the physical location of the equipment anyway so he would have to ask where the equipment was physically located. This would open the door to embarrassing questions, which might lead to many of the legal problems they were trying to avoid. His conscience was clear, and he opted for no action.

The discussion began in earnest with a variety of alternatives being presented, but the question of financial exposure continued to be the stumbling block. No one wanted to take money fraudulently (an ugly term in the best of circumstances), but how do you identify the people who legitimately should have a refund from those who see an opportunity to reduce their operating expenses by claiming a refund they do not deserve? Beyond the refund issue was the question of how to stop collecting money from people who may be unaware they are paying for a service they are not receiving? Eventually the discussion led to a tentative solution, which was to do nothing. It was incumbent upon the customers to cancel the coverage, and if they did not then that was their problem. At this point the vice president of legal said that in his opinion that solution was bordering on conspiracy, and he would have no part of it and he left. The vice president of product marketing then spoke up and said that, legality aside, it was unethical, and he could not accept "do nothing" as a solution. In his opinion it was wrong to take money from someone for a service that they did not need and probably did not know that they were paying for. He suggested that they write all of their customers and ask them to verify what equipment was covered under the maintenance agreement.

The vice president of finance and several others opposed this solution as not only simple minded but financially risky for the company. This was tantamount to telling all of the customer base that the company had no idea of what was covered or what they legitimately owed. This was an open invitation for the customers to cheat, but more probably they would not actually do a physical inventory. They would simply reply with what was in their agreement. Worse, if they did do an inventory and find out they had been overbilled, possibly for years, the financial and legal exposure was immense.

Eventually a compromise of sorts was reached. The executives agreed that the existing process and contract would be modified to ensure that this situation would not continue. Identifying the customers who were affected was impossible without incurring substantial cost and risk, therefore, it was agreed that if any customer complained, the company would immediately work with them to identify how much money should be refunded. In effect the squeaky wheel got the grease. Not a very elegant solution and some would argue, not very ethical, but that is the point, isn't it?

How this scenario eventually played out is not as important as how would you have reacted had you been in this meeting? Would you jeopardize the millions of dollars in the revenue stream? Would you have taken the high road and refused to participate at all? Only you can answer this question, and undoubtedly many of you know precisely how you would have responded, or at least you think you know. But teenagers are not the only ones subject to peer pressure, and in situations like this one, the pressure to conform and "go along" can be immense. Until you are faced with the situation and the decision to disagree with your boss on an ethical point, you do not really know how you will react. After all, a contrary decision might jeopardize your job or career and could have far-reaching ramifications. Still, this situation was sort of sterile and abstract so some degree of moral "flexibility" can be understood. After all, it involved a group decision made by top executives in a major corporation that would affect other large and faceless corporations. No lives or careers were at stake, and no one had a personal agenda, therefore, it might be hard for many people to get very worked up over this situation. What about a situation that is slightly more personal?

THE COPY

John works for a supplier to a large manufacturing firm. His company is preparing a response to a request from the manufacturer regarding some components. This is a hotly contested contract, and several of John's competitors are bidding on the business. It is fairly obvious that the contract will go to the lowest bidder, so John and his manager have been analyzing every aspect of the deal in an effort to bring their bid down to a rock-bottom level. While visiting the customer's offices, John asks to use their copy machine. When he returns to his office, he finds among his copies an internal memorandum from his customer. This memorandum indicates the price they are looking for on the proposal and even provides the bid price of one of their key competitors. What should John do with this clearly sensitive memorandum?

There are three obvious possibilities here. John can destroy the memorandum and act as if he never saw it, he can view it as a windfall and pass it on to his manager, or he can return it to the author with an apology and explanation. The first choice might seem logical and attractive to many people. No one knows John has the memorandum so if he destroys it no one will ever know he has some very sensitive and confidential information. Unfortunately for John, this decision carries another ethical decision— What role should he now play in the bidding process? He knows the price the customer is seeking, and he knows what his key competitor has bid. Ignoring this information is equivalent to telling the jury to ignore the elephant in the courtroom. That is pretty difficult to do even for the most fair-minded person. John could go to his manager and ask to be excused from further participation in the bidding process, but this will require an explanation. John can make up some phony excuse (this is called lying) or he could tell the truth, which puts him at the mercy of his boss Snidely Whiplash (this is called dying). Of course, John's boss might be an honorable person and allow him to bow out of the process without punishment, but this is very hard to predict. After all, the manager has pressure to meet certain financial objectives, and for many, finding the memo was a stroke of luck and "finders keepers."

Of course, John can circumvent this whole problem by simply passing the memorandum on to his boss, thereby letting him make the decision on either an ethical or business basis. But does this alleviate John from responsibility? Should he go along with the decision regardless of whatever it is? Only John can answer this question, but it is pivotal to our point, which is that everyone must establish his or her own moral boundary. If John elects to "go along" with his boss, then he has allowed someone else to establish his moral boundary. But we should all recognize that a moral boundary *was* established. Suppose John decides to return the memo to the author with an explanation. At the very least the customer will know that her incumbent supplier has knowledge of some very confidential information. She might suspend the proposal activity, redraw the request, or even drop John's company from the bidding process. She might accept John's explanation or she might not, but in telling her John has assumed an enormous personal risk. However, suppose the memorandum was "planted"?

It is possible John was deliberately deceived because the customer wanted to get the lowest price possible from the incumbent supplier. Suppose the bidding process was a sham and the plan had always been to manipulate the incumbent supplier through "leaked" information. Of course, John would have no way of knowing this, but it is plausible. Therefore, John or his manager might use this rationalization in making their decision. In your opinion should this possibility be considered in the decision of what to do with the memorandum? If you accept this rationalization would you change your price? What if the memo was planted as a test of your honesty; isn't this a greater risk? If you adjust your price on the basis of this memorandum without informing your customer, are you taking a business risk or simply establishing a moral boundary for yourself (and by default your company)?

In this scenario we addressed the possibility of referring the decision to the "boss" and then accepting whatever decision was rendered. Suppose the boss will not make the decision and refers it back to you; then what? That is the very situation that was faced by our friend, "Melvin the Magnificent."

THE SEMINAR

Melvin was a sales representative for a very large pharmaceutical firm, but he was not just any sales rep. He was number one in the nation and known by everyone as "Melvin the Magnificent." He could sell anything to anyone, or so everyone thought, but Melvin was completely unprepared for Dr. Barbara.

Dr. Barbara ran a large clinic oriented to women. Until recently her clinic had been handled by another salesperson, but in a territory consolidation her clinic was given to Melvin. Unknown to Melvin, Dr. Barbara had been doing independent research in breast cancer, which she had been attempting to publish. So far the professional journals had shown little interest, although she had published some small articles.

Melvin's company had recently had a new antibiotic approved and he used the release of this new product as an opportunity to introduce himself to Dr. Barbara. He had hardly gotten through his introduction when Dr. Barbara stopped him in mid-sentence. She pointed out that she wrote $500,000 in prescriptions for his products last year but she was not going to write anymore. Furthermore, she did not care how wonderful his new product was; in fact, it could be the ultimate cure for cancer and she still would not write prescriptions for it. Melvin was dumbfounded by this diatribe and asked what he could do to change her mind. Without missing a beat she told him that his company regularly conducted seminars where various doctors reported on their research. She wanted to present her research at 30 of these seminars over the next 12 months, and her fee for each appearance would be $2,000 not including expenses. If Melvin could arrange for her to present her research at these seminars, she would continue writing prescriptions for his products, otherwise she would begin using his competitors' products. So what would you do at this point if you were Melvin?

Before you jump onto your moral bandwagon and begin beating your drum of righteous indignation, let us add a few background facts. First, Melvin is a young married man with two small children and a wife to support. He is an excellent performer, but his company is noted for placing a very high value on customer relationships. Melvin is concerned that even though he has a proven track record, bad reports from this customer could damage his prospects for promotion. Furthermore, the customer profiles indicated that Dr. Barbara had actually written slightly more than $250,000 in prescriptions, not the $500,000 that she claimed. Also, the company ran these medical seminars as a means of rewarding doctors who prescribed their products. It allowed the doctors in the area to get together, exchange information, and catch up on the latest research. These seminars were provided by the company at no charge or for a modest fee. The speakers at these company-sponsored seminars were paid, and the requested $2,000 by Dr. Barbara was about the average fee.

So there you stand with clammy hands, butterflies in your stomach, thinking about your children in that fancy private school, your mortgage payment, car payments, and your wife's Imelda Marcos shoe collection imitation. What do you do? Have you been asked for a kickback? Should you go along to get along? It seems there are several courses of action our Magnificent Melvin might take. First, he could take the position that this request was morally corrupt, and he would rather move himself and his family into a cardboard box than to take this deal. This is a firm decision that draws a definite boundary between right and wrong or at least a version of right and wrong. Another decision might be to simply accept the deal as a quid pro quo or simple exchange of services. Yet another alternative might be to make no decision (an ever popular alternative) and seek guidance from that ultimate source of wisdom—the boss.

So which alternative did you select or did you come up with something else? In the actual situation Melvin thanked Dr. Barbara for her candor, acknowledged that she was a valued customer, and promised that he would look into what could be done. Melvin immediately called the District Manager who was his superior, who immediately called the Regional Manager. After explaining the circumstances and the actual amount of business generated by Dr. Barbara, the Regional Manager said, "Do what you think is best." Click—bzzzzzzz. The District Manager called Melvin and said "This is no big deal. Do what you want." At a stroke the management team had established a moral boundary for the company, but where was it? Given the circumstances, Melvin went back to Dr. Barbara and said, "Your business is valuable to us, and we are willing to include you in our list of available speakers, but we cannot guarantee any specific number of engagements over any specific period of time."—and he left. I would like to say Melvin left wrapped in the cloak of self-righteous moral glory, but alas, Melvin's motives were not quite so pure.

The 30 seminars at $2,000 each came to $60,000 plus expenses over the next 12 months. Dr. Barbara was writing $250,000 in prescriptions, so the fees exceeded the profit (approximately 20%). Therefore, the company (and Melvin) would have sustained a dead loss, and the decision was a pure business decision. Melvin did concede that the deal had a little bit of a smell to it, but there was a legitimate exchange of services so, in his opinion, it was not a kickback, at least technically. Furthermore, the reluctance of the company management to take a stand indicated that they wanted to rise above this deal in case it became a problem later. Although there was an exchange of services, the unusually large number of seminars and the associated "fees" could be construed as a "kickback" if it became public knowledge. Melvin felt that by not taking a position his managers were probably protecting themselves and the company at his expense. If this deal became controversial, the decisions were his, and he had no protection. Taking all of these factors into consideration, Melvin opted to pass, not on the basis of legality or ethics, but on the basis of personal and business risk. What would you have done?

Everyone in this scenario drew a moral boundary, whether they knew it or not. Dr. Barbara certainly had no doubts that a quid pro quo was morally acceptable. Melvin wanted something she had, and he had something she wanted. To her it seemed logical and fair to tie the two things together. Melvin's boss undoubtedly thought he took the moral high ground, but did he? Is not taking a position the same as taking one? Is not stealing the moral equivalent of publicly stating you are opposed to stealing? Leaders are expected to set an example, and in this instance, Melvin's management did not display a great deal of moral leadership. They drew a moral boundary through inaction and indecision, apparently driven by greed. They were willing to let Melvin do anything he wanted to do in the hopes that he would bring in substantial profits. They lifted their moral skirts and tiptoed around this question leaving everyone unsure of where they would draw the line between money and morality, if it became an issue. Among the players Melvin probably displayed the most moral sensitivity, simply because he thought to ask the question of whether it fell within the moral boundary of the corporation. When his management refused to draw that line, he was left on his own. Instead of resting his decision on the morality of it, he opted to make a "business" decision. Because his management would not guide him, he was left in this moral wasteland. Although his personal morality said Dr. Barbara was wrong, he was not sure of his management. Therefore, the business decision left him in the same ambiguous position as his management. There are other dimensions to this situation, but before exploring those, let us move on to another Doctor and an entrepreneur.

THE CLAMBAY PROTOCOL

Jessica is a pharmaceutical salesperson working for a mid-sized company. She has the usual bag of antibiotics, ointments, pills, and assorted potions that most pharmaceutical salespeople peddle. She also has a public relations budget of approximately $1,400 per month that she uses to buy birthday cakes, lunches, small gifts, and sundry items for the doctors in her territory. One of her doctors, Doctor Barnum by name, is a very personable fellow with a successful practice; also he is a Clambay dealer, which means that in addition to his successful medical practice, he sells Clambay Health and Home Care products as a side business. Over a period of weeks, Dr. Barnum has made it very clear that he works best with those salespeople who work with him. He never misses an opportunity to explain the value and merit of Clambay products to patients and the pharmaceutical sales representatives and to explain how his distributors are making an excellent second income. Finally he tells Jessica once she becomes one of his Clambay distributors he will select her drugs over those of her competitors. With this *suggestion*, Jessica agrees to become a distributor, and she expenses about $200 in Clambay products, which she then gives away to her other doctors. Dr. Barnum begins to use her products, and she improves her quota performance. After several months she has second thoughts about the situation and goes to her district manager and asks for direction. Her district manager listens to her story, laughs, and essentially tells her to do whatever she needs to do. That is what that the expense money is for. So rather than buying Dr. Barnum cakes and cookies, she is buying Clambay products. Furthermore, he tells her that if she is getting more Clambay products than she can sell or give away, she should hold a garage sale and dispose of them that way.

This is virtually the same situation as the one that confronted Melvin, with two exceptions. First, the products are tangible unlike the speeches offered by Dr. Barbara and secondly, the amount of money involved is much less. Do these differences change anything? What are the moral and ethical issues here? Certainly, the ethical differences between Dr. Barbara and Dr. Barnum are virtually invisible because they both have tied their actions to those of the salespeople in a classic quid pro quo. The moral position of Jessica's management was certainly clear. The district manager did not see any difference between giving Dr. Barnum $200 in free lunches and goodies and spending an equivalent amount on Clambay products. In his eyes these were the same things. If I give you a gift because I choose to, is that the same as giving you the gift because you asked me to give it to you? Clearly the district manager did not see any difference.

What about Jessica in this scenario? Obviously she had some moral discomfort or she would not have gone to the district manager for guidance. Yet she bought the products, expensed them, and gave them away even though she was not sure of the ethics. Conscience or no conscience her actions established her moral boundary, which incorporated buying (if not selling) Clambay products. Furthermore, we can assume that Jessica had excellent garage sales.

It is worth noting that both of these scenarios pivot on the ethics of a quid pro quo. In both of these situations there was a feeling that reciprocity was somehow unethical, yet in both cases there was a legitimate exchange of services. Is that wrong? Am I somehow without principal if I tell you that I will buy your oranges if you buy my apples? Consider that many large companies enter into exchange agreements. A car rental firm agrees to buy a fleet of cars from a manufacturer, and in exchange, the manufacturer agrees to rent cars from that firm. A furniture manufacturer buys technical services from a consulting firm, and in turn, the consulting firms buys furniture from their new client. Are these kickbacks? Are these deals unethical? What distinguishes these deals from the ones proposed by Drs. Barbara and Barnum? Of course, the good doctors had to look someone straight in the eye and announce in a clear voice that some reciprocity is expected. On the other hand, the corporate deals are handled abstractly by executives who do not profit directly from the exchange of services, and perhaps this is the difference between ethical and unethical. Does it matter if these exchanges benefit an individual or benefit a corporation? Is a faceless corporation somehow morally superior to an individual entrepreneur?

These issues become very gray very quickly, especially in situations where money is involved, unless, of course, it is someone else's money. In those cases the clarity of the ethical decision can be remarkable and moral boundaries somewhat "flexible." After all John Dillinger and Jesse James robbed the rich and powerful who were viewed as oppressors of the poor and they are practically folk heroes. Taking money from individuals is stealing but taking money (or goods) from a faceless corporation or an obscenely wealthy person is somehow more like "sharing" and not condemned quite as soundly. But what about simply "diverting" goods to another and perhaps "nobler" purpose. When you want things done and done quickly, sometimes it is best not to look too closely at either the result or the circumstances leading to success.

THE DESKTOP

Mary Beth was a second-tier manager with four groups reporting to her for a total of about 100 people all of whom used desktop computers. Unfortunately the computers being used by one of her groups were obsolete and beginning to affect productivity. They needed to be replaced, and she was on the list, but so far down that it would be at least a year before she got the replacements, if then. In the meantime her superior was pressuring her for better performance, better turnaround times, and more rapid response. In a discussion with her Technical Assistant, Paul, she expressed how she felt trapped, very insecure, and desperate. Paul asked her what the problem was, and she explained how she needed the equipment now but was unlikely to get it before she was replaced for inefficiency or poor performance. Paul said he thought he could help her if all she wanted was new equipment. He explained that he could get the equipment within the week if she wanted it. Obviously she wanted it, and if he could get the equipment for her, he should do it immediately.

Within the week a truck arrived loaded with brand new computers. These were unboxed and installed by Paul, working with some of the other staff members. Mary Beth's boss asked where the equipment came from, she told him Paul ordered it, and she guessed he had expedited it somehow. Mary Beth's boss congratulated her on her initiative and said he expected a lot from her now that she had all of this new equipment. Mary Beth and her staff did not let him down. Productivity increased, morale improved, turnarounds improved, and within the year Mary Beth was transferred and promoted.

This is a real success story and everyone seems to have come out a winner. So what is the problem? This may be one of those situations where the problem only exists if you want to go looking for it, and in this case it looks like no one really wanted to go looking. Mary Beth did not do anything wrong. The equipment was corporate property and was so labeled when it arrived. On the other hand she did not exactly scrutinize her good fortune (we call that looking a gift horse in the mouth), and her boss questioned her good fortune even less than she did. Therefore, no problem existed and no ethical or moral issue needed to be addressed. So the question now revolves around the issue of: Are you morally culpable for not asking questions?

If a friend gives you a gift, are you obligated to ask where it came from? Suppose a friend hands you a box of money with the name of the bank on the box, and the bills are banded and covered in dye. Are you morally culpable for not questioning the source of the gift or do you simply thank God for your good fortune and start preparing a shopping list? These are obviously extremes. We all understand that it is bad manners to ask a friend if the gift was stolen or paid for, and likewise, most of us would be reluctant to accept a box of money that looked more like loot from a bank robbery than an inheritance from Uncle Bob. But there is a lot of ground between these two extremes, and that is where we are with these computers. When do you ask, and when do you select ignorance as the best course of action? Mary Beth was faced with a situation where she felt jeopardized by her inability to meet performance objectives. In this situation she had to choose between knowing and not knowing when knowing could place her in a position of having to take action against her own best interest. What about Mary Beth's boss. Did he have any moral culpability? He casually asked where the equipment came from, but did not respond to a general answer supplemented by the belief that it had been "expedited." It certainly appears that he, too, suspected that the equipment was expedited outside of normal channels, but he did not want to know any more for fear he would have to take action. After all, he, too, is being measured on profit and productivity.

In this case, several months after Paul retired and Mary Beth had been promoted and left the company, a physical inventory was conducted of all company assets. Not unexpectedly this inventory revealed that the computers being used by Mary Beth's former team had been earmarked for someone else. When last seen, they had been sitting on the shipping dock waiting to be delivered, but they never arrived at their destination. It seems someone had called the shipping clerk on the dock with an address change. The boxes were re-addressed and shipped to Mary Beth's department rather than the department who was expecting them. Of course, at this point no one knew why the computers were redirected, who authorized it, or where they were sent, and the key players who might have known (as usual) were gone. Was the equipment stolen? The company certainly thought so because it was recorded as stolen even though no formal complaint was ever filed with the police. This equipment never left the possession of the rightful owner (the company), and it was employed in the legitimate business of the company; so was it stolen or simply redirected?

Actually, from our perspective, the larger issue is what culpability did Mary Beth and her boss have? Did they have a moral responsibility to question how equipment that was not available could suddenly become available? By not asking the hard questions, they were able to meet their personal objectives and the company's objectives, to improve morale and to enhance their careers. Had they investigated and found out that the equipment had been "redirected" and was viewed as "stolen," they would have been morally obligated to return it. By turning their heads, they avoided this decision, and both they and the company prospered. But what about the department that had been expecting the equipment? What impact did the "redirection" have on their objectives, morale, and the careers of their managers? Does this have some relevance to the issue of ethical conduct? Is it possible that Mary Beth inadvertently harmed the career of another manager? So where is the moral and ethical boundary now? This brings us to the fundamental question, which is, if you fail to ask hard, probing questions are you guilty of an ethical breech? Suppose the shipping clerk had gotten fired when the equipment disappeared? Does this make Mary Beth and her boss guilty of unethical conduct or by not asking are they protected from guilt?

In this case the motive was personal performance but where are the boundaries when the motives are power over others or the destruction of a rival manager? Business between corporations is very competitive, but as we all know, sometimes the most competition is between groups, departments, or individuals within the same company. What constitutes ethical and unethical conduct then?

THE EXECUTIVE COMMITTEE

The executive committee of Acme Manufacturing met weekly to review sales performance, financial status, forecasts, sales proposals, and the usual agenda items. The Executive Vice President of North American Operations chaired the meeting. The members of the committee included the Director of Product Marketing and the Director of Field Administration. Each week the Director of Product Marketing reported on the sales performance against forecast for each product line. The sales information was collected daily by the Director of Field Administration and summarized by product line. The figures were given to the Director of Product Marketing the Thursday evening prior to the committee meeting on Friday morning. This schedule allowed the product line managers Thursday evening to analyze and prepare their reports. The Director of Product Marketing picked up these charts on his way to the meeting each Friday morning. This had been the procedure for some time, and no one anticipated any changes. Then a new person was appointed as the Director of Field Administration. This newcomer had gone from new college recruit to Director of Field Administration in just five years. Very few people knew him other than he was a "fast tracker" with a reputation for "getting things done," although no one seemed to know precisely what he had done.

At first, nothing changed. The procedures continued as they had before, and the Friday morning executive committee meetings were uneventful. Then one Friday as the Director of Product Marketing was making his presentation, the Director of Field Administration objected to some of the sales figures. The sales figure for one of the products was incorrect. These things happen, but no one could remember the last time an error had been made in these presentations. The chart was corrected, and the presentation was concluded. The following week another error was pointed out in the figures for another product. The Director of Product Marketing pointed out that these were the figures provided by the Director of Field Administration the night before. The Director of Field Administration denied that these were the figures provided by him or his staff, and he produced a written report that showed the correct numbers. Of course, the figures provided the evening before had been provided in a telephone conference call.

The following week the Director of Product Marketing insisted that his product-line managers get the sales figures in writing from the Director of Field Administration. However, when the product-line managers met with the Director of Field Administration, he did not give them anything in writing, claiming he was too busy to write a special report just for them. However, he had the sales figures right here on a note pad, and they were free to copy them down. Naturally, at the next committee meeting the figures were incorrect due to the inability of the product-line managers to copy the data from a clearly written report. The Director of Field Administration then handed the executive vice president a carefully printed spreadsheet. The Director of Product Marketing then met with the superior of the Director of Field Administration and explained that he was not receiving the same report that was being given to the executive committee. That seemed to solve the problem of getting correct information on Thursday night.

Over the next several meetings things seemed to have returned to normal, then the charts were again incorrect. The Director of Product Marketing produced the spreadsheet, which had been provided to the committee, but the Director of Field Administration simply pointed out that he had more current information that superseded what was on the spreadsheet. From that point on, the data provided to the Director of Product Marketing was never as timely as the information possessed by the Director of Field Administration. In desperation the Director of Product Marketing created blank charts and stopped at the office of the Director of Field Administration on his way to the executive committee meeting to get the most current information. Nevertheless, the Director of Field Administration always managed to have some correction or new piece of data.

Within six months the Director of Product Marketing was viewed by most of the executive committee as not being very efficient and certainly not on top of his products. Questions regarding financial performance and performance against forecast were being directed to the Director of Field Administration because he had the most accurate information. Finally the responsibility for tracking and reporting financial and sales performance was transferred to the Director of Product Administration. The role of the Director of Product Marketing was redefined as being responsible for market analysis, promotion, product introduction, sales support, and so on. In effect, substantially reducing his power and influence, while greatly increasing the power and influence of the Director of Field Administration.

Are there ethical issues here or was this normal healthy competition among executives maneuvering for promotion? Did the Director of Product Marketing have a right to expect accurate sales figures or was he naive? Was the Director of Administration unethical for using his control of vital information to discredit a colleague or was this normal competition between executives seeking advancement? These are very pivotal questions, because they define the basis of ethical conduct. Some of you, perhaps most of you, may think this is a figment of someone's imagination and that this type of ruthless corporate competition does not go on. Others may accept that these kinds of things happen but that they are unethical. And if a person is caught doing them they should be fired. Well and good, but if you got caught you did not do it very well, and perhaps firing is simply the Darwinian law of survival of the fittest. After all, in a fight between a lion and a tiger do we view the victor as unethical?

The tendency is to focus on the conduct of the Director of Product Administration because he was the obvious winner and the aggressor, but what about the Director of Product Marketing. Did he have any culpability? Was he naive, stupid, or politically inept? We might agree that he had a right to expect accurate data from a colleague, but once it became obvious that he was not going to get it, what should he have done?

What would you have done? What were the options open to the Director of Product Marketing? He could have gone over the head of the Field Administration and complained to his boss, but about what?—that he was not getting information or that the information was not timely or that it was incomplete. This would be very hard to prove and would most likely look like whining from someone who was not able to get organized. Besides, he already tried that once, and it did not work. He might have confronted the situation directly in an attempt to make peace, but as history teaches us, appeasement never works and only encourages more outrageous attacks. He could have called the sales managers himself and bypassed the Director of Field Administration. This flanking move might have put him in the position of requesting that the Director of Field Administration be removed from the chain of events as redundant. Another alternative might have been a direct counterattack by pointing out that the Director of Field Administration did not seem to be able to obtain the same quality and timely results as his predecessor. This would raise the question of the competence of the Director of Field Administration and whether he should continue being responsible for providing such crucial data. Of course, these attacks and counterattacks can go on for a long time but the issue at the moment is: Where is the boundary for ethics?

It seems clear that the Director of Product Marketing was attempting to play by the rules, and consciously or not, he established an ethical boundary. He was not going to defend himself by breaking the rules (getting the sales figures directly from the field). Instead he continued to attempt to follow the standard procedure and obtain the sales figures from the Director of Field Administration. Therein lies one of the fundamental lessons of corporate competition—understanding the rules.

From his perspective, the Director of Field Administration was playing by the rules. He was providing the information to the Director of Product Marketing as he was obligated to do. All he was doing was attempting to ensure that everyone (including the Director of Product Marketing) had the most current information. From the perspective of job responsibility and standard procedures, he was within the rules. But the larger question is: Was the way he fulfilled his obligations and brought accuracy to the decision ethical? Did he violate any of the rules? Did he not provide the information he was obligated to provide in the time frame required? What precisely did he do that made any of his actions unethical? The answer to this question establishes a moral boundary because, in the strictest sense, the Director of Field Administration simply did his job. However, what was his motive in this zeal to provide the most current information? Was his objective to inform or to embarrass? Suppose the answer to the question is the obvious yes, it was meant to embarrass a competitor. Is that unethical? Is it unethical to deliberately embarrass a colleague if, in doing so, you can gain an advantage?

If you consider the actions of the Director of Field Administration to be unethical, then consider sports competition. Is the physical and psychological intimidation that happens between athletes "unethica"? When a batter crowds the plate or when the pitcher hits the batter for the purpose of intimidation or gaining a psychological edge, are these unethical? When you play poker do you attempt to deceive your opponents regarding your cards or do you tell them the truth? Are not deception and intimidation the very basis of athletic competition? Why should business competition be any different? Of course, even sports have seen changes in what is considered sportsmanlike conduct and what is "cheating." At one time brawling was considered low class and unsportsmanlike, but now it is commonplace and viewed as a demonstration of a drive to win. At one time, personal insults were considered "ungentlemanly" or "unladylike," and now they are simply referred to as "trash talk," as if by renaming it, it gains stature.

There is a difference between personal morality and business morality and attempts to apply a personal moral code to a business situation may introduce enormous stress on an individual. Business ethics focus more on what is legal rather than what is "right," with "right" being that internal ethical code, which is what most of us use to judge our conduct. In business we must consider the well-being of the corporation in terms of productivity, revenues, and cost reduction, but what happens when those conflict with what we believe is morally *right*?

THE VETERAN

Things had been going downhill at the company for some time. The products had aged, revenues were down, and both the stock and the employees were depressed. The company brought in a completely new management team, and Rocky was part of this team. Among his first actions he reviewed the staff to determine if there were redundancies or unproductive employees. Almost immediately the name of John Smith was brought to his attention. It seems John had been with the company for more than thirty years. At one time he had been an Assistant Vice President, but now he was a "consultant" with rather vague duties and a high salary. A perfect candidate for reduction and Rocky recommended that he be put on the lay-off list. Shortly after the layoff recommendations were submitted, Rocky was called in by his boss. The boss wanted to know if Rocky was aware that John Smith had been with the company all of his adult life? Was he aware that John was responsible for some of the early successes that had made the company a success, and that he had two years to go before he was eligible for retirement? Rocky acknowledged that he was aware of some of these things but not aware of all of them. He asked the boss what he wanted him to do? The boss told Rocky to go back and think about it, and then do what he thought was right.

What would you do in Rocky's place? Would you put John on the layoff list or leave him off of it? John is not actually contributing very much, and his current position is simply a placeholder until he retires. If he is laid off, it is a virtual certainty he would not be able to find an equivalent position. On the other hand, he has been a loyal employee for thirty years and practically saved the company when he was a young man. If it had not been for John Smith, Rocky might not have the job he has now. Under these conditions what is right? Keeping John means other younger and more valuable employees will have to be laid off so that John can be retained, and productivity will suffer. What should be done?

This is clearly a choice between the heart and the head. Loyalty and compassion tell you that John should be retained. He will retire in two years, and everyone will be happy. John will have been rewarded for his many years of service. However, business considerations indicate that John is a financial burden on the unit, he contributes little, his skills are outmoded, and retaining him will require the dismissal of at least two more valuable employees. What is your decision?

Rocky's decision was to put John Smith back on the layoff list. Rocky's rationale for the decision was that John had many opportunities to learn new skills, enhance old skills, and to contribute to departmental productivity. Instead, John had elected to wait for jobs that he could do with little effort to come his way. He had not shown any initiative in a long time and appeared to be coasting on his past reputation. He showed no fire, no aggressiveness, and no concern for the company. If he was financially unprepared for retirement, that was a personal situation and not Rocky's responsibility.

Suppose John could demonstrate that he had upgraded his skills, had gone to school, and learned new skills? Would that change your opinion? Suppose John could demonstrate that he had repeatedly asked for more work and new assignments and had been rebuffed. Would that change your mind? Suppose you found out that John had been friends with the company President for more than twenty years and had in fact hired the President into the company. Would that change your mind? It changed Rocky's mind. When he was informed that the President took a personal interest in John's future, Rocky realized what a valuable resource he had in John and the many contributions he could make, politically.

So now what are the ethics of the situation? When he put John on the layoff list, Rocky took the position that his personal ethics were subordinate to business ethics and the good of the company. However, when that decision appeared to carry some personal risk, Rocky reversed himself. Is Rocky's hypocrisy unethical? By suddenly shifting from business ethics to personal ethics, Rocky was putting his self-interest ahead of the company's interests. Does that sudden change in ethical codes constitute an ethical violation? Only you can decide.

In these discussions we looked at two situations dealing with exchanges, one of service and one of goods. We looked at a situation involving an "ignorance is bliss" approach and one that could be described as "competitive." The last situation deals with a decision involving business ethics versus personal ethics. All of these fell within an ethical gray area where each of us would have to establish our own moral boundary. But isn't that the entire point of this discussion, that ethics and morality are not absolute but are established by the individual and influenced by the circumstances? Was Brutus the "noblest Roman of them all" or a common assassin? Did Henry Ford and his assembly line liberate or enslave the common man? The answer to those questions is not clear-cut just as the "correct" decision to the various ethical dilemmas a manager faces are not universal. How you decide and what you decide are determined by your individual sense of integrity and ethical code.

As we all know, everything changes and nothing changes and, as we have already learned, nothing is as it appears. Ethics and morality may be very clear to the individual but that clarity of right and wrong may not be universally shared and blurs when faced with real moral dilemmas. As we have seen, many decisions carry moral and ethical elements that impact our actions. Additionally our decisions are influenced by unseen risks based on unknown information and the unknown motives of others (the human variable). While our motives and objectives may be clear, those of our management, peers, and competitors may not be as easily discerned. It is here that we enter the realm of corporate politics where competition, power struggles, shifting alliances, and unclear motivations and objectives occur. In effect, the world of corporate politics is one of games and gambits, of illusion and misdirection. Certainly, the world of corporate politics is not for the timid.

10

POLITICS
Games and Gambits

Contrary to popular belief, the tortoise did not win the race. In terms of management, the best or most diligent candidate does not always succeed due to the unseen and often overlooked factor called corporate politics. There are those who would argue that business and politics do not mix, just as there are those who believe that rewards will come to those who work hard, are honest, and strive for the success of their company and themselves. These are the loyalists. They are loyal to themselves, their work, and the company. They are also the ones who often fail to achieve the level of success they desire or perhaps even deserve. Like the ostrich with its head in the sand, these loyalists are often either unable to recognize the political activity that surrounds them or they refuse to participate in it.

These are the people who state with pride that "I may be in the rat race, but I'm not a rat, and I'm not trying to win." Many times these people think that by announcing they are not competitors they are safe. This is rarely the case, and, in fact, may send a signal that they are not aggressive enough for the company. Furthermore, their lack of participation not only hinders their progress up the corporate ladder, it frequently leads to a growing dissatisfaction as those of lesser ability are promoted while they languish in the corporate graveyard of also-rans. Loyalists often think the path to advancement is to work harder, to gain more degrees, to be certified, or to expand their ability in some way. Without doubt these improve individuals and increase their value to the corporation, but by themselves they rarely lead to promotion or advancement. The truth of the matter is that form (the ability to sell oneself as an executive) very often triumphs over substance (the ability to do the job) in spite of what we may want to believe.

Of course there are some corporate citizens who are very aware of the corporate politics, but choose not to participate in the political game. Sometimes this decision is based on an inner belief that it is better to be rewarded on the basis of accomplishment than on the basis of perceived contribution. Others decline to participate in the political struggles because they lack the skill, or at least believe they lack the skill, and would not win in this arena. This does not mean that those who are very good at playing the corporate political game are less capable than those who do not. But it does mean that those who are adept at the political aspects of their jobs can go further with less mastery of their jobs.

Regardless of what people think and whether they choose to participate or not, the reality is that corporate politics exists and everyone participates to some extent. Even those who profess to not participate in politics are, in fact, participating every time they discuss who is up and who is down in the corporate power structure. Corporate politics are as much a part of business as balance sheets and customers, and it behooves all of us to at least be aware of what is going on, even if we are observers rather than players. The reason that we should be aware (other than the amusement factor) is that we must always be prepared to evaluate events in terms of our own self-interest, if for no other reason.

In the political arena there appears to be three levels or types of activity. The first is what is usually referred to as *gamesmanship*. This is the least harmful or most benign form of politics, and its objective is usually to have fun or to embarrass a colleague. A good example of gamesmanship is *Buzzword Bingo*. This is a game where the players select a target (victim?). The target is usually selected on the predetermined basis that he or she is fluff, not substance, meaning that there is little respect for the person from the outset. Once the target is selected, each player then prepares a list of buzzwords they expect will be used by him (or her) during the course of the meeting. As the meeting progresses, each player marks off the buzzwords on their list as the target uses each one, and the first person to complete their list wins. If the player invents a new buzzword, interjects it into the discussion, and the target uses it, that is an automatic win. The targets of this game are rarely aware that a game is being played or that they are the targets.

Although the players in this game usually view it as harmless and nonpolitical, it is in fact neither. It is the corporate equivalent of a snipe hunt. The reputation of the target is reduced, perhaps irrevocably damaged as he is made the butt of jokes. Few people can sustain this kind of attack, even when they are unaware it is happening to them. All they may perceive is a gradual decline in their effectiveness and reputation. Eventually they may be forced to move on, and the players then move on to another victim. Another favorite corporate game is to find a person unfamiliar with how their pager works and to page them with a message that says "Lo Batt" or "Out of range." Again this is viewed as just a harmless joke, except it requires a victim whose reputation is damaged. Some people will defend these games on the basis that the targets were lightweights, did not understand the subject, were uppity, could not get the job done, or were dragging others down. Any or all of these things may be true, but does that justify treating these people like this? This is tantamount to all of the popular kids in class picking on the fat kid, the skinny kid, or the dork who plays the violin. As a manager, I oppose these games because they require a victim and ultimately will hurt morale, but just like the teachers in school, the best you can do is drive them underground.

The players in the next level of political action usually view it as just *healthy competition*. The attitude of these players is that corporate politics is just a game, like poker, where some win, some lose, and some lose their shirt. What these players fail to perceive is that poker has an established set of rules that are the same for everyone. And the participants are usually aware that they are in a game where lying and deception are viewed not only as part of the game, but a measure of the skill of the players. This is not true in corporate politics. The rules are unwritten and each player decides what is fair (remember ethical boundaries?). Furthermore, the players in this game may not even be aware of who the other players are or who is on their side. It is in this arena of competitive politics where you will hear statements such as "Yes, I did read John's excellent report on widgets, but it was not up to his usual standard. Didn't you think he glossed over the long range trends and did not address the subject of widget capacity in nearly enough detail?" Naturally this statement is made to John's boss by John's competitor for promotion.

Corporate players often regard anything that is legal as fair, which means they are not above calling a colleague (read competitor) just prior to an important meeting with their boss and telling him the meeting was canceled. Deliberately providing false information and withholding important information are common ploys used by corporate players. Of course these are blatant examples, and the better players are more subtle than this. The more skilled players will take on tasks that are highly visible while ensuring that their competitors grind away in the background. "Remember that excellent report John did on widget capacity? He would be an excellent choice for that task at our factory in Sioux Junction. While he does that I could fill in for him on the Presidents strategy committee." Players are always willing to sacrifice themselves for the good of the company.

Some only take on tasks that are ensured of success while attempting to maneuver competitors into assignments doomed to failure. "We are on schedule to quadrupling our production, but I think I have taken this widget project as far as I can. I think what the project needs now is John's expertise. He certainly cleaned up Sioux Junction so he would really be able to bring this project to a rapid conclusion." Of course, we all know that this project is just a day away from slipping into eternity due to the mismanagement of the incumbent project leader. I am sure the question that springs to your mind is that if it is so obvious, why would John even consider taking on this albatross? Aha! I say. What makes you think John gets a vote? This maneuver was between the opponent and John's boss. John may have just been called in by his boss, given a "do it for the Gipper" pep talk and a pat on the shoulder, and handed a ticket to career oblivion. Of course, if John is a skilled player he will have a counter maneuver to thwart this impending project Albatross. Perhaps he will point out that his wife is about to have a baby (as soon as he can get home and get one started, but you do not have to give all of the facts). John might point out that his opponent is right on schedule, and if the management team is changed now, the schedule would surely slip while he comes up to speed (a slow learner). These strokes and counterstrokes are what make the whole thing into a game for the players. Please note the *me-first* attitude and that the good of the company, benefit of the employees, or value to the shareholders is not even a consideration.

The third level of corporate politics is usually found at the higher echelons where the political struggles take on life and death dimensions. Battles at this level commonly occur between executives in the line of succession for CEO or other senior executive positions. These are very similar to the dynastic struggles between princes that we read about in the history books, with the same intrigue, plots, counterplots, and deceptions. Shakespeare dealt with these people in *Macbeth*, *Richard III*, and *Julius Caesar*. The circumstances have changed, but not the people or their actions. However, historically the losers usually were killed, unlike today where they are given a zillion dollars and forced to retire. However, in spite of the improvement in the outcome for the losers, the battles in the executive suite are just as real and just as vicious as these historical ones.

Although many view these political battles as the corporate equivalent of a poker game, there are some significant differences. Poker is a game of skill and the rules for the Friday night game between friends are the same as those for the professional players in high-stakes games. The difference is that in corporate politics not only are there no rules, but the skill of the players varies just as the stakes vary, with the highest stakes and most skillful players found in the upper echelons.

The following scenarios are based on actual events. Some have been combined, embellished, or simplified to illustrate the point, but all have a grain of truth. Some of these might be described as *gamesmanship* while others are more like a knife fight in an alleyway. It really does not matter how you describe them because none of them are harmless, even though the participants might view their actions the same as they would view bluffing at poker. Although these scenarios are based on actual events, the motives and interpretations are mostly speculation.

THE LOST MEMO

This is actually a very old technique that was quite effective in the paper-dependent society, but it is even easier to employ with electronic mail and is growing in popularity. Most people would describe this as gamesmanship, but in the right circumstances, it can be a deadly weapon.

This situation usually starts as a disagreement between two managers over some action that one supports and the other opposes. Letters are written, studies conducted, and perhaps even a task force is formed. However, the issue is not clarified, and the dispute continues. One of the participants (usually the one accountable for the decision) eventually takes matters into his own hands and writes a memo (e-mail) to the one with the opposing view. This memo will describe the decision and the course of action that the author intends to take, *unless he hears from the other person by a certain date or time*. The decision or course of action cannot be completely one-sided but it rarely reflects enough of a compromise to gain concurrence from the opponent. Naturally the memo is not *actually* sent to the opponent. It is withheld until the time to respond has either expired or is so near as to render a response virtually impossible. When no response is received, the decision is made and the die is cast. The opponent can protest, but it is too late. He did not respond and something had to be done, therefore, the decision was made. The trick is to be able to show that the memo was sent, *but got delayed*. Sort of, the server ate my e-mail excuse.

This gambit has so many variations that it is impossible to name them or give examples. This is used for telephone calls (I must have dialed wrong), pagers (didn't you get my page?), notes (I left a note on your door), and the list goes on and on. This gambit is not only crude, but like a sledgehammer what it lacks in finesse it makes up for in effectiveness. The experienced corporate player will immediately see through this gambit, but unless you are willing to call your opponent a boldfaced liar, it is virtually impossible to correct the situation.

This is a small illustration of corporate politics at work, and, like most corporate politics, it focuses on personal advantage. In the next situation, the motive continues to be personal advantage, but the political maneuvers are less competitive.

JACK THE GIANT KILLER

A great deal has been written about loyalty, especially recently. Usually, these writings focus on how employees are no longer loyal to the company.

Very few of these address the company's loyalty to the employee, presumably because companies are just as loyal to the employees today as they ever were. Until recently no one has seemed willing to ask precisely how loyal was that? Historically companies have always viewed people as an asset, but when the time comes for cost control and retrenchment, the first reaction is "get rid of the deadwood," meaning lay off a set number of people—the amount of *deadwood* being determined by the amount of cost reduction required. The deadwood is never described as *disloyal deadwood*, and no effort is ever made to isolate employees with a high loyalty quotient from those with a low loyalty quotient. Therefore, employees are really not less loyal than they used to be, they are just using the same rules that the companies have used for years. But loyalty between the company and the employee is really not the issue. What is relevant from a political perspective is personal loyalty and reputation.

We learn in school that Benedict Arnold was a traitor who betrayed his country and went off to England. For most Americans the story ends there, but in reality Arnold lived on, despised by friend and foe alike, and with time, these became harder to distinguish as he was shunned by those whom he helped and those whom he betrayed. Arnold forgot that in defeat you can respect the victor for having played superbly, and in victory you can honor your fallen adversary for having been a worthy opponent. But no one can trust a traitor nor respect someone who would betray a friend. This is a lesson that everyone should take to heart when they begin to play at corporate politics.

Jack was on the staff of the President and functioned as a sounding board and troubleshooter. Through the years they had become friends, so Jack was entrusted with some very confidential information. As part of his duties Jack became aware that a major project was failing, and the failure would cost millions. Although it was true that the President was not directly responsible, it was also true that his political enemies would tag him with the failure. The President had done a good job and had many supporters both on the board and within the company, but he had his share of enemies as well. One of these was Mr. Smith, an Executive Vice President and heir apparent for the job of President. Jack was faced with a decision regarding what to do next, considering:

1. He was not independently wealthy like the President, so he needed his job.
2. Although the President was successful, the failure of this project could cause the board to force him to resign.
3. If Smith found out, he would surely lead the attack against the President. If he was successful and he forced the President to resign, Jack would be forced out as well.

4. If he informed Smith of the situation *before* Smith found out on his own then he might survive if the President were forced to resign. If Smith failed to force the President out, then there would be no harm done and no one would know.

Jack had two kids in college and a family to worry about. Therefore, he felt he had no choice but to go to Mr. Smith with the facts. However, the reality was that the failed project might not be enough to interest Mr. Smith because the President was not directly responsible for the project. Jack had to have something else, so he went back through his files and found two instances where the President had used corporate assets in a questionable manner. He arranged to meet with Mr. Smith and explained everything, being very careful to assure Mr. Smith that he had the company's interest at heart. Mr. Smith took the information, had his own team quietly research it, and then, armed with the facts, he went to some board members who were known to be weak supporters of the President. Very shortly the President was forced out, and Mr. Smith was named his successor. Jack continued on in his position as staff to the President (now Mr. Smith). But things did not go quite according to plan.

Corporations have very few secrets when it comes to corporate politics and who is in and who is out. When the topic is who stabbed whom in the back, the news spreads like wildfire. It was not long before Jack realized that he was having trouble reaching people, and his projects were vigorously opposed by people who formerly had been supporters. His Saturday golfing foursome slowly eroded to three, then two, and ceased altogether. He was rarely invited to lunch anymore, and when he attempted to arrange luncheons, he found his colleagues were simply too busy. Not unexpectedly his performance declined as he found it harder and harder to get anything done.

Somehow, word had gotten out regarding his conversation with Mr. Smith and that he had been responsible for getting "his friend" the President forced out. It seemed obvious to everyone that he had betrayed his friend the President just as it seemed obvious to him that Mr. Smith had betrayed him. Only Mr. Smith knew that he had given him confidential information so only Mr. Smith could be the source of the rumor that he had betrayed the President. When complaints began about his unresponsiveness and poor performance, Mr. Smith was forced to call Jack into his office and *suggest* that he resign. Jack had destroyed his reputation. He was viewed as untrustworthy and a traitor. No one would help him or even feel sorry for him. He lost everything in an unsuccessful bid to keep a job. A very poor exchange, in the opinion of most people, because jobs abound for the person with a sound reputation for honesty and integrity. But once you are known as untrustworthy, it is very difficult finding the references necessary to re-establish yourself in another company. Jack derailed his career on the fast track but, as we shall see in the next scenario, getting on the fast track is not as challenging as staying on it.

THE TOO-FAST TRACKER

Some people enter the workplace not really well prepared for the work but nevertheless feel intuitively that they should run things. Commonly these are the new college graduates who have been assured by the campus recruiters that all that is required is that they work like a galley slave for a month or two and their natural abilities will be recognized. Once that happens the next step is getting on the fast track and from there it is only a short hop to becoming an executive. Usually the real world takes over and these newly minted junior executives end up putting their shoulder to the wheel along with the rest of us, but not all give up so easily. So it was with Alicia. No matter what her shortcomings might have been, she was certainly resourceful and creative.

Having graduated from a prestigious university, Alicia prepared her resume, displaying her academic credentials in detail. This was necessary because she had absolutely no work experience of any kind. She had gone to school but spent her summers vacationing because there was no need for her to work. Besides, in her view the only reason for going to a prestigious university was to establish an income without having to work. Not unexpectedly to everyone but Alicia, there was little interest in her resume. However, one of the consulting firms eventually hired her on the basis of her degree from a topflight school and excellent academic record. And so Alicia began her career as a consultant, doing research, re-engineering processes, creating strategic plans, and advising senior-level executives. Things were going well for Alicia, but in her mind they were also going too slowly. Even though she had an excellent job with a fine future, she was decidedly NOT an executive. Her objective was to be an executive and even though the path she was on would surely lead to that, it was taking too long.

After months of circulating her resume, Alicia received several offers for management positions but none with *executive* status. She was told repeatedly by interviewers and recruiters alike that even though she worked with many senior executives and she had been a *consultant to management*, she, in fact, had no management or operating experience. Although she had created many strategic plans, she had never executed one, and although it was true she had submitted many organizational plans she had never managed any organization. Everyone agreed Alicia had worked with executives from many industries, but she really had no industry experience. (For those of us in the trenches, her resume was "fluffy.") As door after door closed in her face, Alicia realized two things: first, she was truly destined for greatness no matter what these petty people said; and second, she would have to be creative in her approach. She was. She hired a press agent.

The press agent was worth her weight in gold. She ghosted articles, which appeared at first in the trade press but later in the mainstream press. She got Alicia booked as a speaker at various events. She arranged for Alicia to be appointed to panels on women's issues and women in business, and this was the breakthrough. Alicia was receiving publicity and being interviewed by reporters on women's business issues. Suddenly this visibility resulted in her becoming a *prominent female executive*. The articles and high-profile visibility brought recruiters like flies to honey.

Alicia was hired as the President for the Retail Division of a very large firm. At last Alicia was where she belonged. She flew in the corporate jet, had a driver, a huge office with windows, two secretaries to fulfill her every wish, and a huge salary and expense account. Of course, she had no idea what the President of the Retail Division was supposed to do since her retail experience consisted of shopping at expensive stores. But her staff had detailed knowledge of the Retail Industry, and that was all that counted. Things went along pretty well and while the Retail Division did not go into a tailspin, it did not take off into the stratosphere either. The quarterly reports were a little more challenging for Alicia because each of the divisional Presidents had to stand up in front of the CEO and their peers and present the quarterly results, position against plan, and forecast next quarter's results. These were not pro forma meetings. These were serious grillings, and it did not take long for suspicions to arise regarding Alicia's understanding of the business and her leadership.

It took over a year, but eventually Alicia's lack of management experience and general lack of retail knowledge caught up with her. She had a handsome employment contract, which the company paid off, and she left amid the cheers of her long-suffering staff. After a short and well-deserved vacation, Alicia cranked up her public relations machine, and within six months she was named CEO of the Electronics Division of a Fortune 100 company. She appeared in the national press as a leading female executive and one of the few female CEOs. She was touted in the national press as a role model for women executives everywhere. Of course, she did not know very much about Retail, but she knew even less about electronics. She could identify a VCR from a TV and more or less knew what a computer did, but she had no knowledge of how they worked. To make matters worse, she was now surrounded by people who talked of nothing else. She attempted to gain control, but in order to get control she needed respect, and that required at least some knowledge of the product. For someone who could not distinguish between a joule and a jewel, it was hopeless. Consequently, she rapidly became a joke and then irrelevant. Within six months of being named CEO and held up as a role model for the press, she was asked to resign. She took the money from her second employment contract and retired.

This is one of those situations where you do not know whether to laugh or cry. I suppose Alicia achieved her objective, because she never really had to slog her way through the operational muck to get to the top. She certainly used one of the most creative approaches I have ever come across, and it worked beautifully. I am not sure how well it worked for the companies that hired her, but then caveat emptor. If she had even a little practical experience and some subject matter knowledge, she might have succeeded in becoming the *successful* CEO of a top-flight company. Instead she got on the fast track but went too fast and crashed. Curiosity may have killed the cat, but, in this case, impatience killed the *too-fast tracker.*

THE BLUFF

Alicia bluffed her way to the top but when the bluff was called all she had was *Aces and Eights.*[1] The lesson here is when you bluff you have to bluff big enough to convince everyone that what you have is real so they will not challenge you. This is precisely what Curtis did.

The Director of Engineering was an old-style tyrant given to ranting and raving and known to fire people on the spot if they displeased him. Altogether he was not a pleasant person, but he was smart and ultimately the boss for hundreds of engineers. Curtis was one of those lowly engineers assigned as the Project Manager for some small project down in the bowels of one of the R&D departments. Curtis was a young, lightly experienced engineer, so his project was small, inconsequential, and barely visible to anyone other than his immediate supervisor. Therefore, everyone in the chain of command was astonished when the Director asked for Curtis to come to his office and brief him on his project.

The Director wanted to see the Project Plan, the Product Specification, Market Research, and so on. In short, this was to be a full-blown project review, and it was to be conducted before the close of business. The Director believed that any Project Manager worthy of the name would have all of this information at his/her fingertips. Curtis's supervisor called him in and asked to see his Project Workbook before they showed it to the Director. Curtis informed him that he had not even started on the project, and there was no workbook. Curtis's supervisor just gave him a blank stare (the stare was blank because he was looking at his career future and there wasn't any) and then he began to babble. This was impossible, there had to be a workbook, there had to be a project plan, there had to be a Product Specification because they had been reporting progress on this project for weeks.

Curtis agreed he had been reporting progress on this project, but it was a dumb project, and he would be able to knock it out in a couple of weeks. In the meantime he was working on some research of his own that was more interesting. At this point the supervisor is pacing the room trying to find some way of not attending the forthcoming bloodbath, because he is sure the Director will burn the hide off of poor Curtis. However, Curtis is very cool and completely in control of the situation. He tells his supervisor not to worry about it. He goes to the bookcase and selects a huge binder filled with hundreds of pages of project plans, market research, and specifications. Of course this was a project from several years earlier and had nothing whatsoever to do with the project that Curtis was to report on. Curtis quickly created a new cover sheet and slipped it into the jacket on the binder, and they were off.

The meeting was small, consisting solely of Curtis, the Director, and Curtis's supervisor. Curtis walked in, placed the huge binder in front of the Director, but did not remove his hand. Curtis pointed out to the Director that there was a great deal of information here and it would be easier if he just explained and summarized it. Without waiting for a response, Curtis launched into a forty-five-minute, extemporaneous discussion of his project. He covered everything from soup-to-nuts. The Director was very pleased and congratulated both Curtis and his supervisor on a fine presentation and their excellent work. As they stood to shake hands, Curtis quietly picked up the binder, shook the Director's hand, and left with the binder of fictitious material. The Director was never aware he had been bluffed, and both the Supervisor and Curtis got promoted for their fine work.

Bluffing in corporate politics is a dangerous game and should only be used with caution. Bluffing and lying are two different things. If you say something that is not true, that is lying, and it will damage your reputation. At no time did Curtis ever say that the binder he presented contained any information about his project. Bluffing is the art of deception, where you allow a person to believe something that may or may not be true. It is one thing to tell a lie, it is quite another to not tell everything you know. This brings us to another point regarding bluffing, and that is the risk assessment. Bluffing is a high-risk proposition from the outset and should never be used for trivial advantage. Because it is so risky, you should evaluate the situation very carefully, paying particular attention to what happens if your bluff fails. This means that your chances of success should be at least 50-50, and if the bluff is called, it should not be a disaster.

Perhaps the most common form of bluffing is regarding salary. This is so prevalent that it is virtually taken for granted by the interviewer that any salary figure is inflated by 20% or even more. Compensation is always a negotiation with each side establishing a starting point. Everyone knows and accepts the starting amount is not only flexible but probably not totally true. The applicant may have included a promised but unrealized salary increase, a future bonus, or similar soft compensation. The interviewer may offer a salary far below what the market will bear as a test of the employee's desperation, courage, or negotiating skills. This is a game we all have played with varying results, but if your bluff is called, you should be prepared to explain. The objective is to offer an explanation without appearing to have lied in the first place. Lying is the kiss-of-death in an interview, because if you are caught you have demonstrated you are not trustworthy.

If you are caught bluffing the best strategy is to come clean. Attempts to brazen things out will only reduce your credibility and may turn the tide against you. Remember, in the world of corporate politics, we are all the same, and the person who found you out has probably run a similar bluff. Therefore, by admitting everything you give him/her the opportunity to accept you as a person of courage, and most importantly, you build credibility. In the long term that may be the most important thing.

BON VOYAGE

Up to this point these political gambits have largely had a dark side or at least created a win/lose situation. But that is not always the case and, in fact, sometimes political maneuvers may create a win/win situation. Furthermore, just as we have seen in the previous cases, not all of the players may even be aware they are in play. This means that one of the winners may have gotten a positive win in the form of a promotion or new job or both without ever realizing there was something other than their ability and reputation at work. That was certainly the case with Peter and Scott.

Peter was the Director of Product Development for a large firm placed in the Silicon Valley. He worked with the engineers to define and develop new products based on the product requirements which he got from the marketing and sales people. Once the product was developed, he was then responsible for getting the marketing and salespeople to support the new product. Ordinarily there wasn't any difficulty with this process and new products were defined, developed, and sold without incident. Then Scott entered the picture.

Scott was a Product Marketing Manager and he actively opposed Peter's newest product. In the product requirements phase he made unrealistic demands, causing weeks of delay while the engineers ran around trying to either satisfy his demands or find some way around them. While the engineers were scurrying around chasing their tails, Scott launched his second attack with a pitiful sales forecast for the new product. With such a low forecast, Peter's product was now under heavy scrutiny and its future was rapidly clouding. Peter realized that any further efforts to convince Scott of the value of his new product were probably wasted. Therefore, he needed to find a more creative solution.

Scott was very competent and well respected, so it was unlikely that any appeal to his management would result in a change of opinion. Going around Scott or simply ignoring him was not possible either so the only solution seemed to be to get him removed from his current position. Although this was the obvious solution, it carried inherent risk because any suggestion to other internal groups or managers regarding the possibility of acquiring Scott was sure to get back to him. Once Scott discovered Peter was trying to get him transferred, he was sure to reject any offers because he would know that he was winning and that he was right about the new product. This left only one possible alternative, and that was to move him out of the company altogether.

Once Peter arrived at this conclusion, he immediately called a few friends and some recruiters. It was not long before he had some people very interested in Scott and one recruiter had a position that seemed tailor-made for Scott. Within a month of Peter making his first call, Scott submitted his resignation. It seems Scott was to be the new Director of Product Marketing at a competing firm. Peter was appropriately shocked and surprised at the news of this *unfortunate* decision to leave the company. Peter helped to arrange the Bon Voyage party for Scott and was pleased to hear Scott explain how these people had sought him out. Scott maintained that he never sent out a resume. The recruiters came to him and offered him such a deal that he could not refuse. Peter's new product development picked up speed and eventually resulted in a moderately successful product. Certainly a win/win for all concerned. Or was it?

At first glance this seems like a great solution to a political problem. After all Scott got a big promotion with a higher salary, Peter got his product program approved and developed, the company seems to have made a little money, so what's the problem? This scenario actually highlights the basic problem with corporate politics in general, and that is, it is usually a manifestation of self-interest. The impact on the company, colleagues, stockholders, or even the other players is viewed as an irrelevant side issue, if any of these are considered at all. Obviously, in this scenario the company is the loser on several points. Peter's job is to work with engineering to define and develop new products, but all too often product planners become emotionally involved with their new product programs. This appears to be what happened with Peter. He had a pet project and he wanted it approved, even though Scott did not believe in it. However, it was Scott's job to protect the interest of the company, which he did through sales forecasting. His low sales forecast was actually his attempt to act in the company's best interest.

Peter thwarted the process and saved his project by getting Scott recruited by a competitor. Although it is true the company made a little money off of Peter's new product, it was not a huge success, and the company lost a valued employee, perhaps one more valuable than Peter. Furthermore, Scott took his experience and knowledge with him to a competitor, which undoubtedly strengthened the competitor and weakened Peter's company, possibly positioning the competitor to take market share from Peter's company. Therefore, I submit that even though Peter got what he wanted and Scott got what he wanted, the company was the loser in the transaction, which is the frequent outcome of corporate politics.

Up to this point these political games and gambits have been mostly just that— games and gambits. But in real life not all of them are. There have been winners and losers in all of them with the company losing something in most of them. Most of these have been political competition rather than career destroying combats, but as we all know political infighting can be brutal, vicious, and a fight to the death.

THE KNIFE FIGHT

Believe it or not, this is a true story. It has been simplified and reduced to its essence, but the basic framework is real. There are five players in this little game, and if you include the CEO who was mostly a bystander, then six: the CEO (tired and ready to retire), the Executive VP who is also getting long in the tooth but who desperately wants to be CEO before he retires; and four young and aggressive Vice Presidents. The Vice Presidents have that precious commodity so necessary for those who want the brass ring and that is time. They are all young, very capable, with proven track records. Each believes (and rightly) that they could one day be CEO. What they do not know, but their boss, the Executive Vice President knows, is that they are good enough that when the CEO retires, one of them could be leapfrogged over him to be the new CEO. Therefore, the EVP is faced with the problem of how to thwart this possibility without being obvious.

Upon reflection, the EVP realizes that the best way to handle the situation is to feed their ambition. Therefore, he calls each one in to his office as part of a friendly discussion that revolves around the probability that the EVP will replace the CEO when he retires. When that happens, he says, as the new CEO he will have to replace himself, and he tells each one he has selected him as his successor. He is telling this to each of them in confidence and explains that if they breach his confidence, he will disavow them and select someone else. Furthermore, because they will soon be sitting in his chair, he wants them to become more involved with the affairs of their colleagues. That is they should learn more about what is going on so they will be better prepared to fill his shoes when he is promoted. This conversation had the same effect on these Vice Presidents as blood does in a pool of sharks, which was precisely what was intended.

At first things were not too bad as each of the secretly selected successors evaluated their colleagues to determine how they would react to the news that they were not selected. Then each of these VPs began to edge his way into the affairs of their colleagues by asking questions regarding daily events, performance of people, and so on. Gradually, the questions became more leading and the observations more direct, and with each escalation the resistance between them grew. With the rising resistance, the meetings and conversations between the Vice Presidents grew more contentious. As the friction increased it spread to their subordinates, and soon there was open conflict raging between departments.

With each escalation each of the Vice Presidents (each believing he was the chosen one) went to the EVP and complained about the lack of cooperation, the antagonism, and the need to announce to everyone that he was the designated successor. The EVP assured them that he would speak to the others and insist on their cooperation. However, it was premature to announce a successor because that would tip the hand of the CEO.

Each of the VPs accepted the explanation and went back to war, and war it was, because very little work was getting done. By this time documents were being hidden and information that used to flow freely between divisions was now withheld, delayed, or heavily edited. The employees were taking sides, and each person was identified with a champion. It was a classic, either you are with me or you are against me scenario. Conference rooms were the battlegrounds, and there was no neutral territory. The real irony is that no one knew how the war got started or what it was about. The Vice Presidents thought they knew but in reality they were unknowing pawns. The struggle between the Vice Presidents continued, but as in all wars, the advantages ebbed and flowed, eventually leading to the realization by one of the Vice Presidents that an alliance might give him the leverage he needed to bring the war to a close. Therefore, he arranged a meeting with one of his colleagues, whom he felt might be willing to work with him, once the colleague knew that he would soon be one of his subordinates. This meeting produced a very interesting discussion because each Vice President was under the impression *he* was to be the successor. Once they realized that the Executive Vice President had told them the same thing, they knew they had been flimflammed. Furthermore, they immediately realized that the probability was that neither would succeed the EVP when he became CEO, and their careers were effectively ended. One of these Vice Presidents immediately resigned.

Mercifully, the CEO decided to retire (I believe in the same spirit that Czar Nicholas II "retired") and was succeeded (surprise!!) by the Executive Vice President. It seems that what was needed was a stabilizing force because company morale was low, turnover was increasing, and the younger executives who might have been considered were *too aggressive and competitive with each other.* Therefore, the Board of Directors decided to promote the Executive Vice President to the position of CEO. They had hoped to get a younger man but on the basis of recent events, none of the internal candidates seemed suitable. Two of the remaining Vice Presidents resigned when the appointment of the new CEO was announced. The weakest of the original four Vice Presidents remained and by default succeeded to the now vacant post of Executive Vice President. The new CEO allowed the new EVP to select the replacements for the four vacant Vice Presidential positions, secure in the knowledge that he would not select anyone stronger than himself, effectively eliminating any threat to the new CEO.

The drain of resources continued as the Vice Presidents who left continued to draw their best people to them. Not unexpectedly, the organization never recovered from this corporate civil war. Even with turnover approaching 100%, the scars remained, and the organizational culture had changed permanently. None of the four high-potential Vice Presidents ever became a CEO, even though they changed companies. Presumably this experience had so damaged their self-confidence and undermined their trust in others that they could not form the relationships necessary to move higher. To be trusted you must not only be trustworthy, you must trust others. None of them seemed to be able to do that. They had become suspicious of everyone and ultimately victims of their own paranoia. Neither the new CEO nor any of his peers and colleagues ever viewed the new Executive Vice President as either effective or trustworthy. When the new CEO retired after two years, the EVP was allowed to retire, never attaining the CEO position that he once coveted.

Jonathan Swift in his trenchant satire *Gulliver's Travels* highlights not only the destructive nature of civil war but the selfish struggle for power that frequently lies behind it. This was certainly the case with this corporate civil war because the motive was the desire for one man to have the power and prestige of the CEO. There was no consideration ever made for the stockholders, the employees, the products, or the staff members who were deliberately turned against each other. This was one man who pragmatically surveyed the political landscape and came to the conclusion that without some sort of intercession, it was unlikely that he would succeed to the corner office. Taking a page from the greatest pragmatist of them all, Machiavelli, the EVP set his own organizational leaders against each other knowing that the ensuing battles would be to the death. This was done with the knowledge that the struggle would weaken the executives who might be candidates for the position of CEO. By instigating this power struggle he hoped (successfully) to improve his chances of getting the top job—a good strategy from the perspective that it achieved its objective, but the human cost was very high, and the impact on the company was significant and permanent.

On the other hand these Vice Presidents were not innocent, naive children being led down the primrose path. These were mature, experienced executives whose lust for power blinded them to possible ulterior motives and the possibility that they were being manipulated. Instead they *trusted* that their boss was telling them the truth and proceeded to take the actions recommended by him rather than stepping back and analyzing the situation. None of them had a qualm about encroaching on their colleagues any more than they considered for an instant the impact their actions would have on their subordinates or the company. Each of these *victims* was so blinded by ambition that they did not care about anyone or anything except increasing their personal power. Clearly they were not familiar with the fates of Macbeth or Othello and certainly had not read Machiavelli. Nothing is ever as it seems, and everything in life has a price. This was a case where the superior turned against his subordinates and allowed them to destroy themselves. However, it can go the other way just as easily. Subordinates can, and often do, undermine their superiors. Usually this is done in subtle, indirect ways but not always. Sometimes the attack can be nothing short of a direct frontal assault, intended to bring the superior down, but always remember the old saying, *never wound a king*.

THE ASSASSIN

The closer you get to the top of the hierarchical pyramid, the fewer the places there are to stand and the fiercer the competition. There are competitors on all sides including behind you, but most of us think of our subordinates as being loyal and trustworthy. For the most part this is probably true, but assassins rarely strike from the front as Caesar, Lincoln, John F. Kennedy, and Mr. Ferretti the Executive Vice President for Worldwide Marketing discovered.

The CEO had worked with Mr. Ferretti at another company, and when the opportunity arose, he hired him as the Executive Vice President for Worldwide Marketing, a post usually viewed as the precursor to being named CEO and a highly coveted position. Therefore, when Mr. Ferretti was brought into the company, there were a number of very disappointed executives, especially the Vice President for North American Sales. Nevertheless, things progressed without incident, and the new EVP seemed to be overcoming any resistance and disappointment that may have existed. However, it is always wise to remember that smiles and camaraderie may be the mask of the assassin.

Every corporation is expected to file anticipated earnings with the Securities and Exchange Commission (SEC). This is a legal obligation and one that the Federal Government takes very seriously. It is also one that is watched very closely by investors and Wall Street Brokerages. Consequently, corporations go to great lengths to make these forecasted earnings as accurate as possible. This was an exercise Mr. Ferretti and his subordinates had done many times in the past. Therefore, gathering and organizing this information were relatively routine. At least it was routine up until the results were reviewed.

After all of the information was gathered, reviewed with the President, and turned over to the Chief Financial Officer for submission to the SEC, Mr. Ferretti called a meeting with his subordinates to review what was submitted to the SEC. A fairly routine meeting attended by Mr. Ferretti's direct reports, including the Sales Vice President, who had submitted a very significant forecasted improvement in sales revenue. The meeting commenced with the Marketing Vice President presenting the material that was presented to the SEC. When they got to the forecasted improvement in sales revenues, the Sales Vice President interjected that the figures were incorrect. The room was instantly silent as everyone present tried to assimilate what was just said. These figures could not be wrong. That was impossible. Not only was it impossible, it could have significant legal ramifications for the corporation as well as those present. After a moment of stunned silence the room erupted into an uproar of questions and calls for explanation.

After Mr. Ferretti had restored order by shouting everyone into silence, he calmly (or as calmly as he could) asked the Sales Vice President to explain what he meant when he said the forecasted sales revenues reported to the SEC were incorrect. How could that be, because these were the figures he had submitted in the first place. The Sales Vice President explained that while it was true that he had *originally* submitted a much higher figure, on reflection he realized these figures were too high so he revised them downward. Actually, he had reduced them by *half*. There was a collective gasp with that news, because that represented a reduction of millions of dollars in revenues, something the President as well as the SEC would notice. With that statement Mr. Ferretti was on his feet shouting that the forecast could not be revised without his approval and that the Sales Vice President could not make that change. "Horsefeathers" (or words to that effect), shouted the Sales Vice President, who was now standing nose-to-nose with Mr. Ferretti; "I not only can, I did, and I reported the changes to the President."

The argument went on for some time, growing more heated each minute. Finally, the Executive Vice President, Mr. Ferretti, stormed out of the room determined to restore the forecast and terminate the Sales Vice President. However, things did not work out quite like that. It seems that the Sales Vice President did, in fact, reduce the forecasted revenues and had informed the President of that fact. The Chief Financial Officer had amended their submission to the SEC, and now the President wanted to know why Mr. Ferretti had inflated the figures to start with? It seems the Sales Vice President had come to the President and told him that he had actually tried to submit a lower forecast but Mr. Ferretti had demanded that he submit a higher number. He was reluctant to do so but Mr. Ferretti had insisted. After he thought about it, he realized that not only was the number wrong but that when the company fell short of the forecast it would affect the stock price and thousands of shareholders. Therefore, he came to the President with a revised forecast, one he felt was more accurate and achiev-.able. In his discussion with the President, Mr. Ferretti produced the written forecast signed by the Sales Vice President. However, the President told Mr. Ferretti that the Sales Vice President claimed he had submitted the forecast under duress from Mr. Ferretti.

The Sales Vice President had been with the company for many years. He had a loyal following and many viewed him as a strong candidate for the Presidency. It seems that since Mr. Ferretti's appointment there had been a string of complaints from his subordinates regarding his failure to listen and to demand things be done his way. What was not obvious was that many of these complaints about Mr. Ferretti started with the Sales Vice President pointing out to others how Mr. Ferretti did not listen and made unreasonable demands. In any case, by the time this situation arose, the President was psychologically prepared to accept that Mr. Ferretti had forced the higher forecast. Therefore, when his protestations were not accepted and he stated that he intended to fire the Sales Vice President, the President stopped it. Mr. Ferretti returned to his headquarters totally defeated and reduced to the status of figurehead.

Within weeks of this event, Mr. Ferretti was promoted to the post of Senior Executive Vice President responsible for Worldwide Product Marketing. In this capacity he chaired the committee on new product releases, proposed worldwide product pricing recommendations, and made funding recommendations for new product development. He moved to the Corporate Headquarters with an office adjacent to the President's. He had use of the corporate jet, a driver, a handsome salary, a secretary, and because no one had been appointed to his committee, he could work when he wanted. The Sales Vice President was made Group Executive for the Asia/Pacific Division, eventually becoming CEO of the company. Mr. Ferretti enjoyed his new position until his employment contract ended and then he retired.

Again we see the price of trust and not being prepared. Mr. Ferretti had been lulled into a comfortable complacency by the cooperation and smiles of those about him. He believed he had established a sense of teamwork and trust with his subordinates. Many people felt that way about the Borgias, with similar (although more permanent) results. Mr. Ferretti made the mistake of assuming a lack of aggression was a sign of friendship. It might be, but just as often it is a sign that your competitors are too weak to attack you at the moment. This was certainly the case here, but should we weep for Mr. Ferretti? I do not think so. This was a garden-variety power struggle, and he lost. Unlike other power struggles, this one did not have much impact on the employees or stockholders. Are there lessons to be learned here?

As we observe the reactions of executives in different circumstances, we can draw some conclusions about events that surround us every day. Perhaps these conclusions can be viewed as lessons and perhaps the lesson here is that power does not lend itself to friendships. The more power you gain, the fewer people you can trust. You learn to read nuances in behavior, glances, and distribution lists. To trust is to be off-guard, and to be off-guard is to be vulnerable. Mr. Ferretti allowed himself to be lulled with bows and smiles and cooperation and so, like King Lear, he was unprepared when the attack came. Naturally, there will be those who view the Sales Vice President as a back-stabbing assassin, and perhaps he was, but he also accomplished his objective, which was to eliminate a competitor.

The world of corporate politics is real, and the motives are almost always power and self-interest. The games are personal, and the penalties for failure are very real. Ironically, at the highest levels, money is really not the issue, other than it may be a method of keeping track of who is winning. Instead, the drive is for power and prestige, with the loser having to carry the bags and kowtow to the winner. The employees, shareholders, customers, products, dividends, and sales are either not considered at all or are just chips to be played as necessary. This view of corporate politics is not really intended to be cynical but rather to show a realistic view of things as I have observed and experienced. These were real people playing with their own lives and careers as well as those of others. These were all professionals, and like-high wire artists, they were frequently working without a net. However, as we shall see, there are people and executives in the corporate world who appear to be working not only without a net but without a brain as well.

NOTE

1. The Dead Man's hand. The losing poker hand that Wild Bill Hickok was holding when he was shot.

11

SEARCHING FOR INTELLIGENCE

What Were They Thinking?

Regardless of what they are taught and sometimes even in the face of their own experience, some people make decisions and take actions that can only be described as strange, if not downright bizarre. When this happens the people on the sidelines usually burst out laughing, but for those directly involved, the inevitable question becomes "have they have lost their minds?" To some extent, all of us at one time or another make less than perfect decisions, but the ones here go beyond just being sub-optimal. A sub-optimal decision is one where there were better but unselected alternatives available. In these scenarios the decisions are so lacking in judgment that there is no way to study them because they do not seem to have any rhyme or reason. In fact, they may not even have any relevance to you as a manager, other than to provide an example of what not to do. But as we all know, sometimes failure is the best teacher.

THE DRIVE FOR NUMBER TWO

A very large manufacturer of electrical appliances was driving very hard to increase their market share. They improved their products, customer service, increased productivity and generally had done all of the things necessary to challenge the market leader, which to them was the number one small appliance manufacturer in the world. Through diligence and perseverance they had firmly established the company as number two in the world and were poised to challenge their competitor for the number one spot. They brought in a new CIO whose objective was to improve the productivity and competitiveness of the enterprise. The CIO took very aggressive action and very soon after his arrival he had revamped the technical infrastructure and greatly improved communications across the entire world. As part of this effort he set up an interactive Internet-based electronic catalog of the company's products. This new catalog would put the company in direct contact with consumers worldwide, reduce the cost of sales, allow for price reductions, improve inventory management, improve manufacturing times, and generally put the company far in advance of any competitor. The results of the pilot program verified all of these claims so the CIO and Vice President of Marketing expected to get complete support from the CEO. However, the meeting with the CEO did not go quite as planned.

After demonstrating the technology and its ease of use, the CIO turned the meeting over to the Vice President of Marketing. The Marketing VP started by showing where the company placed in the industry by product group by country. He then went on to contrast the company's growth and performance to that of their archrival. Having firmly established that they were number two, he showed how with the new technology-based electronic catalog they could pull ahead of their competitor in virtually every market and within two years they could *be number one in the industry*.

After the crescendo, the CIO and Marketing Vice President stepped back waiting for the applause, cheers, or perhaps even the rustle of bonus money, but instead there was silence. No one stirred while the CEO stared with the cold hard eyes characteristic of auditors accustomed to finding flaws in the Sistine Chapel. Others looked up at the ceiling (perhaps looking for manna to fall), afraid to look at the CEO in case he should read support for this crazy idea in their eyes. The others found reasons to carefully inspect their highly polished wingtips (perhaps thinking they might have stepped in the manna). After a long pause, the CEO started asking questions regarding this new (to his credit he did not add "fangled") electronic catalog. Why was it necessary? Who would use it, and what was wrong with the old catalog and the way they were selling their products now? After all, they were already number two and were showing solid growth, so why change? The sponsoring executives assured him that what he said was true, and they were recommending using this crazy electronic catalog because it would (and I repeat) reduce the cost of sales, improve inventory management, increase sales, and so on. The CEO then asked if their primary competitor was using an electronic catalog. The Marketing VP assured him that they were not using an electronic catalog and that was the beauty of the plan. It would take at least a year for them to react (dinosaurs move slowly) and another year to implement. By the time their competitor for the number one spot could react, they would have overtaken them and now we would be number one in the industry. Another long pause ensued while the ceiling and shoes were once again dutifully inspected for manna.

The CEO was singularly unimpressed and rendered his decision. First, he never used the Internet and none of his friends did either. Furthermore, even if he did use the Internet, he would not shop there. Although the idea of using the Internet was creative, it was simply too risky and in view of their steady growth, unnecessary. Therefore, the project would be suspended *until the market leader (their competitor)* introduced an electronic catalog. The strategy, according to the CEO, was to be prepared to react to changing market conditions. Once the competitor started using an electronic catalog, this project would be on the shelf waiting. That way the company could react almost immediately and would not be in the position of assuming the risk of being first in the market with an *unproven* idea. The message delivered to the executives was that the company strategy was to be a follower and not an industry leader. Creativity and innovative thinking were not required because the company strategy was to be *number two*.

Certainly there will be some that believe the CEO acted in a prudent manner in not supporting an "untried" technology. Of course, these are the same people who felt the airplane wouldn't ever be a commercial success or that automatic teller machines would ever be widely used due to their complexity (do not laugh, I remember the meeting.) The world is filled with people who are lacking in vision and are risk adverse. Admittedly, a CEO should act prudently but he should also act with vision. Remember, this technology (the Internet and web pages) is not actually *new*, it has been around for some time. Plus these executives were not proposing a *concept*, they were asking for commitment to release a capability that was already developed, packaged, and piloted. Their forecast relative to how fast their rival could react or relative to the actual sales volumes was speculative, but every decision carries some risk, and the real risk in this one seemed small with the greater risk associated with *not* doing it. Therefore, this CEO, in thinking he was making the least-risk decision, was in fact making a high-risk decision, and was committing his company to a strategy of catch-up.

EXECUTIVE EMPOWERMENT

Obviously all organizations must have some rules, and just as the King is not above the law, neither are executives exempt from the rules governing expenses. All company employees are expected to report their expenses on a formal and procedural basis. Nevertheless there is a certain degree of judgment that must be used, especially with executives. This means that although executives are expected to follow the process and procedure, the cost of their time must be considered when approving expense reports.

After all, if you cannot trust your executives to report their expenses correctly do you tighten your surveillance or get new executives?

One of the legacies of the hierarchical command structure is authorization authority and the policies governing expense reports. The approval authority varies among companies but as we know, the level of expense approval usually increases by position. Consequently, it is not uncommon for executives to have the authority to approve thousands of dollars in expenses, and so it was at this company. Vice Presidents could approve $25,000 in expenses without further review. At the company in question, the policy is ALL expense reports, regardless of amount, require two levels of approval. Furthermore, purchases of software or equipment require a business case. These are not uncommon policies and certainly not unrealistic, but where do you draw the line between following a policy and using common sense?

The Vice President for Product Development authorized the upgrade of the project management tools used by his subordinates. This expenditure was authorized by him and was within his approval level of $25,000. Although he ordered enough for everyone, he neglected to order one for himself. Very quickly this became a problem because he could no longer read the status reports. Without thinking he purchased the tool for $200 at the local computer store and submitted his expense report, which was promptly approved by his superior, the Executive Vice President.

The President (the second level approval required for all employees) sent it back demanding a business case. Not being able to read status reports electronically was not sufficient reason to purchase this tool. The Vice President reworked the expense report, adding text explaining the necessity of reading the status reports on-line, the efficiencies, and so on. Once again EVP approved the expense report, and the President once again rejected it. After all, status reports could be written, the ones the President received were, so there was no reason to require new software computer for such a simple task. A much stronger business case was required.

At this point it seems obvious that it would have been better to have had a subordinate purchase the tool for him. Admittedly this raises some ethical issues but in view of what happened, it would have been more effective. However, that was no longer possible because he had already spent the money and to have a subordinate submit a *false* expense report had more than moral overtones—it was illegal. Consequently, there was no choice but to resubmit the expense report with a new business case, which was (naturally) rejected. Eventually (after five tries), this $200 expense report was approved by the President. It had taken hours of executive time to write and review a business case for a $200 tool. The President was so focused on the procedure that the cost, which had a much greater value than the $200 in question, eluded him. Of course, it did not elude the others involved, and they were mystified as to why the President was wasting his time on the

"Bungee Expense Report." The Executive Vice President was so amused by the whole thing he wanted to write the cost of the tool off to entertainment.

The most incredible thing about this story is that it is true. Certainly there is nothing inherently wrong with the policy requiring two levels of approval, even at the executive level, but to bounce a $200 expense report back and forth between senior executives borders on the absurd. If these executives cannot be trusted to spend $200, then how can they possibly be entrusted with authority to approve $25,000 in expenses? If there was any question regarding the necessity, could that have been handled by a telephone call? If their integrity is in question, then perhaps new executives are needed. It has been observed by others that on many occasions, managers (and executives) focus on the things they understand and feel comfortable doing while ignoring things that they do not. The result is they micromanage things like expense reports while ignoring larger items like the upgrade of management tools for the whole division, which was roughly 50 copies or $10,000. The President never questioned the need for 50 copies, just the need for one.

I'M THE BOSS—AREN'T I?

I think we have fairly well established that things have changed and that those who wish to exercise power must lead rather than command. Naturally this means different things to different people, but in practice leadership means leaders must not only be prepared to explain their vision, they must be prepared to defend it to subordinates who ask difficult and probing questions. Those executives who make the transition from the command-and-control management style to true leadership are in for some very challenging times as the following example shows. In a way you have to feel sorry for this executive, because like the old aristocrats, he confused the perquisites of his position with leadership. It is clear he either could not grasp the change in attitudes or refused to accept them.

In this example, the stock price was depressed, many employees had been laid off, bonuses had been cancelled, and salary increases had been frozen. In short, things were not good. Employee morale was at an all-time low, so something needed to be done to cheer everyone up. Therefore, the CEO decided that he needed to talk to the employees, share his vision for the future, and explain the need for everyone to sacrifice. All of us know that when executives use the word *sacrifice*, it is rarely a good sign and usually translates into less money for the rank and file. The CEO had hardly begun his cheerful upbeat explanation of why everyone and everything (other than the executive team) was at fault when he started receiving unsolicited questions from the audience. At first he attempted to ignore the questions, but the audience became restive and the questions were being shouted so loud that he could not speak over them. There were many different questions but

these could be summarized as demands to know why he and the other executives got raises and bonuses and not the workers *who earned the money*.
Because the company was clearly in disarray, what did *the executives do* to
deserve the money they were being paid? Why were skilled, successful, and
necessary people laid off but no executives? If people were in fact the greatest asset of the corporation, why was the company disposing of these assets?
What *sacrifices* was the executive team making? Taken aback by what could
only be termed a verbal attack, the CEO attempted to defend himself by
explaining that the people who were laid off were nonproductive or redundant. Of course this was not true, and most of the audience was aware that it
was not true, so the response was met with both verbal derision and visible
scorn. On the issue of money, the executive attempted to explain that it was
necessary to restrict bonuses and salary increases because the company was
not performing well. Therefore, it was incumbent upon everyone to recognize that their failure to improve productivity created the situation where
sacrifices were now necessary. However, the employees should realize that
he and the other executives were under employment contracts, and their
compensation was established by their contracts. Consequently, they had no
choice but to take what they were *obligated* by contract to take. The hoots,
hollers, and catcalls that greeted that statement could have been anticipated
by anyone in the audience, but the fact that it both surprised and hurt the
CEO was a clear indication of how out of touch he was with the employees.
He actually felt that he had given a good answer, and his call for sacrifices
on the part of the employees was not hypocritical. He was unable to finish
his speech. The local management team eventually calmed the audience
enough to where the CEO could retire with some shred of dignity.
However, the CEO cancelled the rest of his *motivational* tour and returned
to the safety of the executive suite, presumably to lick his wounds, and re-
read *Leadership 101*.

   This was a vivid demonstration of a manager who was required to display
leadership and did not have any idea of what constituted leadership. Also,
there were two very revealing attitudes displayed in this meeting that
seemed to go unnoticed and certainly unheeded. The first was the workers'
attitude that they actually produced the products and delivered the services
and were thus more deserving of rewards than the management team. The
workers were willing to accept some responsibility for failure and were willing to make some sacrifices, but they expected the management team to
accept some responsibility and sacrifice as well. When this was not forthcoming, it triggered a reaction that led to the second point, which was the
questioning of the *relevance* of the CEO. Specifically, *what did he do* to
deserve any compensation, let alone extraordinary compensation? Other
than being involved in corporate politics and Wall Street, what contributions did he and his colleagues make? More specifically, precisely what did
they do to contribute to the profitability of the corporation? These points

represent a sea change in the attitude of workers in general and a change that executives ignore at their peril. Today's knowledge workers are becoming aware of their value and role in the creation of wealth and expect to be paid accordingly. Furthermore, they expect everyone's compensation to reflect their contribution to the enterprise, and that includes the management team. Executives who cannot point to their personal contributions will come under increasing pressure and criticism from those whom they purport to lead. This does not mean that executives should make less or should fear for their job, but it does mean they must be prepared to articulate their contributions and to share a greater portion of the profits with the workers.

WHERE DO YOU WANT THE PAIN?

As we all know there are situations where pain cannot be avoided, and the only choice available to the manager is selecting where the pain should be inflicted. Furthermore, it is usually prudent to understand precisely what the mission of an organization is before engaging it. For example, the Environmental Protection Agency is chartered to protect the environment, not create or protect jobs, not to enhance or further business objectives, so why do people get upset when the agency puts owls before people? They are just doing the job they were chartered to do. It is the same situation with purchasing agents (well, not always, but often enough). They frequently consider their job to be to specifically purchase what they are asked to buy, and if no brand is specified, to buy the item at the lowest price available in the market (frequently seen in commercials as Brand X). The assumption is that all items with the same functionality have the equivalent quality. Of course, the operative word there is *equivalent*. Sometimes quality is easy to see but sometimes it is very difficult to pin down even by the most experienced person. Take the example of the large petroleum firm that needed to buy a new network server.

Servers are essentially computers with all of the foibles of computers large and small. This means that buying servers on the basis of cost or even functionality can be very tricky. For this reason, many firms specify specific vendors and models to their purchasing department. Many do, but not all, and at this particular firm the network design engineer specified the functionality and recommended a specific brand with an estimated price of $25,000. As the recommendation passed through the various levels of approval, the specific brand was shorn from the request. When it arrived in purchasing the only thing specified was the functionality and a note stating that the purchase price should not exceed $25,000. Purchasing promptly went out and bought a new network server from the V&X Server Company for $10,000. Although this is not a great deal of money for a multibillion-dollar company, it does add up. It also does not buy much in the world of network servers. In due course, the server was delivered, configured, and installed.

The server promptly crashed, and because it was not a *standard* server, it was not included in the maintenance agreement. Therefore, all service was on a time and materials basis. The service technician came to the site, brought the server back to life, and left. Within days the server crashed again, the technician returned, resuscitated the server, submitted his bill, and left. This scenario was repeated almost daily with each occurrence attributed to something different. By the end of the first month, the technician was beginning each repair session by laying his hands on the server, closing his eyes, and shouting, *"HEAL!!"* This was not especially effective in repairing the server but it did convey to the bystanders the relative severity of the problem and the frustration of the technician. The first month's repair bill was $25,000 or roughly the cost of the standard server specified by the network designer in the first place. Thus the out-of-pocket expense at the end of the first month was $35,000.

The network engineer had protested the purchase of the cheap (but functionally compliant) server in the first place but was overruled by the manager of purchasing who was following his mandate of controlling costs. The second month of the server saga began much like the first, with the server down. However, the local team had gotten much better at restoring the server, so the "pay by the call" server healer only had to be called in cases of dire emergencies. However, the emergencies were occurring so close together that the server technician hardly ever left. In fact, he adopted a cube and moved in some of his tools, and other magical apparatus. He even got a badge and kept a running tally of his time and expenses. By the end of the second month, the cheap (but functionally compliant) network server had run up maintenance costs in excess of $55,000.

The network engineer was appalled by the maintenance costs and again raised the issue of the cost of buying cheap. However, this time he did not go to the manager of purchasing, he went to the CIO, who was appropriately chagrined. They went to visit the Manager of Purchasing with the purpose of explaining to him in simple declarative sentences that this cheap server was made from tinfoil and bubble gum and must be replaced forthwith. The Purchasing Manager was very cooperative and pointed out to the deputation that his charter was to purchase the best quality at the least cost. He had purchased this V&X server against *their* specification, which was functional. No specific brand or model number was provided and the only other guidance was to keep the purchase price below $25,000. The purchasing agents had fulfilled their charter, but if the new V&X Server could not be stabilized, that was the fault of the Information Technology Department and their network design, not the equipment, which was functionally compliant to their specification. However, if they would now like to *retire* this new server after only two months of operation, he would be very glad to purchase a new one at an additional $25,000. Of course, he would have to file a report explaining how the Information Technology Department had revised its specification and was now requesting a *new* server with the same functionality but at roughly two and a half times the cost.

The message was clear, so the deputation retired with as much dignity as they could and went back to watching the server waver and crash with painful regularity. In the meantime, the server healer had brought pictures of his family to his adopted cube, added a few decorative items, got a picture badge, had a telephone installed, and began to use this as his base of operations. Billings were now monthly, and the company was getting a volume discount. Nevertheless, by the end of the third month, the maintenance charges had climbed to a total of $92,000 for the first three months of operation. During this period the network engineer and the network designer had reconfigured the server, balanced the load as best they could, removed all critical functions, and basically were using the server for as little as possible. By the fourth month they had managed to reduce the maintenance charges to about $25,000. In effect, by not buying the better server at the outset, the company was now effectively purchasing a new server every month in the form of time and materials maintenance. Eventually this situation was corrected, but not before a great deal of money was lost.

There are so many lessons to be learned from this little scenario that it is hard to know where to begin. Certainly it is important for everyone to understand precisely what motivates individuals, groups, or departments. In this case the purchasing department was not given specific instructions regarding brand or performance. They were only given the functional requirements, which they fulfilled with a low-cost item, thus fulfilling their charter. The disastrous result was not their responsibility, and when the technical staff attempted to rectify the mistake, they encountered the second lesson in the scenario.

There is an old saying to the effect that "success has many fathers, but failure none," and the larger the corporation the more true this is. When determining who should be rewarded for a corporate success, there are usually more claimants than the people actually assigned to the effort. However, finding the person accountable or responsible for a mistake in most large corporations is about as easy as finding diamonds. This scenario really described an oversight (mistake) that needed to be rectified but the problem became who was to take the blame. The Purchasing Manager was happy to correct the problem, but intended to shift the blame to the technical staff. The technical staff did not want to have the problem corrected if they were to be held accountable for not specifying the brand of server in the first place. Therefore, nothing was done, and the maintenance costs continued.

In effect this problem was simply buried until it became so encrusted with other problems that it was hard to establish the root cause. When the pain of the low-cost server became so great that something had to be done, the pain of going back and establishing responsibility was greater than just fixing the problem and moving on. Any attempt to actually establish responsibility under these circumstances is usually dismissed as witch hunting. Of course, you never know who might be the next witch, so most managers accept this explanation and let the current witch move on to the next brew. Remember, corporations rarely promote those who are associated with failure, so this scenario merely demonstrates this.

NATURE BOY

It is not a secret that computer programmers are creative as well as being a free-thinking lot, and for this reason they are rarely exposed to customers, or even daylight in extreme cases. However, there are times when there is no alternative, and the sales team must expose the technician to the customer (or is it vice versa?). When this happens, everyone involved is on edge until the ordeal is over. This scenario describes what can happen when the salesperson does not expect the worst.

The ABC Company had been wooing the federal government of a large European country for sometime and the company was now a finalist in the selection process. The head of the Social Services Ministry for the country was visiting the headquarters of each of the finalists. The purpose of the visit was to hobnob with the corporate executives and to get a demonstration of the computer program that formed the basis for the service being proposed. This was a new application with a new demonstration, so none of the sales team had yet been trained. Therefore, it was decided that the chief designer of the application would come to headquarters to demonstrate it and explain all of its features. Of course no one had ever met the chief designer and had no idea what he looked like. They asked around and were assured he was presentable, and some even considered him quite good looking. Because they had spoken to him on the telephone and he spoke very well, there did not seem to be a problem. Of course, there should not have been a problem, but, as we all know, Mother Nature is a jokester and can put a crimp in the best plan.

Actually the chief designer of the application was looking forward to the presentation. This was to be his debut into corporate society. He bought a new blue suit, matching tie, a (believe it or not) white shirt, wingtip shoes, and, making the supreme sacrifice, got a haircut that actually exposed his ears to sunlight. He even shaved, but that was on the Friday before the big presentation on Monday morning. It seems our hero was also a Boy Scout Troop Leader. A task he took very seriously, so he was always prepared, but not necessarily for everything.

This was the weekend for his big campout, which he and his scouts had been looking forward to for a long time. Therefore, our hero carefully packed his new suit, tie, and all of the rest of his new corporate uniform, including new underwear, shaving kit, and all of the other sundries into his new suitcase, which he carefully placed in the trunk of his car. He arranged his travel so he would depart on the last flight on Sunday evening. That would permit him to spend maximum time with his scouts and still arrive at his hotel with enough time to get a good night's sleep.

Friday evening came and our hero rendezvoused with his scouts. He was dressed in his scout uniform, knapsack, hat, compass, knife, and hatchet—all-in-all a picture-perfect scout leader. The camping trip went very well, right up until Sunday afternoon when it began to rain. Soon it was raining very hard so our intrepid scouts struck camp, packed up, and headed home. Of course, with the rain, the dirt roads leading to the highway were a mess so the return trip to the main highway took longer than expected but they left early so not to worry. At this point things began to go down hill. The trip back to town was one long traffic jam. Dropping the boys off took longer than planned, so there was no time to change clothes at the airport as anticipated, just enough time to check his bag and race to the security gate.

Picture what our hero now looks like. He has three days' growth of beard, a wrinkled, dirty scout masters uniform, a muddy knapsack, a hatchet, a knife, and a wild look in his eyes because he is about to miss his plane. Naturally, the guards at the security checkpoint were suspicious and not very amused by the six-inch hunting knife and hatchet. Once inside of the little room kept for these purposes, our hero quite logically pointed out that these were not *weapons* but tools. Furthermore, he was not a member of some paramilitary organization but a scout leader. BOY Scouts, you nitwit, not a reconnaissance group. By the time the search was finished, the police appeased, and the knapsack returned, the plane was long gone, along with the new clothes, which were on board or at least somewhere else. Fortunately there was an even later flight on another airline, which our hero took. This flight would still arrive with just enough time to allow him to shave, wash, change clothes and race to the meeting. However, this flight was also late due to weather, the earlier flight had been redirected to an alternate airport, and no one had a clue where his baggage might be.

We are now at that fork-in-the-career path that separates greatness from notoriety. What can be done? What should our hero do? What would you do? Quick now, the clock is ticking. It is 6 A.M., the meeting is miles away and begins at 8 A.M., and a decision must be made—NOW! Quick, make a decision! There appear to be three choices: (a) call and cancel out of the meeting; (b) stop somewhere and buy a clean shirt, pants, and razor; and (c) go straight to the meeting. Well, going to the meeting dressed as he was really isn't a choice, is it? No one would meet a minister from any country unshaven, dirty, and dressed in a boy-scout uniform. Who would do that?

Our intrepid hero rushed to the taxi stand and raced to headquarters, arriving breathless, dirty, in uniform, and after the meeting started. He burst into the room like Superman emerging from a telephone booth, creating quite a stir in the process, because the minister and members of his staff leaped to their feet, obviously thinking they were about to be attacked. Once order was restored and the minister was assured that assassination was not part of today's plan, the salesperson asked our hero to step outside for a moment. The full text of the conversation you can imagine, but it was the tagline that raised our hero to the status of a sales legend. When the salesperson paused for breath, our hero offered in his defense, "It could have been worse. I could have had my hatchet."

This scenario certainly illustrates our starting point, which was searching for intelligence. But as a manager, is there a lesson to be learned here? Actually this little anecdote illustrates a point that most managers know but probably do not think about very often and that is the lack of understanding between technical people and salespeople. In this case our hero was motivated to provide the very best service and support to the sales team that he could provide. In his heart he knew that only he had the knowledge necessary to demonstrate the new product at its highest potential. If the salesperson could have done this, he would not have asked for support, so in the eyes of our hero the entire sale and success of the company were dependent on him being at the meeting. Therefore, he could let nothing stand in his way, apparently not even good judgment. But in his defense we should note that the salesperson neglected to place the meeting in the proper perspective. He never explained what he was expecting from the meeting or that sales are built on relationships as much as products. All the salesperson did was point out the importance of the customer and the necessity for impressing him with a razzle dazzle demonstration of the product. He assumed the technical person would understand the basics of sales just as the technical person assumed the entire deal was dependent on a product demonstration. This failure to understand each other led our hero to his infamous debut and subsequent notoriety. For years the phrase "at least he didn't have a hatchet" was used to excuse actions that fell short of the mark.

THE PROTECTOR

The following situation is so common that I am not sure that it even belongs here. In fact, the larger the company the more probable it is that this situation has occurred because it really represents the division between field operations and headquarters bureaucracy. It always begins with the sincere desire by the headquarters team to support the field, and it almost always ends with frustration on all sides. This situation has many forms, but usually involves the headquarters task force, the need by field operations for a tool, and the desire to protect an intellectual asset.

This particular incident began with a competitive problem of a large telecommunications service provider. This is a very competitive field with many companies vying for the rights to provide voice and data communications service to large companies. Many times the difference between profit and loss is in the ability of the field implementation team to quickly plan and install the network with a minimum of rework. Therefore, having a proven and repeatable process is necessary if the company has any hope of being both competitive and profitable. The logical conclusion is to establish a task force to investigate best practices and then to develop a repeatable process to be used by field operations that will ensure a profitable quality service. A simple objective and one suited to a task force.

The corporate task force was duly formed and immediately began its search for best practices. Because the field team was the one with the problem, looking there for a best practice seemed like searching for gold in a salt mine, therefore, the task force leader did not see any need for field people on the task force or to examine current practices. Since competitors were having similar problems, looking at their practices did not seem to have any potential either. This led to the obvious conclusion that because the task force was composed of brilliant staff members with years of planning experience, the solution was to develop an original repeatable process. Once the process was developed it would be reviewed with representatives from field operations, revised based on their review, and then released for use by field operations. A simple but elegant plan and work began immediately.

It took months of struggling but the standard process was finally completed. It was duly reviewed by a series of field managers who gave it the usual fish-eyed review that field people reserve for anything coming from corporate headquarters. After several weeks of wrangling, the field managers eventually agreed that the standard process was bureaucratic but at least standard and it would meet its objectives of improved service quality and profitability. With this endorsement by field operations, the task force leader realized that the company now had a significant intellectual asset. This repeatable process would yield a quickly installed quality service that would improve profitability and give the company a competitive edge. Therefore, this asset must be protected from falling into the hands of competitors.

The field operations managers instructed their teams to begin using the new process immediately. Copies of the new process could be downloaded from the headquarters server. The complaints began immediately, because a password was needed to access the process. Calls to the task force leader determined that the repeatable process was a significant corporate asset and therefore could not be made generally available. Field operations personnel would have to request the password and demonstrate their need to have access to the process, but in any event passwords would be restricted to field managers. Appeals and protests to the task force leader were to no avail. The password policy stood. Upper management eventually modified the policy so that passwords were available to anyone who needed to know the process. However, by the time the policy was modified, the field team had written the whole thing off as another corporate fiasco and returned to their original inefficient but familiar process.

WHERE DO I PUT THE DUNNAGE?

Reputations are funny things. Sometimes you meet people who are buried deep in the bowels of an organization who are brilliant but have a reputation that prevents them from rising. Others have reached the pinnacle of the corporate ladder and have a reputation for brilliance that never seems to reconcile their actions with their results. This was certainly the case with the new Vice President of Purchasing for a large manufacturer. Mr. O'Leary was recruited from a large European firm where he had earned an international reputation as a cost-cutting, penny-pinching, purchasing whiz. An executive who had created strategic alliances, reduced the total number of suppliers, and clubbed the remainder into an ever decreasing spiral of cost reduction by simply informing them of the price he was willing to pay. He had a number of personal foibles including a passion for healthy (as determined by him) foods, exercise, meditation, and a drive to control everything and everybody—an altogether charming man, as you can imagine. He castigated subordinates in public and rarely listened to anyone about anything. Consequently, he very rarely heard bad news or was given any facts that might possibly indicate that he was (God forbid) wrong or even slightly out-of-touch with the reality of a situation. However, his reputation indicated that he was rarely wrong and had demonstrably reduced the manufacturing costs of competitors, prior to joining the firm. Therefore, he went unchallenged as he set about remaking his new employer into a lean and mean low-cost manufacturing machine.

Large pieces of equipment like bulldozers, ships, trucks, airplanes, and even automobiles have thousands of parts supplied to the manufacturer by hundreds of suppliers. These suppliers are scattered across the globe with multiple locations, thousands of employees, and perhaps hundreds of customers. Consequently, parts are streaming into factories scattered around the globe from suppliers scattered around the globe. Scheduling and monitoring this movement are extremely complicated and when you realize that most manufacturers today use JIT (Just In Time), the materials scheduling is even more complicated. To control all of this requires very tight control and rigidly defined processes. In this case, each supplier had an identification number, and in turn, each of their factories or points-of-shipment had a number. As a result each supplier had multiple numbers residing in the database. It is important to note that these numbers served a variety of purposes. They were used for tracking, lot control, billing, and for dunnage control.

Dunnage is not something that people outside of the manufacturing area think about very much, but it is very important to manufacturers. Essentially *dunnage* refers to the customized containers used to ship awkwardly shaped parts. For example, when you buy a VCR it arrives in a box filled with foam pellets and held in place by molded foam packing materials. This is a simple, low-cost, non-reusable form of dunnage that prevents damage from dropping, scratching, or other misadventures. It also allows the shipper to efficiently pack the parts into containers or trucks. Suppose you are shipping bumpers, radar cowling, or airplane wiring harnesses. These require the same sort of customized packing. If you are a manufacturer shipping parts by the thousands to the same locations, this dunnage is expensive and must, therefore, be reusable. If it is reusable, then it must be returned to its starting point, which is identified by vendor and location, usually bar coded on the container. Since each supplier has multiple locations, each of these locations has a unique identification code. It is a simple but effective system and one that allows for the control and accountability of parts, scheduling, inventory management, and dunnage. At this point, Mr. O'Leary enters the picture, determined to not only bring order to this *chaos (?)*, but to reduce costs as well.

The first step in his crusade to reduce waste and improve performance was to instill the *warrior creed* into the staff. This consisted essentially of substituting yogurt for doughnuts at the meetings and forcing everyone to shift their wristwatches to the other wrist. The relevance of this Zen-like order was never fully explained, but to Mr. O'Leary warriors wear their watches on their sword arm. Once the warriors were properly motivated and equipped, Mr. O'Leary was ready to attack the enemy, which he defines as too many suppliers charging too much. Therefore, his first objective was to reduce the number of suppliers and the cost of the parts they supplied. Unfortunately many of the suppliers felt he was attacking them. Very few of these suppliers rely on a single customer, so when Mr. O'Leary informed them of what he was going to pay them for their products, many simply laughed and eliminated him and his firm from their customer list. This put the team on the way to achieving the first objective, which was to reduce the number of suppliers.

Once Mr. O'Leary got the list of suppliers it did not take long for him to discover the obvious need to reduce the number of supplier identification numbers. His reasoning was that the only supplier identification number needed was for the headquarters because that is where the checks and correspondence were sent. When the directive went out to purge the database of multiple identification numbers, there were some protests from the ignorant and uninformed, but it did not take long for everyone to realize Mr. O'Leary knew exactly what he was doing because he repeatedly told them that he did. Thus the database was purged, and business went on more or less as usual. Mr. O'Leary and his warrior band continued on in their holy crusade against waste and mismanagement.

The first symptoms of a problem began rather quietly. There seemed to be some problems with dunnage. Some suppliers were complaining that their dunnage was being misdirected, was late, and in some cases missing altogether. At first there were a few complaints as factories were overwhelmed with empty dunnage while suppliers were short of dunnage, but gradually the chorus grew in size and intensity. Finally the whole thing blew up when an eighteen-wheeler filled with dunnage arrived at the New York City Fifth Avenue headquarters of a major supplier. The truck driver proceeded up the elevator to the executive suite where he asked the well-tailored and efficient executive receptionist where he should deliver his load of dunnage. Of course, the ever-charming and unflappable executive receptionist wanted to know "load of what?" The trucker pointed out that he had a load of dunnage and wanted to know where to deliver it. The receptionist, apparently not knowing the difference between dunnage, tonnage, and cabbage, tapped her pen on her desk and said that if he had something to deliver then he should just deliver it. Tempted though he was to fill her lobby with a load of dunnage, the trucker was a gentleman, and after looking around the reception lobby, pointed out that he had a full load and did not think it would fit in the lobby. Once she understood that he was trying to deliver a complete truckload of dunnage (whatever that was), she went to the CEO and asked what she should do. Thus began a series of phone calls, each one at a higher decibel level until it reached the ears of Mr. O'Leary personally.

Actually, it never reached the ears of Mr. O'Leary, it reached the ears of his replacement, because Mr. O'Leary had been recruited by an even larger firm to head their purchasing department. His reputation as a wizard at revamping, reengineering, and reducing costs had captured the attention of another CEO, who was willing to pay him even more to reduce their costs. However, the successor to Mr. O'Leary immediately realized what had happened and why there were all of these problems with missing and late dunnage. It seems that all of the dunnage was being sent back to the headquarters addresses of the suppliers where they were forced to see that it was redirected to the appropriate destination. When they could not determine their factory of origin (and this was frequently the case), they sent it back to the manufacturer, thereby creating storage problems at the manufacturer's factory and a shortage of dunnage at theirs.

Suppliers usually supply more than one customer from more than one location. Therefore, when a load of dunnage arrives on the doorstep of their headquarters, they really have no easy way of determining who it is from, what factory it came from, or which of their factories owns it. This was a very aggravating problem for the suppliers, but being suppliers and not willing to alienate a customer, they did not complain too loudly. Instead they just tried to muddle through. However, once the problem was escalated high enough at a major supplier, the problem was immediately recognized and action taken. In the meantime the successor to Mr. O'Leary abandoned the health food and the warrior creed, put his wristwatch on his non-sword arm, and restored the old tracking system. It took a while to put the old system back together again, but the donuts arrived the next day. Many of the improvements installed by Mr. O'Leary were valuable and useful and did indeed result in reduced costs and a more efficient operation, but dunnage management was clearly not his strong suit.

To put this in perspective, the decision to reduce the number of identification numbers was just one decision among dozens of decisions, and when put into context, it did not even seem to be a very important decision. Naturally this raises the question that if this were such a small decision, why did no one stop it from being implemented? Why did not one of the *warriors* point out to Mr. O'Leary the ramifications of eliminating the multiple identification numbers? Probably no one really knows the true answer to this question, but consider the context. Mr. O'Leary was a very quirky outsider. He made it very clear at the outset that he was the man with the answers and they were the ones with failure written all over them. Remember they *did* try to point out to him that this was not a good decision. Admittedly, they did not press the point. They just wanted to clear their consciences. This was a very clear case of *malicious obedience*. Mr. O'Leary would not listen, made no effort to garner their support, forced them to do idiotic things, called them his *warriors* in public, and generally failed to lead or inspire them. At no time were they motivated to avoid or even correct this situation. It seems apparent that the unspoken plan was to simply do what he said and thereby let him hang himself. However, Mr. O'Leary got the last laugh by leveraging his vast (and some would say undeserved) reputation into an even more lucrative position.

KING TUT

Up to this point these scenarios have been built on situations described to me by other managers. Some have been embellished, others consolidated into one scenario, and others abbreviated to make a point. I realize that in reviewing and critiquing these situations and the good and bad decisions made by the parties involved, I might appear as either one of those people sitting in the bleachers telling others how to do it or worse, to be a smug "I've never failed" manager. Therefore, I feel compelled to describe one of my own less-than-splendid decisions. I like to think of this as the incident when I learned to play nice with the other kids.

At one point in my career I held a position where I was responsible for the marketing and promotion of several product lines. Although the promotions team did not report to me, I was a major consumer of their service and thus had a great deal of influence over the materials they used to promote my products. Like others in this position, I had a limited budget to promote and market a very large number of products; hence, I was always after the biggest bang-for-the-buck. This meant scrutinizing brochures, trade shows, advertisements, videos, and direct mail pieces. This brought me into frequent conflict with the artistic community, which generally viewed me as having the same level of culture and class as any barbarian chieftain, while I viewed them as a bunch of simpering, mincing, uncreative, artistic wannabes. An altogether excellent working relationship, as you might imagine.

We reviewed the results of our advertising and promotions every quarter and revisited our programs annually. Every meeting was a donnybrook, with me complaining about their lack of creativity, the poor quality of the artwork, and the miserable results. They complained that all of my products were just ugly boxes with complicated names and that Michaelangelo could not have made them beautiful nor could Shakespeare have given them verbal imagery. But, the real battles raged over the direct mail campaigns. I hated them. I hated spending money on boring pieces of paper that cost a ton of money and were nothing more than wastebasket filler (my term). Naturally the direct mail people came prepared for this battle and would always show me that our campaigns were among the most successful in the nation. I could not refute the figures, but I was unconvinced and still considered their campaigns to be boring, uncreative, and completely lacking in artistic interest or excitement. Finally, the Director of Direct Marketing came to me with a new campaign. One he hoped would meet my expectations.

This new direct mail campaign was truly spectacular. This was when the King Tutankhamon exhibit was touring the United States, and Egyptian art was everywhere you looked. The new direct mail campaign was built around the King Tut exhibit and consisted of four mailings. Each mailing included a solicitation letter written on a papyrus-type paper and suitably decorated, a response envelope, and a 16 × 20 gold foil (suitable for framing) embossed picture of one of the Tutankhamon art treasures. Naturally the last one of the series was the famous gold mask of Tutankhamon. These were truly beautiful and were admired by everyone, including the advertising community. The awards began to pour in. This direct mail campaign was recognized by virtually every professional advertising association and won the annual award for the best direct mail campaign. The office of the Director of Direct Marketing was lined with these awards when he invited me over to see the results of his work.

I was certainly impressed when I saw all of these awards, letters of commendation, and articles describing the quality of this direct mail campaign. At last we had achieved what I wanted. We had created an award-winning direct mail piece that was artistic, creative, innovative (it had a whole theme of items associated with the campaign). Once I had congratulated everyone and explained to the Director that at last he had met my expectations, he played his trump card, which was the only measure that mattered. He brought out the response figures. It seems this campaign was an award winner. It had not only won numerous awards for its creativity, it had set a new mark for responses. It had the fewest responses ever recorded by the Direct Marketing Department. From a promotions perspective, it was a disaster. The campaign was the most expensive direct mail program ever launched by the company, and it had the lowest response rate, which translated into the highest cost per response ever recorded. This information was provided to me in beautiful multi-colored charts (suitable for framing).

To his credit the Director of Direct Marketing did not say "I told you so," nor did he gloat. He simply provided me the facts and let them speak for themselves. I retired with as much dignity as I could and chose to ignore the gales of laughter and thrashing sounds as the Director apparently rolled around on the floor clutching his sides, after I closed the door.

Although this was humiliating, it was also a learning experience. It was through this event that I learned to manage creative people and those from different disciplines. Actually, what I learned was how to delegate responsibility. In this case, I had been attempting to tell an expert how to do his job. I was attempting to dictate colors, format, and style with the objective of the exercise getting lost in the detail. The real objective of the direct mail promotions was to generate sales leads, not win artistic awards. The Director of Direct Marketing was always aware of the objective, but it was only when he switched his focus to my objective that I realized that I was the one who had lost focus. The lesson here is that delegation requires a clear understanding of the objective. That it is the objective that is being delegated, not the technique. *How* the objective is achieved is usually not relevant. Attempts to govern how an objective is attained constitute micro-management, and this is how I learned that lesson. The question I have for you is: Have you learned that lesson too? If you have not, then you may find yourself struggling in the new world of management.

In this chapter we have reviewed some situations that defy description. These were events that could either not be predicted or were the result of a manager acting in the old command-and-control model, or certainly without clear thought, and oblivious of the changes that were obvious to others. Evolution will gradually eliminate these obsolete managers, just as nature eliminates species that fail to adapt to changing conditions. As leaders replace these obsolete managers, we must remember that leaders are people oriented and as these scenarios showed, people can be very unpredictable. This unpredictability, as we discovered earlier, is compounded by the changing organizational structures.

Our overall purpose was to view management, not from the perspective of theories and classical structures, but from the pragmatic viewpoint of actual situations, alternative solutions, and the results actually experienced by the managers involved. Through our examination of practical managers faced with practical problems, we have observed the evolution of management techniques from the hierarchical command-and-control model to the new. We have seen real managers in real situations, and in this chapter we have seen some managers in rather unreal situations. There have been many questions asked but very few answered, at least in any definitive way, and that brings us to what is perhaps the most fundamental question of all, which is "So what?" So what does all of this mean and why should you care?

12

SO WHAT?
Observations and Reflections

So what is the lesson here? What can we learn from the managers in our scenarios? Perhaps what we can learn is that in the world of leadership and human events there is never a single answer, because both human beings and events are unpredictable. Therefore, the effective leader must look at every situation from different perspectives and be prepared to react to changing circumstances, behavior, and unanticipated events. I have attempted to apply that lesson here by showing real situations, without establishing THE answer. Instead, we examined possibilities, actions taken, and decisions made, and then we looked at the outcomes with the understanding that different decisions and actions might have yielded different, but not necessarily better, results. I am not sure that there is ever any ONE answer to management or leadership problems. Therefore out of the many possible alternatives, only the participants can determine the one best suited for their situation. In order to do this, the leader must not only be prepared to select the best tools and understand how to use them, but he/she must also be aware that in many situations all of the relevant data may not be apparent. It is this unknown factor that frequently causes the best-laid plans to go awry. This awareness was one of the fundamental objectives of the scenarios presented here.

We started by examining the differences between leadership and management. These are terms that some view as separate and distinct abilities, while others see them as interchangeable. Management and leadership are not only different, but as we discussed, they are also inseparable. Nevertheless, as you may have observed, I have used these terms more or less interchangeably not because they are the same but in an effort to illustrate the subtle differences. If the manager cannot inspire confidence and articulate the vision and direction, all the organizational ability in the world will not yield success. Conversely, an inspirational leader devoid of management skills will be unable to bring his vision into reality. However, this dichotomy between management and leadership is as theoretical as the dichotomy between good and evil. Neither exists in the pure state and everyone has good and bad just as they have management and leadership skills in varying amounts. The trick is to develop these skills and then know when and how to apply them. The operative word being "trick" because the ability to appropriately respond to a situation is what raises management and leadership to an art form.

In our discussion on ethics, we focused on the ethical questions facing Melvin the Magnificent rather than the leadership of his management. However, this scenario could just as easily have been used to illustrate the art of leadership. When Melvin turned to his manager for guidance, he was told to do what he thought best, which, in effect, was no guidance at all. In fact, it was a rather transparent attempt by his manager to shift any failure or future problem onto the shoulders of the employee. Whatever that response was, it certainly was not leadership. However, it would not have required very much of an effort by Melvin's manager to display leadership. What could Melvin's manager have done to shift from *nebbish* to leader? After listening to Melvin describe the situation, his manager could have explained that although the situation was ambiguous, it was not technically illegal. Certainly it violated the spirit of the company's seminar program but it did not actually violate any company policy. Therefore, Melvin was free to take whatever action he felt appropriate, but he (the manager and presumably the company) *would stand by whatever decision Melvin made*. The difference between this response and the one that Melvin was actually given is the final phrase committing the manager and the company to his support. This response not only empowered Melvin, it displayed courage and leadership on the part of the manager. He did not make the decision for Melvin, but neither did he abandon him. He assured Melvin that he was not alone in this and that the manager was willing to share any repercussions from Melvin's decision. This was an excellent opportunity for Melvin's manager to display leadership through a simple decision with limited risk.

The very foundation of leadership is the willingness to take responsibility for decisions and assume accountability for the results. Conversely, an unwillingness to assume risk demonstrates a lack of leadership, which is what was displayed by Melvin's management. When you think about it, there are really only two ways of leading. You can lead from the front, meaning: Follow me. I'll set the example and you do as I do. The other is to lead from the rear, meaning: I'm behind you and you can rely on me to be there when you need me. Of course, in the latter case, the quality of leadership is sometimes dependent on exactly how far behind you the leader is.

Historically, leadership skills were most necessary at the higher organizational levels, but the need for leadership is in increasing demand at the threshold levels of management. Consequently, as we move more and more into the new team structures, the team leader must be more of a leader than a manager. The Captain Bligh approach to management is not only in decline, but it must ultimately be replaced by a more democratic team leadership style. How these new team leaders are selected was not discussed here, but it is certainly a subject worthy of consideration. In the old paradigm, bosses selected new managers on the basis of friendship, longevity, experience, or availability. But whatever process was used, it rarely, if ever, included a consultation with those to be supervised. As we saw in the Emancipated Worker scenario, this arbitrary selection process is no longer universally successful. In our scenario, the workers resigned en masse, but more commonly the workers drift away, morale suffers, work quality is affected and ultimately many of the workers do resign. Eventually, the team either disappears entirely or is reduced to a second-class team. Given that this is a problem, the question then becomes: How do you select a team leader? I am not sure that I have an answer, but history may once again provide us an example of how it might be done.

During the American Civil War, a man could earn his commission by raising a platoon, cavalry troop, or regiment. In effect, the troops elected their officers by agreeing to serve under their command, and in many cases, the troops actually held an election to elect their officers. However, once the officer was elected, he carried the full authority of his commission, meaning he was viewed as a commissioned officer the same as any regular officer. This is very analogous to what is happening in many organizations today. We have not gotten to the point where the employees are electing their managers, but we certainly are at the point where the workers can and do refuse to work under specific individuals. From this I conclude that not only are strong leadership skills needed at the very first layers of management, but the people selected to lead must be recognized as leaders by those whom they propose to lead. I will not go so far as to say an election should be held, but before a person is selected to lead a team, the manager should be confident that the candidate has (or can earn) the respect of the team.

Regardless of our selection process, it is clear that someone must be in charge and empowered to make the decisions, with the operative word being "empowered." What is changing and to some extent may still be unrecognized is that the workers are empowering their leaders. While this empowerment is informal and invisible, it is nonetheless real. Empowerment has generally been thought of as something that the manager delegates to subordinates, but employee empowerment is a new concept, or is it?

Actually, it may be a revival or extension of Theory Y. This participatory style of management slowed the decision process through interminable discussions, but it also brought the workers and management closer together by involving the workers in the decision process. Although participative management was not very successful, it did give the workers an opportunity to participate in the decision-making process, and the workers became reluctant to return to simply taking orders. At one time, the decision to retain or replace an unpopular manager would not have been an issue but that is not the case with our knowledgeable and empowered employees of today. If there has been any consistent theme here, it has been that the workers themselves are causing significant changes in our organizational structures.

Most of the observations regarding employees are from the perspective of the workers, but there is obviously another side. When corporations speak of their employees as their most important asset, they truly do view the employees as such. However, what many employees fail to recognize is that like all assets, they can be depreciated, written off, and disposed of, especially when times are bad. The lesson that many workers (of all ages) fail to recognize is that being a thinking asset carries a responsibility that non-thinking or inanimate assets do not have. A thinking asset must continually improve through education and training or risk being replaced. At one time a college degree was all that was required to ensure a career. Gradually, it became necessary to have an advanced degree, and for a while it seemed the entire world was determined to get an MBA. Although degrees are still important, they no longer guarantee a long and successful career. What is required today is continuing education, and those workers who fail to continually refresh their skills become just another depreciating asset subject to disposal and replacement.

Somewhere along the line, the workers lost track of the fact that they were a company asset, and they confused the management of thinking assets with loyalty. The people assets came to believe that there was some form of unwritten social compact between them and the company. Employees came to believe that if they were loyal to the company (i.e., did not quit), then the company should and would be loyal to them (i.e., no reduction in force). But the fact is that this unwritten compact between the company and the worker never really existed. The reality has always been that, until recently, of all of the corporate assets, the people have been the most replaceable.

Historically, management has protected its machine assets rather than the people assets because the people were more easily replaced than the machines. Computer technology has created an environment where the machines are quite generalized (not necessarily simplified), but their operators are quite specialized. For the contemporary manager this means that when times are bad, layoffs should be a last resort, because people may be irreplaceable. Naturally, we can hear that old refrain, "nobody is irreplaceable," but it increasingly has a hollow ring to it. Certainly, if you lay off your CAD specialist, lab technician, sound mixer, or computer graphics technician, you can eventually replace them, but not necessarily at the same level or same cost. When you lay off one of these knowledge workers, they walk out of the door with years of experience, knowledge of the company culture, and a familiarity with the standard processes that cannot be replaced—at least not replaced quickly or easily. Therefore, the lesson here is that people truly are the most important asset of most companies and that managers need to more carefully protect this asset than they have in the past. It also means that those knowledge workers who fail to maintain their skill and knowledge levels will, like all other assets, decline in value, and the manager should not hesitate to dispose of them. Contrary to what some employees may think, it is not up to the employer to maintain the skill level of the employee. That is the employee's responsibility. It is the manager's responsibility to provide the organization infrastructure that allows employees to apply their expertise, not necessarily to improve their skills. Granted that many employers use the prospect of training and education as an inducement for the employee to remain with the company, but that is a voluntary commitment on the part of the company and not an obligation.

The workforce today is not only intellectually different, it is culturally and socially diverse as well, which means that if a universal moral code ever existed, it doesn't any longer. The workforce is no longer a homogeneous group, composed exclusively of heterosexual males with nonworking spouses. Not only is the workforce increasingly composed of dual-income and single-parent families, many of these are same-sex couples. As if these changes were not enough, there are growing issues with cultural diversity as well as various religious and cultural issues that are brought about by the spread of business across the globe. The lessons here are that managers must be much more cognizant of the personal situation of their employees than ever before. The fact is that it is not just their management style that managers must modify, they can no longer apply their personal value system to their workers either.

Aside from the obvious need to address the people issues, today's managers are required to assess risk, make timely decisions, develop and implement processes, and establish organizational structures. Of all of the lessons here, organization may be the most challenging. Historically organizations have been hierarchical, with tiers of leaders cascading downward. However, the effectiveness of this organizational model began its decline with the introduction of business computers and the supporting specialists. This group did not really fit into the company as a whole and certainly did not fit easily into the organizational structure. The problem was (although unrecognized for a long time) that the information systems were not a core competency of the company. Eventually companies came to the realization that the solution was to outsource all areas that were not core competencies. As is so often the case, the solution to one problem creates another. Outsourcing created a virtual enterprise, the virtual workplace, and virtual employees, and this created the need for new management techniques and new organizational structures.

However, creating a problem does not necessarily create the solution, just the need for a solution. By balancing what we have, what we need, and what others have tried, we are left with an organizational structure that includes strategic partners, suppliers, internal services, outsourcers, employees, and, possibly, customers. As we saw earlier, even though the organizational structure may retain the look of the traditional hierarchy, in reality it is not quite the same. It has many dotted lines, some boxes appear disconnected from the rest, there may be customer boxes, and the employees on the chart may not report administratively to the managers in the boxes. With this greater organizational complexity, the management team is faced with more complicated decisions as they grapple with varying corporate cultures. These management decisions must now be rendered within the boundary of a clear moral and ethical code and an awareness of the existing political environment. These management elements are the building blocks to leadership. But above all of these, there is the need for a plan.

I was given the opportunity to learn the value of a plan as a young Lieutenant. I was asked by my commanding officer to prepare a plan. This was the first time I had ever been asked to write a plan, so I spent a considerable amount of time preparing and polishing it. When I finished, I felt the plan was tactically sound, well written, and clear. In my opinion, I had done a good job for a first effort. I presented the plan to my commanding officer with considerable pride, comfortable in my work, and assured that he would agree that it was an excellent plan. Things went extremely well right up until he asked me for my alternate plan. I was thunderstruck. I did not have an alternate plan. I had just given him THE plan, which he had agreed was excellent, so why was an alternate plan needed? The military does not encourage explanations (read excuses) for failure, so I snapped to attention and stated loudly and firmly that I did not have an alternate plan. My superior fixed me with a steely-eyed gaze and handed my plan back to me. He then delivered to me a lesson I have carried for the rest of my life. He said, "Don't ever bring me THE plan. I expect you to bring me THE plan, an ALTERNATE plan, and a BACKUP plan!"

Success is not just arriving at a point through some random or accidental process, but getting there through a plan with clearly defined objectives. A plan is critical, be it a personal mission statement, a vision of the future, or a detailed list of objectives, because it tells you not what you are doing, but where you are going. And to paraphrase the Cheshire Cat, "If you don't know where you are going then how will you know when you get there?"

BIBLIOGRAPHY

Ackoff, Russell L. *The Democratic Corporation*. New York: The Oxford University Press, 1994.

Davidow, William H. and Malone, Michael S. *The Virtual Corporation*. New York: Harper Business, A Division of HarperCollins, 1992.

Drucker, Peter F. *Managing for the Future: The 1990s and Beyond*. New York, Truman Talley Books/Dutton,1992.

Drucker, Peter F. *Managing in a Time of Great Change*. New York, Truman Talley Books, 1995.

Drucker, Peter F. *Post Capitalist Society*. New York: Harper Business, A Division of HarperCollins Publishers, 1993.

Hamel, Gary and Prahalad, C.K. *Competing for the Future*. Boston, Massachusetts: Harvard Business School Press, 1994.

Harvey, D.F. and Brown, D.R. *An Experiential Approach to Organizational Development*. Englewood Cliffs, New Jersey: Prentice Hall, 1992.

Jay, Antony. *Management and Machiavelli*. New York-Oxford: Pfeiffer & Company, 1994.

Luthans, Fred. *Organizational Behavior*. New York: McGraw Hill, 1992.

Makridakis, Spyros G. *Forecasting, Planning and Strategy for the 21st Century*, New York: The Free Press, A Division of Macmillan, Inc., 1990.

Mintzberg, Henry. *The Rise and Fall of Strategic Planning*. New York-London: The Free Press, A Division of Simon & Schuster, Inc., 1994.
Ouichi, William. *Theory Z: How American Business Can Meet the Japanese Challenge*. Reading, Massachusetts: Addison-Wesley Publishing Company, 1981.
Wren, Daniel A. *The Evolution of Management Thought*. New York: John Wiley & Sons, Inc., 1994.

INDEX

Accountability, 97, 212
Ackoff, Russell, 102
Animal Farm, 25
Arnold, Benedict, 176
Assembly line, 48
Authoritarian management style, 25–28, 92

Battles, executive, 174, 184–90
Birthday lunch, 80–84
Bluffing, 180–82
Books, 1–3
Boundaries, importance of, 79–80
Boxes and Bubbles organization, 106–9
Buzzword Bingo, 172–73

Change, 31–32
    process control for, 54, 55–56, 57
    rate of, 37
    resistance to, 90–91
Chaos management, 40–42, 126

Chaplin, Charlie, 48
Circular organization, 102–3
Code of honor, 152–53
Command and control model, 93, 125–26, 152
Command presence, 10
Communication with employees, 68, 95, 101
Competition, internal. *See* Politics
Computers, personal, 94
Consensus management, 27, 29, 33, 214
Consultants, 95, 113–14
Contractors, independent, 113
Corporate clones, 5
Corporate politics. *See* Politics
Corporate training programs, 3–5
Critical thinking, 5, 6

Dangerfield, Rodney, 153
Deadwood, 176

Decisions, 133–49
    alternative, 211
    analysis of, 139
    barn burner project example,
        140–43
    drive for number two example,
        191–93
    executive empowerment example,
        193–95
    executive sacrifices example,
        195–97
    immediate, 135–37
    King Tut example, 207–10
    nature boy example, 200–2
    password protection example,
        202–4
    risk and, 131–34, 138–39, 145
    server specifications example,
        197–200
    super computer example, 137–40
    timing, 21–22, 134–37
    undeserved reputation example,
        204–7
    Wizard example, 143–46
Delegation, 53–54, 96–97, 209
The Democratic Corporation, 102
Diana, Princess, 14
Dishonesty, 181
Dominance struggles, 71–77
Drucker, Peter, 30, 93

Egalitarianism, 25
Eisenhower, General Dwight D., 19
Employees
    attitudes toward management,
        112–14
    changes in workforce, 91–94, 215
    communication with, 68, 95, 101
    expectations, 67–68
    with hidden agendas, 147–49
    invisible, 119
    knowledge workers, 63, 91, 93,
        113, 117, 215
    loyalty to, 169
    management, relationship with,
        25–26, 34, 116
    managing, 67–87
    as resources, 129

    retaining, 92
    as robots, 63
    temporary, 33
    veteran, 168–69
    virtual, 113, 119, 124
    See also Human variable; Politics
Empowerment, 53–54, 96–97, 128,
    193–95, 213–14
Enterprises, virtual, 107–8, 125–32
Ethics, 151–69, 212
    business morality, 152, 168
    Clambay products example,
        160–62
    computer conversion example,
        154–56
    computer replacement example,
        162–64
    copy of memorandum example,
        156–58
    employee competition example,
        164–68
    personal morality, 152, 168
    seminar example, 158–60
    situational, 153
    tests, 153
    veteran employees example,
        168–69
Excellence, searching for, 39–40
Executive battles, 174, 184–90

Fads, 2
Failure, fear of, 20–21
Fast food industry, 49–50
Fast tracker, 115, 178–80
Figurehead leaders, 14–15, 115
The Five Rings, 2
Foremen, 12
Functional managers, 36

Gamesmanship, 172–73
Globalization, 96–101
Gulliver's Travels, 186

Hawthorne Experiment, 42
Healthy competition, 166, 173–74
Home office, 119, 123–24
Honesty. *See* Ethics
Human variable, 6, 50, 64, 65, 67, 71

Indecision, 133
Independent contractors, 113
Influence, 90–91
Input Units, 105
Inspiration, 4
Integrity. *See* Ethics
Internationalization, 99, 100
International Petro-Chemical
    Corporation (IPC), 97–101
Internet, 96

Japan, 32–35
Just-in-time (JIT) manufacturing, 33

Keiretsu, 33
Kennedy, John F., 14
Kestin, Hesh, 103
King, Martin Luther, Jr., 14
Knowledge workers, 63, 91, 93, 117

Leaders, 129
    authority exercised by, 26
    characteristics, 13–14, 15
    control shift to, 92, 111–12, 129,
        213
    ineffectual, 14–15, 115
    managers compared, 9–22, 67, 212
    need for, 11, 24
    responsibility assumed by, 212
    selection, 213
    successful, 18
    virtual, 112–13
Leadership skills/management skills
    ratio, 16
Leading by example (from the front), 4,
    10, 129, 213
Leading from behind, 4, 213
Life, quality of, 68, 84–87
Lifetime employment, 33
Loyalists, 171–72
Loyalty, 169, 175–76, 214
Lying, 181

Magic bullets. *See* Theories
Malicious obedience, 207
Management
    theories, 23–45
    training, 1–8

virtual, 111–32
Management by objectives (MBO),
    30–32
Management skills/leadership skills
    ratio, 16
Managers, 11–13
    attitude toward organization, 114
    characteristics, 10, 11
    critical thinking by, 4, 5, 6
    employees, relationship with,
        25–26, 34, 116
    leaders compared, 9–22, 67, 212
    levels of, 12–13, 101
    roles, 12, 106
    successful, 18
Managing by walking around (MBWA),
    38–39, 120
Market Units, 105
Master/apprentice relationship, 49
Matrix management, 35–36
McDonald's Corporation, 49–50
McGregor, Douglas, 25–27, 28–30
McProcess, 49
Military leadership, 27–28, 152–53
Modern Times, 48
Morale, 15
Morality. *See* Ethics
Multi-dimensional organization, 104–6

Nonmonetary rewards, 6–8

Odiorne, George, 31
Organization. *See* Structure
Orwell, George, 25
Ouchi, Dr. William, 34
Output Units, 105
Outsourcing, 63, 113, 216

Paralysis by analysis, 134
Participative management, 27, 29, 33,
    214
Password protection, 202–4
Patton, General George S., 14, 19
People. *See* Employees; Human variable
Perot, Ross, 19–20
Personal computers, 94
Policies of predecessor, 81–84
Politics, 171–90

assassin example, 187–90
attitude in, 174, 183
bluffing example, 180–82
bon voyage example, 182–84
company loss in, 183
executive committee example,
    164–68
knife fight example, 184–87
levels of, 172–75
lost memo example, 175
participation in, 171–72
too fast tracker example, 178–80
traitors example, 175–78
Procedures. *See* Process
Process, 47–65
automated, 62
change control, 54, 55–56, 57
contract review, 61–62
in corporate training programs, 4
customer communications exam-
    ple, 51–63
dehumanization, 48–49
failure to document, 49
flexible, 64
incomplete, 57, 58–61
lack of, 72
legal, 55
need, 65
repeatable, 49, 50, 62–63, 64
service delivery, 63–65
standard, 49–50, 62–63, 64
Project managers, 36
Promotion, 5, 116–18
Pyramidal organization, 89–90, 101–2,
    125–26

Quality of life, 68, 84–87
Questions, refusal to ask, 162–64
Quid pro quo, 159, 161

Repeatable process, 49, 50, 62–63, 64
Reputation, 172–73, 176, 177, 204
Resources, people, 129
Respect, 153
Responsibility, 97, 212
Rewards, nonmonetary, 6–8
Ring structure, 103–4
Risk assessment, 133–49

Robots, 62–63
Roman Empire, 126–28

Sacrifices, financial, 195–97
Salary negotiations, 181
Searching for excellence, 39–40
Self-interest, 174, 175, 183
Situational ethics, 153
Smith, Roger, 19–20
Standard process, 49–50, 62–63, 64
Status, struggles for, 71–77
Steuben, Baron von, 16–17
Strategic planning, 36–38
Structure
Boxes and Bubbles, 106–9
circular, 102–3
globalization effect on, 96–97
multi-dimensional, 104–6
need for, 24
pyramidal, 89–90, 101–2, 125–26
ring, 103–4
support, shift to, 91–94
Style, 19–20
authoritarian management, 25–28,
    92
changes in, 119
chaos management, 40–42
consensus management, 27, 29,
    33, 214
Success, 17–18, 217
Suits, 5
Supervisors, 12
Swift, Jonathan, 186

Technology, 94–96, 215
Temporary workers, 33
Theories, 23–45
chaos management, 40–42, 126
management by objectives, 30–32
managing by walking around,
    38–39, 120
matrix management, 35–36
rules for, 42–45
searching for excellence, 39–40
strategic planning, 36–38
Theory X, 25–28, 102
Theory Y, 28–30, 102
Theory Z, 32–35, 102

Theory X, 25–28, 102
Theory Y, 28–29, 102
Theory Z, 32–35, 102
Time off, request for, 77–80
Training programs, 3–6, 8
Traitors, 176–77
Truman, President Harry, 19, 20
Trust, 119, 120, 123, 125, 189
21st Century Management, 103

University training programs, 3, 6

Virtual employees, 113, 119, 124
Virtual enterprises
    instability of, 112
    leadership in, 129–32
    Roman empire and, 126–28
    structure, 107–8, 126

Virtual leaders, 112–13
Virtual management, 111–32
    emancipated worker examples,
        114–18
    employee supervision example,
        121–25
    of scattered employees,
        121–25
    trust in, 119, 120, 123, 125
Virtual workplace, 118–20, 130–31
Vision, 13–14, 15

Washington, General George, 16–17,
    151
Window cube, 71–77
Workers. *See* Employees
Workplace, virtual, 118–20,
    130–31

ABOUT THE AUTHOR

ROYCE L. CALLAWAY is division manager at Electronic Data Systems, Troy, Michigan. He has more than 20 years of management and leadership experience with a variety of companies, including Burroughs Corporation, NCR Corporation, and Tally Corporation. Mr. Callaway also consults on technical management and planning and lectures on management issues at the university level.